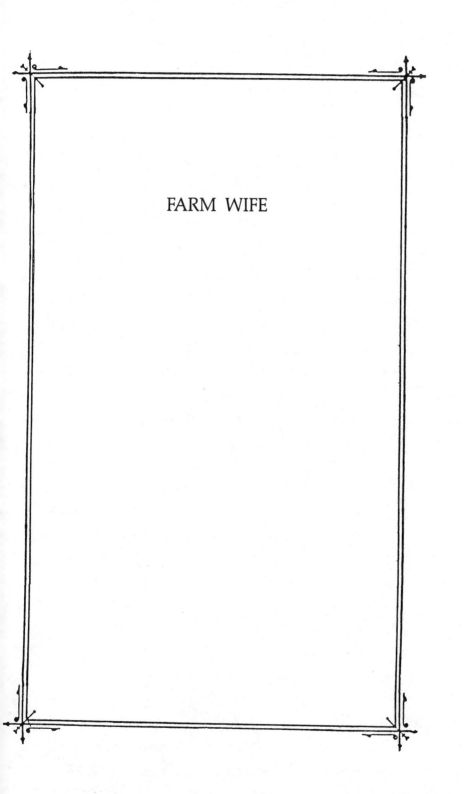

FARM WIFE

Farm Wife

A Self-Portrait, 1886–1896

Edited by

VIRGINIA E. McCORMICK

Iowa State University Press / Ames

Virginia E. McCormick has been a county extension home economist in Ohio, a program leader on the 4-H staffs at Pennsylvania State and Ohio State Universities, and a home economics administrator at Ohio State and Iowa State Universities.

© 1990 Iowa State University Press, Ames, Iowa 50010

Manufactured in the United States of America

⊛ This book is printed on acid-free paper.

First edition, 1990

Library of Congress Cataloging-in-Publication Data

Gebby, Margaret Dow.
    Farm wife : a self-portrait, 1886–1896 / edited by Virginia E. McCormick. — 1st ed.
      p.   cm.
    Includes bibliographical references (p.).
    ISBN 0–8138–1212–7 (alk. paper)
    1. Gebby, Margaret Dow—Diaries. 2. Farm life—Ohio—Bellefontaine Region—History—19th century. 3. Farmers' wives—Ohio—Bellefontaine Region—Diaries. 4. Bellefontaine Region (Ohio)—Social life and customs. 5. Bellefontaine Region (Ohio)—Biography. I. McCormick, Virginia E. (Virginia Evans), 1934– . II. Title.
F499.B4G43   1990
977.1'463—dc20
                                                   90–35046

CONTENTS

v

COMMUNITY

PREFACE

I ntense identification with the welfare of the "family farm" is somewhat surprising today when less than 5 percent of our national population live and work on farms. But millions of Americans share
childhood memories, or stories from parents and grandparents, that
weave myth and reality about rural life into a legend of shared heritage.

If the story of a nineteenth-century farm family has twentieth-century relevance, it is perhaps in presenting a comforting reality somewhere between glorified myths of good old days when life was simple
and problems were solvable and horror stories of dawn-to-dusk struggle
for survival.

The role cluster of a nineteenth-century homemaker was largely
defined by family and community relationships: wife, mother, daughter,
sister, neighbor, church member. Historical researchers are often frus-
trated by the realization that the commonalities of these roles were
shared by an overwhelming majority of the female population, but rich
details of individual experience are usually underrepresented in historic
narrative simply because most were considered too mundane for preservation.

Recent emphasis in women's history has quite appropriately given
priority to issues such as women's legal status and educational and economic opportunities. Biographies usually feature women who have
played leadership roles in social movements such as temperance or wom-
en's suffrage; were pioneers in professions such as medicine, education,
or the arts; or recorded dramatic experiences of pioneer life or wartime
service. As the knowledge base of women's history expands, more focus
is and will be devoted to the individual experiences of ordinary women.

Margaret Dow Gebby was such a woman, one whose name was
unknown beyond her family and community. Her husband owned and
operated a grain and livestock farm near Bellefontaine, Ohio. Her
household during most of the period covered by these diaries included
three sons and her widowed mother-in-law. Because she was unusually
faithful in keeping daily records of family activities and farm and household income and expenses for more than a decade, she left a private

record that illuminates concepts that are currently referred to as the "extended family" and the "family farm." Such terms often conceal within their statistical averages the individual diversity that is the heart and soul of groups such as full-time homemakers or farm wives.

This account is a housewife's perspective, but it is more than an edited diary.[1] It is a story told by two voices: a nineteenth-century recorder and *a twentieth-century interpreter*. Separated by a century, neither can question the other. Each voice leaves readers the task of determining the representative value of the experiences one chose to record and the other to interpret.

The strength of these diaries lies in spanning a decade of varied physical, economic, and political environments. They provide an opportunity to evaluate what are common practices or unusual events within one family. As individuals grow older, readers can observe changing responsibilities and relationships that would not be revealed by a single incident vignette.

Current history almost always depicts nineteenth-century farm housewives devoting long hours to the physical labor of housework and farm chores, feeding and clothing family members, and caring for the young, elderly, and sick. In eleven years of daily entries Margaret Gebby confirms such images overwhelmingly, but she simultaneously reveals sociability with a network of female relatives and a psychological satisfaction with the homemaking role that most twentieth-century writers fail to capture.[2]

The decision to present this story in topical rather than chronological form risks depriving readers of the rhythm of labor and leisure, but it appears necessary if one is to write social commentary rather than a family saga. Work cycles such as planting and harvest, spring housecleaning, and fall butchering might be obvious, but few readers of the original diaries would pursue the tedious repetition of daily events long enough to discover subtle but equally strong rhythms of leisure. In the Gebby family, the Fourth of July might be celebrated with fireworks or completely ignored by crews busy in the hayfield. But year after year there would be days after corn was laid by and before hay was ready for cutting when men would go fishing and families would go visiting.

No account can capture all the nuances of individual experience, but this story will remind readers that families have always been three dimensional and unique. The Gebbys are presented neither as a typical nor an exceptional nineteenth-century farm family. The size of their home and farm, their crop and livestock operation, their home furnishings and farm equipment are slightly above average but quite representative of western Ohio in this time period. But they could just as easily have been chosen from many communities throughout the midwestern Corn Belt. The proximity of the Gebby farmhouse to their county seat presents an interesting view of farm and town interaction, but their pattern of shopping, church attendance, and social visits would not be shared by farm families in more isolated locations. The fact that the husband and wife of this family were past thirty when they married was unusual in the post–Civil War era, and it affected the size of their family and the particular generations of extended family with whom they and their children interacted.

The detailed financial records of this farm and home span years of economic prosperity and depression in the agricultural Midwest. Some of their most surprising data relate to the amount of money earned by homemakers in an era that officially considered married women unemployed.

Some noteworthy perspectives of this Ohio housewife's record are

- a private record written daily as events occurred rather than memoirs written years later for publication;
- a woman's viewpoint of farm work and daily life;
- a family record that reveals dynamics of changing relationships as youths become adults and grandparents die;
- detailed financial records over a decade of fluctuation that reflect family adjustment to agricultural prosperity and depression;
- a record of technological innovations adopted by one farm and home that can be contrasted with patent and advertisement data.

Few of those who lived on family farms a century ago spent time recording the experience, and those who did were usually too mundane to interest historians. But the farther our society is removed from certain shared experiences, the deeper we must search for understanding of clichés such as family farm, full-time housewife, and extended family.

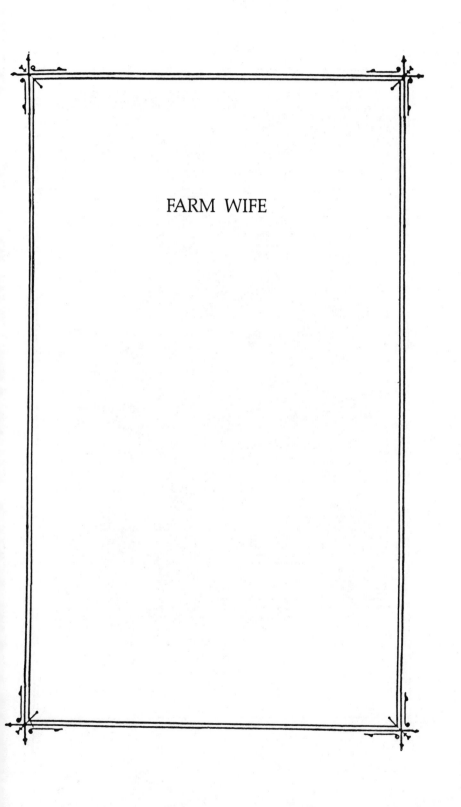

FARM WIFE

Margaret Dow about the time of her marriage
to Jeremiah Gebby in 1868.

THE GEBBY FAMILY FARM

Margaret Dow was born 14 April 1835, the third daughter of Peter Dow and Sallie Campbell Dow. Her father had been born in Perthshire, Scotland, and immigrated to the United States with his parents as a boy. Sallie Campbell was born in New Jersey shortly after her parents immigrated from northern Ireland. They met near Marietta, Ohio, where Peter Dow was teaching school. After their marriage in 1829 they moved to Logan County, an area in northwestern Ohio that was just opening for settlement. Peter Dow farmed and taught school during Margaret's childhood, but in the 1850s moved to the county seat of Bellefontaine where he served on the County Board of School Examiners and later operated a drugstore. The family was devoutly religious with Peter Dow serving as an elder of the Associate-Reformed (later United Presbyterian) Church from its founding in that neighborhood until his death.[1]

Little is known of Margaret Dow's childhood but it appears she was called Maggie by family and friends.[2] She undoubtedly attended the local one-room school and perhaps the Union School established in Bellefontaine in 1854. Family legend suggests that she taught school during some of the years prior to her marriage 30 September 1868 at age thirty-three.[3] It is interesting to speculate but impossible to know why she did not marry at least a decade earlier like her two older sisters. Was she less attractive, more reserved, more independent, more pampered by her parents after her younger sister's death, or might she even have lost a love in the Civil War? She would certainly have been considered an old maid with few prospects for marriage by the time she married Jeremiah Gebby.

3

The Gebby family late in the 1880s; left to right,
George, Elmer, Margaret, Orra, and Jeremiah.

Jeremiah Morrow Gebby, more than three years younger than his
wife, had been born near Monroe, Ohio, 24 December 1838. He was a
fourth-generation descendant of Scots-Irish immigrants, named for his
grandmother's brother who served as Ohio's first congressman, and later
as U.S. senator and governor. Jerry's parents separated when he was a
baby and his mother, Mary Robeson Gebby, lived as a widow, raising
her two sons. Jerry Gebby had a brief previous marriage but was living
with and caring for his mother and brother when he married Margaret
Dow, whom he would have known through the United Presbyterian
Church. Margaret must have accepted from the beginning that her
mother-in-law would be part of the household as long as she lived.[4]

Jerry and Margaret Gebby became the parents of four boys: Orra
D., born in 1871; Elmer R., born in 1872; John C., born in 1874, died in
1875; and George H., born in 1878.[5] The extended family network re-
vealed in these diaries includes Margaret's Dow-Campbell relatives and
Jerry's maternal Robeson relatives. The closest interactions on
Margaret's side are her sibling's families, particularly the family of her

next older sister Martha Aikin, who lived on a farm less than a mile away. Her sister Jane Cook lived farther away, but the Gebbys were especially close to her oldest son Charles, who had married Jerry's cousin Elizabeth Harner, and her daughter Mary McCracken, whose husband had a nursery in Bellefontaine. Among Margaret's cousins she was closest to Duncan Dow, a lawyer in Bellefontaine, and Anna Wolfe, Lyman Doan, and Joshua Doan, daughter and sons of her mother's sister Martha Campbell Doan, who lived several miles west near Degraff.[6] These diaries consistently reveal particularly close relationships between sisters and their descendants.

Jerry's father died in Iowa before these diaries begin and there is no evidence that the family ever interacted with any Gebby relatives. Jerry's only brother, John, died of consumption in 1875. Mary Gebby's mother had died in childbirth when she was two years old, but she was quite close to her stepsisters and brother. She moved to Logan County to be near her sister Martha Harner's family, and her brother, John, moved within walking distance in 1889. Jerry also visited frequently with his aunt and uncle Clara and John Kitchen, who lived near the old Robeson homestead west of Lebanon, Ohio.[7]

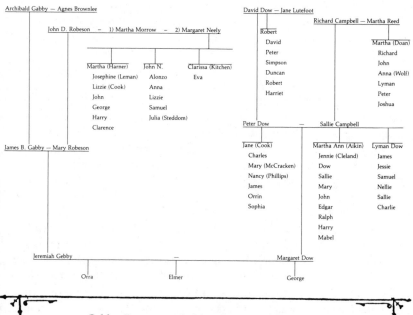

Gebby-Dow extended family network, ca. 1890.

Jerry Gebby was eighteen when his mother moved to Logan County and purchased a farm near her brother-in-law Abraham Harner, which her two sons operated. They benefited from rising land prices and wartime demand for agricultural products, and by the time of Jerry and Margaret's marriage they were farming a 168-acre quarter section seven miles southwest of Bellefontaine. It may have been Margaret's desire to live nearer her family that prompted their purchase of sixty-one acres just west of town in the fall of 1872, shortly before the birth of their second son. During the next five years, the Union Township farm was sold and two parcels west of the Gebby home were purchased, completing the unit of 286 acres that the Gebbys were farming when Margaret's journals commence.[8]

The Gebby home had been built prior to their purchase in 1872, but the style suggests it was relatively new, probably one of several in that neighborhood referred to as "wheat houses" for its origin in grain profits from the war economy.[9] The Gebby farm was above average for Ohio in the 1880s and 1890s. In its neighborhood it was neither the largest nor the most profitable, but it ranked among the top 10 percent. In 1880 its land and buildings were valued at $17,800, its equipment at $2,500, and the value of agricultural products produced at $4,085. Of 107 cultivated acres, 28 acres of corn produced 1,200 bushels and 58 acres of wheat produced 1,500 bushels. The remainder was in hay, pasture, woods, an acre of potatoes, and an orchard of seventy-five fruit trees. At the census enumeration it contained seventy-four cattle and twenty-two swine.[10]

Harrison Township late in the nineteenth century was considered excellent for agriculture, containing relatively flat land and productive soil underlaid for the most part with limestone gravel from its glacial heritage. Blue Jacket Creek, near the Gebby home, bore the name of a famous Shawnee chief, one of several Indian tribes that maintained villages in this area prior to white settlement.[11] Because of its proximity to the county seat, the township remained entirely rural, developing no villages of its own. Its 1890 population of 978 had been static for decades, and it consistently had one of the lowest tax rates in Logan County, but its seven one-room school districts in the 1880s served over three hundred scholars.[12]

Logan County was completely agricultural in orientation with a population of 27,386 in 1890, only 3,998 of whom lived in Bellefontaine, the county seat. Its topography is quite varied, containing Ohio's highest point above sea level and the headwaters of the Miami River. The Greenville Treaty line, which opened land north of the Ohio River to white settlement in 1795, was three miles north of the Gebby home. The last Indians left their reservation in this area in 1832, and the largest of

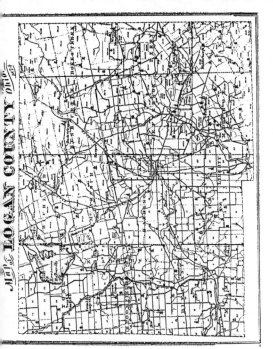

Map of Logan County, Ohio, showing location of Gebby farm and hired man's house (F) and the Gebby home farm (G) (in Harrison Township just west of Bellefontaine). (From D. J. Stewart, *Combination Atlas Map of Logan County, Ohio* [Philadelphia: D. J. Stewart, 1875])

several glacial lakes was expanded to serve as a reservoir for the Miami and Erie Canal.[13] By the late 1880s Bellefontaine was a crossroads for east-west and north-south rail lines, a thriving county seat with two newspapers, two banks, eleven churches, several general stores, physicians, attorneys, carriage manufacturers, lumber and grain mills, and a school enrollment exceeding one thousand. Its prosperity was distinguished by an imposing three-story high school completed in 1878 and an elegant Italianate courthouse on a well-manicured square enclosed with wrought-iron fence.

Like communities of comparable size and diversity throughout the Midwest, Bellefontaine experienced a golden era late in the nineteenth and early in the twentieth centuries. For farm families like the Gebbys it was the center of their educational, social, and religious universe. Like Margaret Dow Gebby, many lived their entire lives within such orbits.

Her diaries for the years 1886 through 1896 are legibly written in pencil in leather-backed commercial diaries. Expenses are noted daily and summarized monthly in the back of each book. Excerpts quoted in the following topical sections retain original spelling and abbreviations and generally reflect a well-educated farm housewife.

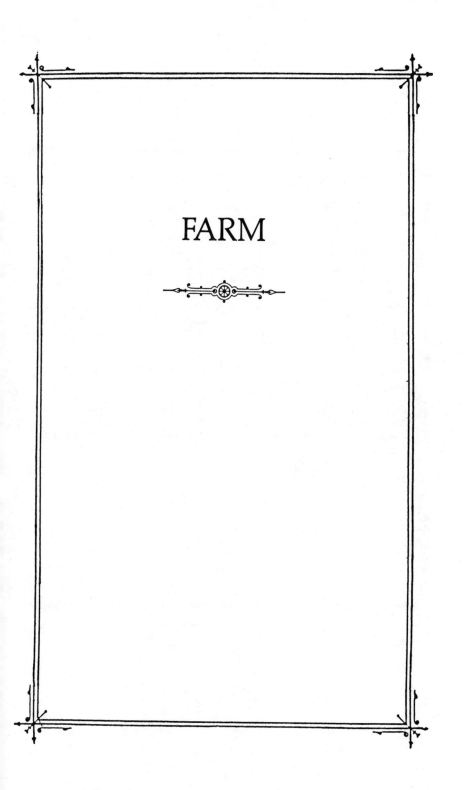

FARM

Exceedingly warm all day
the warmest day this
season at one time this
afternoon the mercury
was 102 on the porch in
the shade, looks like
rain this evening a good
rain gone north.
The men not doing
much around the
pickles, I pickled.
My? dress skirt
father and Mother
here for dinner Arthur
and Tommy McCracken
here for supper.
finished Ora's shirt
commenced making
my blue calico dress
Mrs Krouse and Mit
here over this evening
to hear Ora play.
churned, Blacksmith
$4.50 repairing sickle
60 total $1.94.

very warm, rained a
good shower this after
noon, is raining now
went to town this morn
had 13 lbs of ? butter
6 doz of eggs. took can
peaches 80, 6 gingham
43 shirting 24 corn
15 fish 20 got tomato
at Miss Miller $2.50
Grandma $8.50 George
pants 75 cal Murdock
$1.00. Hammock $1.00
kit fish 35 shot 25
Levy, Ora and Cal
stacked some lumber
and fixed the barn
doors at the farm
Seeded some set
out 18 cabbage plants
and 49 pepper plants
this evening Ora & one
to prayer meeting.
$9.57

June 20–21, 1888, entries from Margaret's diary.

WEATHER

Each day began with a look at the sky and the thermometer. It was the weather which determined crop growth, livestock care, and farm worker comfort. Margaret began each day's entry with a brief notation about temperature or weather condition. Like their neighbors the Gebbys walked, rode, and worked in heat and cold, rain and sun. Weather was far more important to them than the twentieth-century population who live, work, and ride in artificially heated and cooled environments. Most of the time Margaret accepted weather as a given that she could not change, but occasional entries express joy, worry, or humor.

Northwestern Ohio weather can be quite changeable, varying considerably from day to day and year to year. Summer of 1890 brought drought and spring of 1892 brought flood, but season after season weather and farm work dictated patterns of survival. Modern readers may be surprised that nineteenth-century rural families were so mobile during severe winter weather, but in many ways their horse and sleigh was more reliable transportation than a modern automobile attempting to drive on icy or unplowed streets.

19 January 1890: Cloudy raining again this eve. almost Egyptian darkness[1]

7 January 1893: The men not working to day, too cold, 8 above. Orra went for the clothes $1.00 [*washing*] . . . *10 January* The coldest day so far this winter, 8 below A.M. . . . *12 January* Another cold day, 4 below A.M., snowing this evening, splendid sleighing could not be better. We went to town this afternoon, at Boals I got calico dress 63 cts, thread 4, yarn and Saxony 25, cheese 28, called at Mr Harners, also at Fathers, he has a cold his gas stove did not keep him warm the gas having frozen, set up a coal stove . . . *24 January* Rather pleasant morning, 18 above, Jerry and I visited at Milton Wolfs today had a nice visit. Jerry did not get any cattle. We came home this afternoon in a regular Nebraska blizzard.

3 January 1895: Rather pleasant winter day, getting colder to night the cold and snow signal out this afternoon . . . *12 January* Very cold, 7 deg below zero here, at the newsstand 14 below, a great many suffered from frost bitten ears, fingers & toes. A Mr Pool had his face badly frozen coming from Degraff to Bellefontaine. a colt and two cows frozen to death about 6 miles north. the cold is reported general over this & Europe.

20 February 1891: Wet, Wet, everything wet, still raining this evening.

13 February 1892: A splendid Aurora Borealis this evening

4 February 1893: Cold, 6 below A.M., east wind this evening, broke our thermometer, cannot tell how cold it is, everything a glare of ice. Orra and George was skating in the field this forenoon. Jerry was at the farm found one hog on ice so it could not get up, another in the field west of the railroad, they got the rope and hauled it across to the barn where it could walk. I went to town got the mail, called at Fathers

19–20 February 1896: very strong cold west wind, we find it very hard to keep the house warm . . . last night the mercury was 8 deg below zero, everything froze in the kitchen, the first for this winter

23–24 March 1891: Cloudy though warmer, Frogs singing this evening . . . Orra and Bob threw down the remainder of the straw stack this A.M. the barn yard is knee deep in mud, mud everywhere.

10 April 1886: Warmer, snow gone except in the drifts

28 April 1887: Rain and stormy the greater part of the day went to Mr Kaylors funeral, rain, hail & wind quite a large funeral too wet to plow not doing any thing of importance today.

18 April 1889: Very pleasant, warm, no fire in the grate all day.

25 April 1892: Ice in the horse trough!

3–4 May 1892: Rained considerable to day, entirely too wet to work in the ground. Orra gathered some mushrooms . . . George was hunting mushrooms this A.M. got quite a number of small ones.

14–16 May 1892: Rained last night and very, very hard this afternoon, the big 4 railroad crossing at Columbus St flooded two feet deep, the lower part of town flooded, gutters all full. Tuckers run and Blue Jacket roaring this evening. the railroad culvert over possum run was washed out delaying trains both directions . . . Orra and Bob opened a ditch then repaired the damaged fence along the pike. Jerry was at the pasture, everything was all right, the flood on Saturday had washed the fence across the ditch away. was at the farm this afternoon some fence was washed entirely away there.

16 May 1894: still dry, looked like rain, but passed by. Jerry was at town got 20 feet of hose to water the garden $2.00

21–22 May 1895: A very heavy frost this morning some ice in water trough, vegetation and fruit much injured, grapes about all killed, also strawberries . . . the field at the farm first planted was up nicely but is so badly frost bitten they thought best to plant it over again, got considerable of it done this afternoon.

4 June 1886: Considerable frost this morning

20 June 1888: Exceedingly warm all day, the warmest day of the season, at one time this afternoon the mercury was 102 on the porch in the shade, looks like rain this evening . . . the men not doing much ground the sickles.

1 June 1889: rained quite hard this morning too wet for the trip to the reservoir.

8 June 1889: a very beautiful rainbow this evening

2–3 July 1889: the men working at the hay, very bad hay weather rains every day. We with Uncle John, Aunt Hannah, and Aunt Clara visited at Harry Harners to day took Aunt Clara to Ed Lemans, waited there till after a heavy rain, and supper, got home about seven Oclock, raining again this evening . . . considerable cooler this evening wind from the northwest, a red sunset[2]

21 July 1890: Still exceedingly dry, vegetation suffering, very dusty . . . *30 July* Still very warm, 96 in the shade, quite windy, a little cloud but does not rain, everything drying up . . . *1 August* Exceeding hot, no appearance of rain. Orra & George took 36 pigs to the farm put them in the clover field, thereby saving the corn . . . another very warm day 96 under the sugar tree . . . *3 August* 101 deg a while this P.M. attended S.S. & church . . . *6 August* Jerry looking for pasture for the cattle did not succeed in getting any, saw Kaufman and Mrs Case will know tomorrow. the gravel engine set fire to the track on the switch run out in the field some. the boys saw it in time to control it before doing much damage . . . *7 August* the switch took fire again to day. burned some dried grass, Orra and Cal put it out. Jerry saw Gardner this eve. he promised to send hands in the morning and burn both sides all off . . . *8 August* they brought the cattle from the pasture took 20 of them to Kaufmans pasture, put the rest of them in at the farm. the railroad men burned the track off this morning. John Kaylors barn burnt this evening . . . *9 August* Jerry began feeding green corn to his cattle. the pasture is dried up . . . *17 August* had a nice rain this eve. much more than we have had since the first part of June . . . *19 August* Rained last night and another good shower this morning, things seem revived somewhat.

12 July 1894: A very warm day, hot wind, the men worked at the hay, we washed, churned and Ironed. it is too hot to work but we have to . . . *18 July* they plowed 6 furrows in the wheat stubble and 3 in the timothy stubble along the Railroad it being so very dry fire is liable to break out any time

12 July 1895: Very, very dry and dusty. Orra and Jerry was at the pasture to see what could be done for water, it is getting low.

31 August 1886: Earthquake at half past nine[3]

14 August 1891: had a very severe hail storm this evening. the hail was quite large and a good deal of it. the boys gathered up several bucketsful and made ice cream.

13 September 1886: Quite cool, some frost last night . . . *21 September* considerable frost this A.M. . . . *27 October* Raining and colder, commenced snowing about noon, is still snowing . . . *28 October* Snow about five inches deep broke a great many trees, moved the stove into the kitchen this morning . . . *29 October* thawed some . . . *30 October* snow all gone

21 October 1890: a very heavy frost, cut the tomato vines, moved the stove in this morning.

31 October 1895: An earthquake was distinctly felt this morning at 5-15 A.M. we did not notice it[4]

11 November 1888: This is the time to look for falling stars

17 November 1889: Very wet, Sleeting, the trees covered with ice. the boys and I went to S.S. and church, not many there . . .

BUILDINGS, EQUIPMENT, AND HIRED HELP

Although the Gebbys had been farming at this location for more than a decade before these journals begin, Jerry was expanding his operation as his sons matured. In 1887 he purchased additional land for summer pasture and increased the number of cattle that would be fed corn to fatten them for market. Margaret's diary records the process of consulting with relatives regarding the value of this prospective acreage, buying it at sheriff's auction, paying off the mortgage, and initiating improvements to fences and buildings.

This land was evidently not exactly what Jerry wished, but it was all that was available close enough to drive cattle to pasture and regularly monitor their progress. The fact that cattle were turned on to this pasture before the fences were rebuilt suggests just how badly additional land was needed. The property obviously contained some old farm buildings, including a sixteen-foot log house, which had probably been the first dwelling on this land. Its salvage by the Gebbys for use as hog houses and feed boxes no doubt suggests the fate of many such structures at the hands of persons more concerned with thrift than history.

1 March 1887: Went down the Liberty pike to see the Miller land . . . *7 April* Jerry & George Aikin[1] was looking at the H.I. Miller farm did not like it as well as they expected . . . *13 April* Jerry with Dunk Dow[2] and Orra went to see the Miller land this afternoon . . . *30 April* The H.I. Miller farm was sold this P.M. Jerry bought the first & second lots at $52 pr acre . . . *2 May* Jerry went to the Miller land and closed the fences keeping the stock off the pasture . . . *3 May* Paid first

15

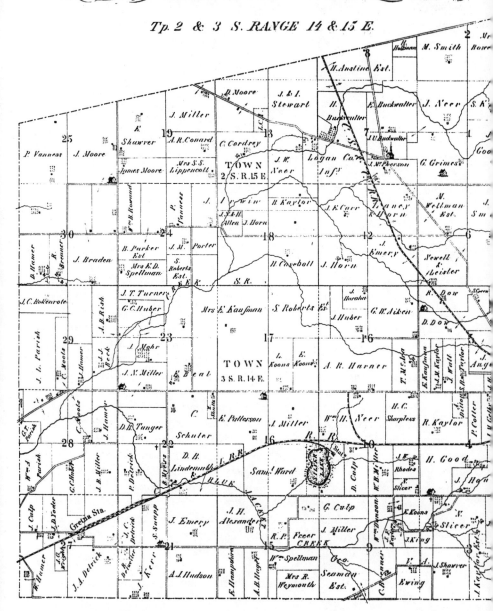

Harrison Township map. Gebby home farm is in northeast part of section 4. The farm where the hired man lived is in section 11 (incorrectly labeled as another 16 on this map), shown here as the A. R. Harner farm. The J. M. Kaylor farm between them is where Jerry's uncle John Robeson moved. (From D. J. Stewart, *Combination Atlas Map of Logan County, Ohio* [Philadelphia: D. J. Stewart, 1875])

payment on the H.I. Miller land $1703.83 . . . *4 May* Jerry went to the farm fed the last corn, turned them out to pasture, went to see those on the Miller lands found them all right . . . *19 May* were at town this afternoon got the deed for the Miller land (Sheriffs fee $2.00) gave a mortgage on the land (fee $1.50) . . . *20 May* Jerry and Orra went to the Miller land measured the fence they are to build . . . *23 May* Cal, Orra, Elmer & Hover built fence on the east of the Miller land . . . *24 May* the boys, Hover & Cal built fence on the Miller land . . . *25 May* Cal, Hover & the boys were at the Miller land building fence . . . *26 May* Orra, Elmer & Hover worked at the Miller land . . . *30 May* Hover was here this morning brought all home paid him $7.50 for building fence.

15 December 1887: Jerry and Cal went to the pasture this morning tore down the old springhouse and brought it to the farm to make a smokehouse of it . . . *27 December* Jerry was at town paid the taxes $187 had the deed for the Miller land recorded $1.60, got 3 pts oysters 45, crackers 25

2 April 1888: Jerry settled with Sheriff Loyd, paid him $1805.53 the second payment on the Miller land.

5 November 1888: Jerry and Orra went to the pasture took most of the roof lath and rafter off the cabin preparing to taking it down to build hog houses at the farm and here . . . *6 November* Jerry, Orra and Cal went to the pasture Cal had 13 logs 16 feet long, and Jerry had 3 logs and lath and rafters, came home through the rain

22 February 1889: Jerry and Cal went to the pasture brought to the farm four long logs and eight short ones from the old house to make feed boxes for the cattle.

30 April 1889: Jerry settled with the Sheriff for the last payment on the H.I. Miller land, paid $1907.73, got the Mortgage canceled and the note.[3]

While Margaret was aware of every phase of the Miller land purchase and perhaps discussed its pros and cons privately with her husband, her diary gives no hint that she shared in the decision-making process. A surprising comparison a year later is the decision of Jerry's Uncle John Robeson to move from Darke County to Logan County. This clearly involved his wife's money and, while the men were involved in deciding about the quality of the farmland, it was Aunt Hannah alone who finalized the purchase.

Although the Robesons considered moving as early as the winter of 1887–88, it took a year to locate property in a suitable location at a satisfactory price. When they moved a distance of approximately fifty miles, Margaret's journal gives a fascinating glimpse of the intricacies

involved in transporting farm and household goods by train and wagon. Neighbors helped the family settle into their new home with firewood, plants for the garden, hay for the livestock, and help with the hauling and redecorating. But, as their closest relatives, the Gebbys were their sponsors in the new community, providing liaison on the real estate transaction, credit reference for a bank loan, assistance in finding workers such as a plasterer, and introducing them at church.

15 February 1888: John Gabby[4] called here this morning to see about trading lands with Uncle John Robeson. Jerry wrote for them to come and see about it themselves . . . *23 February* Jerry went to the Depot and met Uncle John and Aunt Hannah Robeson at the train, rode up and looked at Mrs Taylors place then rode past John Gabbys to look at it . . . *24 February* Uncle John and Aunt Hannah rode with us to the farm to see the stock were weighed Grandma weighed 102, Uncle John 150, Aunt Hannah 175, and I 120 . . . *25 February* the Judge Taylor farm was sold to day to I.F. Miller at $98 per acre Uncle John bid 95.50 Mrs Houts bid 96, called at Fathers rode out to look at Mrs Anders place did not like it . . . *27 February* Uncle John and Aunt Hannah Robeson left on the noon train for Pemberton, were going to Mrs Bonners then look at property about Sidney . . . *5 March* received a letter from John Robeson this evening stating that they did not find a home at Sidney. Jerry wrote to them the Kaylor property is for sale at $100 pr acre

10 August 1888: Uncle John and Aunt Hannah came here this afternoon . . . *11 August* Jerry, Uncle John, Aunt Hannah & Grandma went to the pasture called at Tylers to see about trading Darke Co land. Went to John Gabbys to talk trade Darke Co. land no success . . . *13 August* Uncle John and Aunt Hannah went home on the noon train they bargained for the Kaylor property to pay $200 when the deed is made and $2000 April 1890. David Kaylor to sow all the wheat and timothy seed.

17 September 1888: David Kaylor called saying they wanted to make the deed for the property next Saturday. Jerry wrote to Darke Co. this evening asking them to come over on Friday . . . *21 September* Aunt Hannah Robeson came this afternoon to finish the writing for the Kaylor place . . . *22 September* Went to town this morning with Mrs Robeson who settled her business with the Kaylors all right . . . *24 September* Aunt Hannah went home at noon[5]

23 January 1889: Met Aunt Hannah Robeson at the depot at 1.30. D.M. Kaylor called. Settled for the bank notes $2,000. They want to move the first of March if they can get possession of the property . . . *7 February* Jerry wrote to Uncle John telling them that they can get their house the first of March

5 March 1889: Orra brought a letter from S.H. Robeson this evening saying that the Friends would be here on the nine Oclock train this evening . . . *6 March* Uncle John, Aunt Hannah, Annie and Lizzie Robeson here last night. Jerry and Uncle John went to the farm took a load of wood to their home. We went to their house found everything dilapidated enough . . . *7 March* Jerry & Uncle John went to the farm got 15 hhd & 30 lbs of hay, put it in their stable. Aunt Hannah and I went to town saw Tom Stillwell to patch the plastering in their house. Lon and Sam Robeson came about five Oclock. Jerry went to Cals then to Dave Kaylors to get them to haul out their goods, the car [*rail freight*] came this afternoon . . . *8 March* Jerry, Cal, Dave Kaylor, Lon and Sam emptied the car of Uncle Johns goods, hauled out eight loads. They were all here for dinner. Aunt Hannah and the girls went home after dinner, Lon and Sam came back got their trunks . . . *10 March* [*among eleven joining church by certificate*] John, Hannah, Anna, Lizzie, A.H. & S.H. Robeson and [*among five by profession of faith*] George H. Gebby . . . *11 March* Sam Robeson got the step ladder and the papering board . . . *12 March* we helped paper at Uncle Johns a while this afternoon finished the sitting room . . . *26 March* Uncle John got some raspberry sprouts and a few Blackberry roots also wineplant

Even when farmers were not interested in buying land, farm auctions were a regular source of neighborhood interaction. Relatives and neighbors were expected to attend and often as not found something they needed to purchase.

2 April 1889: All went to Neers sale. Jerry bought a set of buggy harness $18, horse blanket 60 cts, 2 clevis, 2 wrenches 25 cts

11 October 1893: were at Tommy Cooks sale.[6] There were a great many people there, things generally sold high. Jerry bought a colt for $40.00 . . . *16 November* Tommy Cooks moved to town to day in Lockharts new house. I helped them put away things this P.M.

28 March 1896: Jerry attended the Robeson Bros sale this afternoon bought some chains 25 cts[7]

BARNS AND OUTBUILDINGS

Although carpenters were universally used for home construction, the neighborly practice of getting together to help someone raise a barn

still survived in this community late in the nineteenth century. But transitions were under way and the daylong social event with neighbor women helping prepare dinner for the crew seems to have disappeared.

24 *April 1886:* Jerry helped raise Mr Neers barn this morning
16 *April 1887:* Jerry helped John Marsh raise their barn this A.M.

Farm barns and outbuildings needed constant repair or remodeling to suit changed needs. Most farmers developed some basic carpentry skills and were usually quite thrifty about cutting timber from their own woods or reusing timber from old buildings. This was especially true when the Gebbys purchased the Miller farm for pasture, but it was a continuing process year in and year out.

12 *October 1888:* Orra making an ice house of the granary.
30 *July–3 August 1889:* the boys and Cal cut eight saw logs today . . . Cal hauled seven logs to the mill hauled back one of lumber (joists) . . . Orra and Cal hauled one saw log and one load of lumber home . . . the boys and Cal took up the floor of the barns to put in new joists the others having rotted . . . Cal and the boys put in the joist in the barn floor, laid some of the boards.
25 *September 1990:* Jerry went to town this P.M. had the house[8] & barn at the farm insured in the Royal of Liverpool Eng. paying $15, the house valued at $500, the barn $1000, Cory Lame Agt. . . . *8 December* Jerry blazed four trees for sawing
14–29 *May 1891:* Orra and Bob worked at the barn floor . . . Orra hauled a log to the mill, got lumber paid $2.25 . . . Orra and Bob finished the barn floor . . . the men hauled two saw logs to the mill . . . Orra and Bob hauled two saw logs, took home a load of boards left it at the farm . . . Orra and Bob hauled home a load of lumber . . . the men hauled three loads of four logs to the mill, brought home one load of joists . . . Jerry and Orra brought home the rest of the lumber, took up the old joists of the west mow, put down some new ones . . . Bob hauled the old lumber of the barn floor home for wood. Jerry paid his saw bill $10.19
17 *October–1 November 1894:* Moon was here this morning about moving the stable, agreed to move it for $25.00 and dinner, to commence next Monday . . . Moon and hands came on this morning to move the stable . . . the men got the west end of the stable on blocks at the right place, worked at the other part some but one got sick and they all went home after dinner . . . tore down the cow stable moved the timbers away. Ben Goff was here prepared the sills for putting under the

stable . . . the men fixed the fence where the stable stood, cleaned up things around there . . . Jerry was at the mill paid the saw bill $11.48, took Ben Goffs auger home paid for the carpenter work done last Wednesday $1.25 . . . the men worked at the stable again this afternoon, got the new sills under it . . . Old Moon got the remainder of the barn moved today took his traps and went. Glad he is gone a fearfully dirty old chap and very greedy at the table. Haven't been giving our own folks very good meals lately[9] . . . paid Moon $25.00 . . . the men worked at the stable this afternoon got it leveled have it in pretty good shape . . . the men worked at the stable all day. Jerry took Moons lifting jacks home this afternoon.

28-29 October 1896: This afternoon the men threw down the colt stable & moved it to the pasture field to rebuild it . . . the men got the colt stable raised but not finished.

FARM TOOLS AND REPAIRS

The varied equipment necessary on a farm, the cost of maintenance and repairs, and the distance from mechanical expertise created a legendary self-sufficiency among farmers. Slack seasons found them sharpening tools and repairing equipment. The Gebby men were constantly remodeling something from one use to another to avoid buying something new. This called for a variety of basic tools and a range of skills from carpentry to plumbing, roofing, welding, and harness making. The ethic was clearly to wear it out or use it up. When the requirements were obviously beyond their skills, the Gebby men still saved by tearing down old and doing preliminary work for skilled craftsmen.

2–5 June 1886: Orra and Jerry hauled shingles $35.00, nails $1.77, knocked the shingles off the barn at Cals . . . Jerry and Orra working on the roof of the Old Barn, Orra got two thousand more shingles $7.00 . . . Jerry and Orra went to the farm this forenoon took out two carpenters to shingle the old barn . . . Carpenters finished roofing the barn, paid $11.20.

26 September–28 October 1887: The men went to the pasture to bring the scales to the farm had two wagon loads . . . took the roof & siding off the scale house and brought home two loads . . . the men went to the pasture took the frame of the scale house apart and hauled it and the fencing home . . . Jerry, Orra & Cal plowed and scraped a cellar for the scale house, Orra & Cal finished it this afternoon and hauled stone for the foundation . . . Cal & Orra hauled stone and sand to build the foundation of the scale house . . . Jerry & Orra & Cal worked on the foundation of the scale house today . . . Jerry helped the Evans men with the scale platform all day . . . Jerry, Orra and Cal worked on the scales finished the platform. Went to the scales were weighed. Sallie Murdock weighed 110 lbs Mont 26, Grandma 96, George 66, Jerry 132, Orra 140, Cal 170, I 116, Rover 45 [*big dog*]

11–17 December 1888: Jerry stopped at the tan yard bought a side of harness leather 12 lbs at 35 cts pr lb $3.90 . . . Cal helped Jerry cut and make eight halter straps, repaired one halter, took five straps home with him, Jerry kept three.

17 May 1890: Jerry ordered a set of double harness from the Murray Co of Cincinnati, sent a draft on New York for $20.00

15 August 1892: Jerry bought two pitchforks $1.30

26–30 October 1893: Elmer worked in the Machine house, making a shop of part of it . . . Elmer was making a Buckboard out of the old Eureka buggy

20 September 1894: Jerry got two corn cutters 65 cts, Hardware 60 cts, Twine $1.00, a bushel of Peaches $1.90

15 March 1895: Orra went to Huntsville and bought a pair of floor scales from Will Orr, paid $5.00 for them and counter scales $1.00 they were badly rusted but he got them cleaned off nicely so they are almost as good as new . . . *15 June* Jerry got two mowing knives $9.00

1–24 July 1896: The men worked at the hay, George mowed but unfortunately broke the mower, had to get a new tongue paid 75 cts . . . George mowed nearly all day . . . George broke the mower about 10 A.M. Jerry took it to town for repairs . . . The men fixed the mower . . . Jerry mowed, George & Wellie ground the sickles and hauled in some hay, broke the loader. Jerry came home to repair it . . . George broke a casting of the mower had to send for one to Springfield . . . Jerry got the casting for the mower, got it fixed at Bowmans, mowed some . . . Settled with George Rife for mower repairs $6.45

Growing up on a farm did not guarantee the youngest son would be mechanically inclined!

WINDMILLS

Water for livestock was a daily need that required hard physical labor pumping it from wells into troughs except when cattle and hogs were on summer pasture with a stream. It is not known whether the wind wheel that the Gebbys installed in 1889 was their first, but Margaret's record of difficulties suggests a lack of experience with such equipment. Over the course of its first year one can clearly see why this technology was cursed as frequently as it was blessed.[10]

2 September 1889: Lew Emery called this eve to see about putting up a wind pump . . . *12 September* Lew Emery called this eve bargained of a wind wheel pump 25 ft of 1¼ inch drive pipe 150 feet of conducting pipe, three way force pump, point fan $100 . . . *24 September* got a letter from L.J. Emery wanting to dig the well next Monday . . . *28 September* Jerry went to the Depot got well pipe and tools . . . *30 September* Jerry met the well digger at the train, they drove down about 20 feet, broke the pipe four or five feet below the ground, have not succeeded in getting it out . . . *1 October* The men with Mr Wilcox worked at the well all day did not succeed in getting water yet, Mr Wilcox went home this evening . . . *3 October* measured the water in the well pipe 6 ft 6 in . . . *4 October* Lew Emery & Mr Torrence called here will come Monday to fix the well . . . *5 October* Jerry got the wind engine and Derrick at the depot this P.M. . . . *7 October* Cal, Wilcox and Jerry worked at the well pipe all forenoon, failed to move it, tried it again with chains, broke one large ring then quit. concluded to set up the wind wheel at the barn well . . . *8 October* the men walled the well and laid the platform this forenoon . . . *14 October* The well men Lewis Emery, Mr Torrence and Charlie worked all day at the derrick got it up this evening. Mr Emery went home . . . *15 October* the men finished the windmill this evening went home on the eve train to Bellecentre. the new pump works very well.

The men enjoyed the luxury of water being pumped for the livestock and Margaret benefited from a new water tank in the kitchen, but the equipment's vulnerability soon became apparent. The windmill reappeared frequently in Margaret's diaries with one problem after another.

3 February 1890: Lew Emery looked at the Wheel found a casting cracked . . . *28 March* An exceedingly stormy day, very high winds, rained, thundered & lightning with wind all night, this forenoon turned to snow, colder now, froze and still snowing. the storm is general reports from different places of great destruction of life and of property. Our wind wheel is again broken . . . *8 April* Mr Torrence and G.H. Poe of Kenton put up an entirely new mill on the pump. Jerry went to the depot this P.M. for the mill. they finished it in time to take the evening train for the north . . . *9 April* very windy, exceedingly stormy night, a great deal of thunder, sharp lightning, quite a hail storm about half past 11 Oclock, hail stones as large as hickory nuts, some places larger, did considerable damage to windows, broke five panes for Krouses, 25 for John Canby injured the Green houses. the wind blew down the wheel breaking it badly also the castings . . . *11 April* G.H. Poe was here looking at the broken wind wheel, was here for supper, Jerry took him to the Depot for the evening train. said they would put up a new mill as soon as possible . . . *26 May* Jerry wrote to Emery & Co why the delay in fixing the wheel . . . *27 May* received an answer from Emery & Co expect to fix it next week . . . *31 May* Mr Poe of Kenton put up a new wind mill, Elmer helped him, paid him 60 cts, Freight on wind wheel 25 cts

10–11 October 1890: Mr Mussulman with the help of Jerry, Orra and Cal took up the pipe in the well took off the old point it having no screen, it pumped up so much gravel that caused it to leak badly, giving a great deal of trouble, put on a point with a screen, took all day to do it . . . paid Mussulman for fixing pump and pipe $4.45

The wind wheel continued to be a problem, but it was such a labor-saving device it was worth the attention it demanded. Margaret's diaries reflect growing ability among the Gebby men to make their own repairs as they did with other farm equipment.

18 November 1892: The high wind broke a casting of the wheel . . . *19 November* Ordered a casting for the broken wheel from Kenton . . . *21 November* took the broken castings to the bridge shop for repairs[11] . . . *22 November* Jerry got the pump repairs at the Buchannon Bridge Co. shop $1.25, put it on this evening does very well, it is made of malleable Iron will not break . . . *23 November* Jerry sent a dispatch to Kenton this morning countermanding the order for a casting for the wind wheel.

29 January 1893: The wire that holds the wind wheel broke last night. Orra had to repair it this morning had nothing to keep it from pumping.

24 February 1896: Jerry & Orra went to Frank Culps to see a wind wheel belonging to John March he wanted to sell it. Jerry bought the whole outfit wheel, derrick & tank for $40.00, delivered & put up at the farm.

Now the Gebbys had windmills for pumping water at both sets of buildings. They apparently valued the equipment despite its problems and now had enough confidence in their ability to bargain for used equipment.

HIRED MEN

Young men who wanted to get started in farming but were not in position to inherit a farm often began working as hired hands. During the period covered by Margaret's diaries the Gebby hired man was Cal Murdock from 1886–90; Bob Wallace, 1891–93; and Bob's brother Wellington Wallace, 1893–96. In some communities the contract for farmhands was renewed annually in the spring, but on the Gebby farm and probably in this geographic area changes occurred after harvest. December 1 was standard with Cal Murdock, but when he was able to purchase a farm he was released early and the contract with each of the Wallace brothers renewed annually the first of November. Payment remained the same throughout this period at $20.00 per month plus a house for his family and space to raise a garden and keep chickens, pigs, and milk cow.[12] Money was often paid in quarterly installments with adjustments for any purchases such as beef or flour on the Gebby account. Like family members the hired man worked long hours six days per week and fed livestock as needed on Sunday. But there was time off for emergencies or special occasions, and like family members, the hired man might go hunting or fishing when work was slack. The relationship between the family and the hired man was a business agreement, but it was also a friendship, distinctly closer than the relationship with seasonal hands hired to make hay or cut corn.

30 November 1886: Jerry and Cal settled today, Jerry owing him $116.25 cts paid $16.25 gave check for $100 in four months 8 pr cts[13]

1 December 1888: Jerry settled with Cal for this years work paid him $137.68

2 December 1889: paid Cal Murdock for the year $209.05

19 September 1890: Mrs McCormack and a Mrs Salsberry called to

see Cal about buying his Aunts property . . . *22 September* this P.M. Jerry went to C.C. Cooks looking for some one to take Cals place, Sallie and Mont Murdock was here this P.M. . . . *23 September* Jerry and I went to Cherokee this eve, saw Jim Horner about taking Cals place when he leaves, got home about nine Oclock . . . *7 October* Jerry went to Mr Dennys to see about a hand to take Cals place when he leaves. he then went to see a Bob Miller who lives north of the Reservoir took dinner with him. he is to decide in a few days . . . *16 October* Jerry settled with Cal for 10½ months work ($206) deducting $4 for Beef, he expects to prepare for moving in about two weeks . . . *31 October* Grandma and I called at Cals this afternoon . . . *1 November* Cal here for dinner . . . *4 November* Cal moving to the farm of Joe Wallace. J. Longfellow, Dave Kaylor, Andy Koons, and Lon Robeson helped. Bob Wallace of Stokes Tp. moved into the house this afternoon . . . *5 November* Orra was at the farm this morning saw Bob, intends to begin working tomorrow, he went to town got a cupboard, hauled firewood . . . *6 November* Orra and Bob husked corn.

8–9 June 1891: Cal Murdock & family are visiting with us to night . . . Jerry & Cal Murdock walked around here then drove to the pasture this A.M. Cal & family went home about 2 Oclock

30 May 1893: Orra went to Cal Murdocks this P.M. on the wheel . . . *9 June* Grandma, Jerry and I visited at Cal Murdocks to day.

20 October 1893: Jerry settled with Bob paid him $80.00 all he owed him . . . *25 October* Bob moved to their farm in Stoke Tp to day. his brother Wellington works for us in his place. he moved yesterday

30 October 1894: Wellie and Jerry settled this afternoon paid him $16.60 cts what was due him October 26, has paid him for the year $240

17 August 1896: Wellie gave notice of his intention to leave when his time expires . . . *4 November* Wellie moved to day to Dennis Dennys farm in Stokes Township. his brothers brought their wagons and hauled his goods for him had three loads.

The hired men appear to be recruiting their own replacements, so one can assume that the Gebby farm offered a comparatively desirable situation in terms of salary and living and working conditions. The Murdock's overnight visit the summer after Cal left strongly suggests that he had developed a proprietary interest in the productivity of this farm and was interested in seeing how it was doing without him.

FARM CHORES

Although planting and harvest required the heaviest commitment of farm labor, routine farm work went on all year. Margaret's diaries reveal an interesting process as her husband focused more and more on farm management as their sons assumed more and more of the physical labor. The pattern is quite similar to what one expects in an organized apprentice program.

Maintaining and repairing buildings and equipment was usually worked in between more pressing jobs, but emergencies required immediate attention. One of the most time-consuming tasks a century ago, when most fields were fenced to confine livestock, was the building and repair of fences. During these years the Gebby property used rail, barbed wire, and board fences simultaneously. Rails were gradually yielding to the utility of barbed wire, and board fences were preferred where appearances mattered or horses were confined.

Rail fences were used because they were inexpensive on a farm that still had timber. They could quickly be erected for temporary pasture without digging postholes, but they were vulnerable to storms, fires, and shoving cattle. Barbed wire was effective for cattle but did not hold hogs or horses. Board fences required milled lumber but were considered more attractive along the road and around farm buildings. By law line fences between two different owners were jointly maintained so neighbors had to agree on the type of fence to be constructed. Margaret's reference to the improved appearance wrought by new fences and the use of barbed wire around the back sides of a pasture and board fence along the pike suggests that fences were criteria by which a "good" farmer was judged.

11 February 1887: Very windy blew down a great deal of fencing on the farm . . . 12 February Jerry, Orra & Cal put up fence that had been blown down by the wind . . . 15 February Jerry & Cal hauled a load of hay and built up the fence next McAras which was blown down Friday . . . 17 February Jerry & Cal built fence all afternoon . . . 21 February The wind having blown the lane fence down and the lane almost impassable they threw the rails over in the mud making a dry track in the fence row . . . 24 March Jerry and Cal commenced plowing sod, Jerry built fence (Cantwells line) but the high winds this eve blew it down again

27 July 1887: Jerry took Mr. Krouse to the ditch to dig post holes being too warm he only dug one hole came home . . . 1 August George

and Curt Krouse this P.M. dug nine post holes began raining . . . *2 August* the men hauled two loads of lumber from the mill to the Miller land for the fence along the Liberty pike . . . *3 August* Orra hauled a load of posts to the Miller land, Jerry & Cal set posts at the ditch this forenoon, Orra & Cal finished this afternoon, George & Curt Krouse finished the post holes and split posts today . . . *4 August* Jerry, Orra & Cal cleaned the mouth of the ditch on the pasture and drove stakes for post holes along the Liberty pike . . . *5 August* went to town got keg of nails and barbed wire $6.00 . . . *6 August* Jerry and Cal worked the fence at the ditch . . . *13 August* paid George Krouse $5.70 . . . *20 August* Jerry went to the pasture hauled a load of posts for the Liberty pike fence . . . *21 August* Jerry and the boys took a load of ties to the Liberty pike fence . . . *29 August* Jerry and Elmer took two loads of fencing to the Liberty pike fencing

22–24 September 1890: A beautiful day, the men finished seeding here at noon, this afternoon Orra and Cal brought a load of rails from the pasture to fence off the hill, then pasture the field . . . Orra and Cal hauled two loads of rails each from the pasture to the farm . . . Orra and Cal hauled a load of rails from the pasture to the farm then built fence along the gravel bank and cut docks. Jerry laid the fence worm[14]

11–13 September 1892: the fence between us and Cotters was set afire by the cars, burned several rods of it before we got home from church. we soon got it checked . . . The section boss called this P.M. with regard to settling for the fence burned by the railroad yesterday . . . The Section boss called with blank to fill for the burnt fence. Jerrys bill was $10.00

15 April 1893: Bob went to town got Barbed wire for fencing paid $12.00 . . . *18 May* The men worked on the fence between our line & Cantwells, Orra and Bob dug 51 post holes set the posts, put on two strands of wire. Jerry was at town got 200 lbs of wire, didn't pay for it. Jerry & George hauled the posts, hauled away the old rails . . . *20 May* paid hardware bill (barbed wire) $7.03 . . . *31 July–3 August* Orra and Bob finished hauling manure here this forenoon hauled at the farm this afternoon. they had to put out fire in the fence caught from the railroad. hauled a load of rails and repaired the fence. Mrs Wallace told them the horses and their cow had been in McAras corn last night, but were out this morning. Jerry was at the pasture this forenoon salted the cattle, they were all right. this evening Mr Windsor came saying they had got out and had been in his corn wanted $50.00 damage. a number of misfortunes for one day . . . Jerry was at the pasture settled with Windsor for the corn the cattle destroyed yesterday $7.00 Bob took down 27 fencing boards, he and Orra repaired fence. Jerry bought a roll of barbed wire $3.85 put it on the east and north sides of the field east of Bobs house. the horses will break into Dan McAras corn . . . Jerry and the boys went to the pasture put wire across the northwest and southwest corners of the pasture to keep the cattle from jamming against the fence and getting into mischief . . . *23–24 October* Elmer tore down the fence between the yard and the barnyard, then he and Orra reset the posts and made a new fence, did not get quite done . . . the boys finished the fence, cleaned up the barnyard, improving the appearance of things very much.

29 August 1894: Jerry saw Mrs Cotter got her to sign an agreement allowing him to use barbed wire on the line fence

3–5 August 1895: Orra and George was at the sawmill got a load of fencing boards . . . the men repaired the fence on the west side of the orchard and put a new fence across the north side. looks much better than it did.

The glaciated terrain west of Bellefontaine where the Gebby farm was located was naturally marshy in spots, and much of it had required tile drainage when settlers began clearing it for cropland. The fields that had been tiled required occasional additions or replacements, but the installation of a new drainage system when the pasture land was purchased gives a picture of the process with nineteenth-century technology. Margaret's records suggest that it cost $92.65 to survey, buy tile, dig ditch, and lay tile for 168½ rods of ditch or fifty-five cents per rod.

1–3 October 1887: Jerry & Orra went for tile this morning got two loads of tile got home about three Oclock . . . Orra went to the tile mill got a load of tile

8–25 October 1890: Orra and Cal hauled tile to the pasture, Cal hauled three loads and Orra two, 88½ rods . . . Orra and Cal hauled two loads each of tile, two of five inch and two of 6 inch, 54 rods in all, Jerry was at the pasture nearly all day . . . Orra & Cal went to Gretna for tile (25 rods) took them to the pasture. Jerry settled with Huffman for tile $32.65 . . . Jerry and Orra took the Surveyor (Ginn) to the pasture leveled the ditch, paid him $5.00 . . . Jerry went to the pasture saw the ditchers, they have to put a board under the tile in the prairie where it is soft . . . Jerry and Orra finished their part of the Cotter fence except the top riders, they went with Lon and George Harner to measure the depth ditch being dug by Pattons, accepted six divisions . . . Jerry & Elmer measured ditches, one 83½ rods other 85 rods, Paid H.J. Paterson $30.00 and Geo. Krouse $25.00

On a crop and livestock farm the manure that accumulated in the barns over winter was the source of fertilizer for cropland. Unfortunately, it needed to be hauled out to the field after hay and wheat had been harvested. The hard labor of pitching manure by hand from barn to wagon and then from wagon to field must have been exceedingly disagreeable with the smell generated by the heat of an August day. One needs only a brief description of this annual event to picture the scope of the daily effort and the annual job.

17–22 August 1892: the men hauled 35 loads of manure today, used two wagons . . . Orra, George & Bob hauled 29 loads of manure . . . the men finished hauling manure here this forenoon, in all 104 loads . . . the men began hauling manure at the farm this morning, hauled 27 loads.

16 August 1893: finished hauling manure 250 loads altogether

Hauling manure was routine and nearly identical year after year, but many farm jobs got done as needed when time and talent were available. Some entries give clear vignettes of daily chores in the Gebby household, confirming the folklore that the work of farmer and housewife is never done.

21–26 July 1890: Orra helped Dillons thrash. Jerry went to the sawmill got enough hard pine lumber for a floor in the wagon bed, paid $1.25. Elmer helped put it in. Elmer cut the docks in the orchard, burned caterpillars on the walnut trees. [I] baked bread, a green apple pie, and a roll cake, washed sunbonnets, swept the cellar . . . Orra cutting briers & weeds along the fence, Elmer painting the yard fence . . . Elmer painting the wood house.

31 July 1891: Orra, Elmer & Bob cut thistles at the pasture all day

20 February 1893: Orra and Bob threw down the dangerous part of the straw stack at the farm then sawed wood the rest of the day.

13 February 1896: Orra & George took a load of hay (2930 lbs) to Robeson bros $21.97, bought a plow paid $15.55. Jerry took 4 plowshares to the shop for repairs . . . 16 March Snowed again last night. George fixed the tank faucet, oiled the wheel & cleaned his gun with other things.

CROPS

———————✦———————

PLANTING AND HARVEST

T hose who have not relied upon their ability to produce food, either enough for personal use or as a medium of exchange for economic survival, may find it impossible to fully understand the sense of urgency associated with the annual rhythms of planting and harvest. In spite of technological innovations, modern farmers encounter many of the same uncertainties of climate as their predecessors a century ago. But many Americans now take centrally heated and air-conditioned living and working environments for granted. Today, weather is a concern only when it threatens the extreme danger of tornado or blizzard, or the inconvenience of rain on a weekend golf game or picnic. But careful reading of these diaries over a period of years reveals the constant challenge of wet or cold weather, which delays planting or kills seedlings, heat and drought, which gradually turns promise to despair, or a capricious hailstorm, which in moments destroys one crop while leaving others nearby untouched.

Ohio is on the eastern edge of that vast midwestern richness described as the Corn Belt. On the Gebby farm, like most of its neighbors late in the nineteenth century, farmers believed they received the best economic return by feeding their corn to livestock and marketing fat cattle and hogs. Enlightened farmers of the period were using a three- or four-year crop rotation of corn, grain, and meadow. This practice spread their labor-intensive jobs, provided a wheat cash crop that simultaneously allowed them to seed their timothy/clover meadow, while the meadow provided hay for winter feed before being plowed down to enrich the corn ground.[1] The rhythms of planting and harvest

31

began each spring as soon as it was warm enough and dry enough to begin plowing the fields for corn.

During the decade covered by these diaries, the owner-operator of this farm gradually assumed more management roles as his sons did more of the physical labor. An interesting pattern of apprenticeship is revealed as the boys began riding the planter to drop seed and progressed to more difficult tasks such as plowing sod. By the time he was married the oldest son was clearly established in the decision-making as well as the operating phases of the farm enterprise. Technological innovations such as the check-row planter and the corn-cutting sled were his to master and operate.[2]

Major equipment purchased on this farm during this period to improve corn planting and harvest were a surrey plow, a check-row corn planter, and a corn-cutting sled—equipment widely owned by progressive farmers of the day.[3] Hay harvest was expedited with the addition of a new rake and hay loader, and the market expanded with the purchase of a horse-powered hay baler.[4] The harvest of wheat and oats utilized a reaper that tied sheaves automatically and a neighborhood threshing ring with a steam-powered machine.[5]

The gradual progress that equipped each generation to produce more with less time and labor began well before the 1880s, but spotlighting a single farm during a specific time span illuminates the process that changed American agriculture from units producing for self-sufficiency to units competing for commercial viability.

CORN

The Gebby farm required the full-time labor of two men plus seasonal help from the boys and extra hands hired for harvest. At fifteen the oldest son quit school for the season in time to do the plowing and planting work of a man. Completion of corn planting by mid-May and final cultivation by mid-June was about average for this farm. A detailed look at one year's entries illustrates this process.

Twentieth-century farmers with huge tractors and multibottom plows turn soil with incredible speed, but they forfeit days to rainy weather, which was no problem to the Gebby men, who were often in the field behind the team and single-point plow almost as soon as the rain stopped. Plowing sod was hard physical labor, and in 1886 Orra's slow recovery from mumps increased the time his father spent at this task and perhaps influenced Jerry's decision to purchase a Gilpin plow before the job was done.[6] Until this time the farm had probably used only walking plows for breaking sod.

13 April–12 May 1886: Very pleasant and warm Orra and Jerry plowing sod, [*last year's meadow*] Cal plowing on the farm . . . Jerry and Orra plowed sod this forenoon and this afternoon finished plowing and harrowed and sowed the oats . . . Orra plowed sod, Cal plowing on the farm . . . Orra plowed nearly all day, planted some potatoes this evening . . . Jerry went to the farm rolled the logs to the mill, Orra plowed . . . Orra not well [*recovering from mumps*] Jerry plowed this afternoon . . . Jerry plowed, Orra still sick . . . Jerry finished plowing here, plowed the garden in the afternoon . . . Jerry plowed on the farm and cultivated at home this P.M. . . . Jerry finished cultivating field one way this morning, bought a Gilpin plow $42.00 . . . Cultivating and rolling corn ground. Jerry went to the farm and set up the new plow . . . Orra cultivated at the other place . . . Orra worked till noon at the farm then plowed the Briar patch . . . Orra harrowed here this forenoon then at the farm in the afternoon. Jerry and Elmer shelled corn. Mr. Hill wanted to get some seed corn . . . Raining this morning. Jerry and the boys finished shelling seed corn, planted the eight acres at home, ground in nice order, raining again this evening . . . Orra and Cal cultivated this forenoon, began planting about 3 Oclock . . . Jerry and Cal planted corn till noon, Cal and Orra harrowed in other part of field . . . Jerry planted corn this afternoon on the farm . . . Jerry and Orra plowed and harrowed and planted potatoes in the barnyard at the farm the corn land being too wet . . . Rained last night but clear today, the men fixed barn doors and repaired fence this A.M., planted corn this P.M. . . . Jerry, Orra and Cal worked on the farm this afternoon planting corn &c, George was with them.

The amount of corn that had to be replanted in 1886 was unusual. Margaret recorded a heavy frost the last week in May and perhaps it was the cold, wet weather that hindered germination. However, farmers of that period selected their seed corn from the previous year's crop, and germination problems were frequent. Cultivating corn to control weeds certainly required much time and labor by the standards of those who currently do the entire job with herbicides. The hired man was very likely doing cultivating that did not get recorded in Margaret's diary, but it seems clear that the corn was plowed at least three times before it was "laid by" and the men began making hay.

21 May–18 June 1886: Jerry cultivated corn, Orra and Cal replanted . . . Jerry cultivated corn . . . Jerry and Orra at the farm found that part of the seed corn did not grow had to plant it over again, got a bushel of seed corn at Mr Neers, bought a new corn plow [*cultivator*] $21.00 . . . Orra plowed corn . . . Orra and Cal replanting corn, Jerry cultivating . . . Orra and Cal replanting corn. Jerry plowed in the forenoon . . . Orra and Cal plowing corn . . . Jerry and Orra plowed the garden this forenoon. Orra plowed corn this afternoon . . . Orra and Cal plowing corn . . . Too wet to plow corn, Jerry and Orra picked cherries this forenoon, plowed corn in the afternoon . . . Orra plowed corn, plowed garden this evening . . . Orra plowing on the farm . . . Orra plowed corn this A.M., mowed clover this P.M.

Corn harvest also required hard physical labor, and it had to be accomplished as quickly as possible so wheat could be seeded and make sufficient growth before the onset of the Ohio winter.

This farm was still cutting by hand in 1886, and it was backbreaking labor for a man to walk the row gathering stalks in his arm as he used his other hand to slash each stalk near the ground with his sharp corn knife. There was some advantage in beginning as soon as the ears were mature and accomplishing as much as possible before the leaves dried and became as sharp as knife edges.

Margaret does not record how many acres were harvested nor total how many shocks were cut, but it appears an average crop must have required approximately thirty man-days of labor to cut, with the men hired to help paid about ten cents per shock.[7]

But harvest work was far from over when the stalks were cut and shocked. The men hauled cornshocks to the barn all winter as weather permitted. There they could be husked as needed or, if necessary, fed as fodder and the cattle allowed to find the ears themselves.[8]

7 September–4 October 1886: Jerry and Orra tied gallouses for corn cutting[9] . . . Jerry & Orra worked at the farm tying corn, went to D. Langers and Jim Workers for seed wheat . . . Jerry went to town got two balls of twine to tie corn shocks. Jim Coon, Tink Dillon, Scott Kaylor, Ed Foote, two of the Blackwoods and Holland were all cutting corn today . . . Jim Coen, Link & Orra Dillon, three Blackwoods and Scott Kaylor finished cutting corn here, paid Blackwoods $5.40, Orra harrowed and rolled at the farm, Cal drilled . . . paid Holland $4.41 for cutting corn, finished drilling wheat at the farm at noon, began here this afternoon, had to quit on account of rain . . . Orra cut corn all day, Cal drilled the cornfield, not quite done . . . Orra cut corn all day (19 shocks) Cal made their apple butter this A.M. cut corn this P.M. . . . Orra & Cal cut corn all day. Jerry, Elmer & George cut corn this afternoon, in all 55 shocks . . . men cut 26 shocks of corn in the afternoon . . . the men all cutting corn today in all 55 shocks . . . men cut 12 shocks of corn until it rained . . . Orra and Cal finished cutting corn today. . . . *11 November* Jerry hauled down shocks of corn into the barn all day (38 shocks)

21 January 1887: Jerry & Cal hauled nine shocks of corn at the farm leaving 473 shocks still in the field.

Corn harvest was obviously a task deserving mechanical assistance as rapidly as possible. An Ohioan named Peterson had, in fact, patented a corn-cutting sled that same year and was soon experimenting with improvements in the Bellefontaine area. The Gebbys tried it but waited two years to purchase.[10]

29 August 1887: Jerry hauled out the cutting corn machine for Canby to try it in Segmans corn, says it will work in large standing corn . . . *8 September* The men cut corn to day 55 shocks, Jerry was at town this P.M. and ordered a corn cutter on trial tomorrow . . . *9 September* The men cut with the corn cutter cut 60 shocks but did not altogether suit, took it back this evening.

26 August 1889: Bought a corn cutter $25 to pay for it with hay 2½ tons . . . *10–26 September* The men cut 92 shocks of corn to day with the corn cutter . . . Cal and the boys cut corn 97 shocks . . . Cal drilled [*wheat*] at the farm . . . Orra & Elmer cut 66 shocks of corn . . . too wet to cut corn this forenoon, Orra and Cal cut by hand this P.M. 21 shocks . . . Orra and Cal cut 102 shocks of corn, Elmer and Jerry cut middles and tied some . . . Jerry drilling, Elmer tramping weeds, George harrowing, Orra and Cal cut corn east of the house, 91 shocks . . . Orra and Cal cut 95 shocks, Jerry and Elmer drilled and harrowed in the field east of the house . . . Orra and Cal cut 98 shocks, Jerry and Elmer finished drilling at the farm this evening . . . Orra & Cal cut 98 shocks, Elmer, Jerry & George cleaned up, drilled and harrowed . . . finished cutting corn and seeding for this year.

Without knowing the acreage involved it is difficult to evaluate, but enough corn was cut to form nearly 800 shocks and the ground worked and seeded to wheat in two weeks without hiring outside labor. Compared to the $24.50 paid to four men to cut corn in 1888, the first season with the $25.00 corn sled appears to have been an outstanding economic success.[11] *There was still handwork to be done in tying gallus centers,* *cleaning up fallen stalks, and tying finished shocks. It is unlikely that sales agents ever dwelt on the problems caused by wind or rain.*

5–12 September 1892: The men worked in the cornfield today. Orra & Bob cut with the sled and Old Charley [*horse*] 75 shocks of corn. Jerry bought a muzzle for the horse and a rope to tie the shocks . . . Orra and Bob cut 130 shocks of corn to day. Elmer and Jerry tied the shocks . . . Orra and Bob cut 133 shocks of corn to day in the field north of the orchard . . . Orra and Bob cut 49 shocks by hand, the rain yesterday softened the ground so that the wind blew down the corn so badly they could not use the sled.

It is not surprising that a housewife would not describe the farm equipment in detail in her diary, but over the years as new purchases were made one gains a perspective of the equipment needed to keep at least three men working most days during planting and harvest.

7 February 1890: Jerry went to town bought two new plows (Sidney) ($26)
23 February 1891: Jerry took three plows to the shop for repairs, preparing for spring plowing. . . . *15 April* Jerry got a Disc harrow tried it a while, think it will work . . . *22 April* Jerry paid for the disc harrow $24.00. . . . *4 May* Orra harrowed with the disc, Bob with the drag harrow, Jerry rolled. . . . *12 May* Orra and Bob finished planting corn this forenoon, took the implements to the machine house at the farm. . . . *18 May* bought a corn plow from J. Canby $25.00
4 April 1893: Orra commenced plowing sod this afternoon, uses the riding plow, has Bill, Selim and Fan for a team.
1–10 May 1894: The men commenced planting corn this P.M. in the field east of the house. Jerry drove, Orra dropped, Wellie harrowed in the other field . . . Orra and Wellie finished planting corn this forenoon, Jerry and George finished planting the lot this morning which closes up the planting for 1894.

It seems clear the Gebbys were still using a corn planter that was some modification of the Brown two-row model. This required a driver and a boy to trip the seed release at appropriate intervals. As the boys grew up and cultivated acreage was expanded, the oldest son was evidently anxious to try an automatic check-row planter, which had been on the market for a number of years.

27 March–9 May 1896: Jerry bought a corn planter ($45 with $5 for the old one) . . . Orra commenced plowing the prairie this morning. Jerry & George helping pry up stumps and stones, haul them off the ground they expect to plow . . . Orra, Wellie and George finished hauling stumps and stones off the field they are plowing. Jerry plowed this afternoon, he is very tired . . . Orra and Wellie plowed in the prairie all day. Jerry has not been well all day, overworked himself yesterday . . . George and Wellie finished plowing for this spring brought the plows in and put them away . . . Orra and Wellie worked here preparing for planting corn, Jerry brought out the check rower bought some time ago. Jerry and George shelled the seed corn . . . Orra planted corn with the new planter, a check rower, got along tolerably well, does not understand how to work it yet . . . Jerry got some more chain for the corn planter, the field is so large had not enough chain[12] . . . the men working at the farm, Wellie harrowing, George rolling and Orra driving the planter, got over half done with the field.

9 September 1896: The men finished cutting corn for 1896, they have nearly 1400 shocks.

HAY

Depending on the weather, there came a point about mid-June when the corn was "laid by" and everyone turned to making hay, which was interrupted only by harvesting wheat. In the 1880s this required much hand labor and extra men were hired by the day.

17 June–9 July 1886: Orra plowed corn this forenoon, mowed clover this afternoon . . . Orra plowed and mowed clover again today Jerry used the tedder this afternoon . . . Too wet to haul this forenoon hauled seven loads this P.M. George Wallace helping . . . The men are scattering and hauling hay this afternoon. Rained about 4 Oclock and stopped them left out 3 loads of hay . . . Finished hauling hay at the farm at noon, Jerry mowed some at home hauled some hay this P.M. Wallace and Cal here for supper . . . Jerry mowed this forenoon, the rest hauled what hay was ready, paid George Wallace for work $3.15 . . . the men hauled hay, mowed and raked all day, all very busy with the hay, George Wallace and Cal was here for dinner and supper . . . Jerry mowed some this forenoon, broke some guards took them to the shop for repairs paid $1.00, hauled ten loads of hay, it being in nice order. George Wallace and Cal here for dinner & supper . . . *30*

June Working and hauling this forenoon, paid George Wallace $3.75 . . . *7 July* finished cutting wheat this forenoon, cut hay till supper . . . the men worked in the meadow hauled seven loads of hay into the barn . . . still dry and warm, finished the hay this evening.

Considering the importance of hay being well dried before it was stored in the barn, it is significant that this family did no fieldwork on the Sabbath even though that might be the only sunny day during a rainy week. It is also interesting to note that wheat harvest had priority over hay even though the hay crop might require only another two or three days. Year after year, this farm interrupted hay making to cut and shock the wheat when it reached its prime.[13]

The size of the hay crop may have been related to the capacity of the barns for it seems remarkably consistent from year to year in spite of varied weather conditions for growth.

12 July 1890: finished the hay for 1890, in all 110 loads without getting wet.

20 July 1891: the men finished their hay hauled in 6 loads today making in all 100 loads.

23 July 1892: The men finished the hay, hauled in 9 loads making 104 loads in all.

18 July 1893: the men finished the hay today hauled in nine loads making in all 102 loads.

This was obviously more hay than the farm needed for its own livestock, and Margaret recorded regular hay sales around the neighborhood. Late in 1887 the price was evidently eleven dollars per ton picked up and twelve dollars delivered, and an average wagonload usually weighed something less than a ton.

1 November–30 December 1887: George Henderson got a load of hay this morning $9.63 . . . Robb got a load of hay pd $10.00 . . . sold 1080 lbs of hay $5.90 . . . sold two loads of hay to Henry Powell 3230 lbs at $11 pr ton $17.76 . . . Orra & Cal hauled a load, 2140 lbs, $12 pr ton to Hosaac Downs.

In 1886 the Gebbys were using a mower, a tedder, and a rake; probably a sulky-style spring tooth rake that allowed the operator to dump piles that would later be pitched by hand to the wagon. They clearly used a horse-drawn trip fork to carry hay from the wagon to the barn mow. During the decade Jerry purchased a new rake, probably one of the popular new side delivery models that made a neat row for an automatic loader, and a loader that delivered it to the wagon.[14] *Orra seems to have encouraged the latter purchase, small wonder when he and the hired man did most of the pitching from field to wagon. Such loaders had become commercially successful only recently, and as one of the first in the neighborhood, the Gebby loader attracted numerous visitors.*

14 June–12 July 1890: Jerry got his new hay rake home took it to the farm . . . Elmer put up the trip rope in the barn, the windpump men having taken it down . . . Jerry settled some bills, Hay Rake $19.00 . . . George rode the horse to unload the hay.[15]

23 April–30 June 1892: Orra went to Tommy Cooks on his wheel [*bicycle*] to see a hayloader . . . George Rife left a hayloader in the barn here this afternoon, The Rock Island . . . John Kiser & Tannehill with Jerrys help set up the hay loader . . . the men hauled in the hay 8 loads, used the loader, it does very well. George Rife was here to see it start . . . Father walked out here to see the hay loader work, also Jim Dow and others . . . John Williams & John Riddle was here this P.M. looking at the hay loader.

The economic depression of the 1890s evidently forced this farm to search farther away for hay markets. This made it necessary to bale leftover loose hay for shipping.

11–28 April 1894: Jerry was looking for hay balers, heard of them but did not see them . . . Jerry and I was at the Mathew Bros to see the Haybalers, they promised to come next Tuesday . . . [*Tuesday*] Jerry was at Degraff to see about the Balers did not get much satisfaction. Orra was looking up hay balers at Rushsylvania and vicinity could not get Royer Bros until Wednesday, then went to Huntsville to see a horsepower baler, said they could come on Monday . . . [*Monday*] Balers did not come as expected. Jerry went to Fickengers to see Hannahs they said they could not do it this week . . . 25 April The Hay balers came this evening very unlooked for, there are six of them . . . the men baled hay to day, Wellie and Orra helped them, we have 14 to cook for, we baked bread, pies and a cake, busy all day. they baled about 20 tons finished the west mow this forenoon . . . the balers finished the hay in the barn here at noon, had about 30 tons, moved to the farm baled about 7 tons this P.M. Jerry received a letter from Forest offering $8.50 for the hay . . . Hay balers finished at noon, left after dinner had 46 tons of hay, paid them $69.00, $1.50 pr ton with board.

The size of the work crew strongly suggests that this was a steam press baler. This was an expensive operation and Jerry evidently checked out every known baling crew within a ten-mile radius. This was clearly unsatisfactory and it became evident that Jerry must purchase a hay press of his own if he intended to continue shipping hay to eastern markets. Railroads had captured the agricultural freight business, and by the 1890s Ohio farmers had a wide range of market options.[16]

13–15 June 1894: the men hauled 4 loads of baled hay to the railroad, filled one car and put some in another . . . the men finished hauling hay, loaded 4 cars, billed to T.L. Todd, Richmond, Va. by the way of the Chesapeake & Ohio through Cincinnati.

25 February 1895: Jerry ordered a Hay baler from Ann Arbor, Mich.[17] . . . *18 March–27 April* Jerry was at town, came home reported the haybaler was at the depot. Wellie brought the team in. Jerry & Orra took the team and brought all to the barn. paid $13.20 for freight from Ann Arbor, Mich. 25 cts for freight for a bale tie machine . . . Orra, Jerry and Wellie make Bale ties, made about 1000. the agent came this eve to set up the Baler . . . the men worked at the Hay baler but did not get one bale finished till they broke a brace and sweeps, went to town got repairs but did not get anything done . . . the men baled hay got along very well. had no trouble baled 122 bales, Irvin Naugle helped this afternoon . . . the men baled hay, 144 bales. they got along very well, the agent John Christiansen went home to Ann Arbor this morning . . . the men baled hay this forenoon, 70 bales, made bale ties this P.M. Jerry attached a tongue to the power so as to be easier on the horses, tried it thinks it a great improvement, paid Irvin Naugle $2.00 for working at the hay . . . the men were baling hay, C. McClain helping them. got 130 bales about 6 tons, got along very well . . . the men baled hay, about 130 bales . . . the men baled hay got 120 bales. I helped Jerry make bale ties, George and Elmer helped this afternoon. Sent a draft to Ann Arbor, Mich. to pay for the baler $200.00 . . . the men began baling hay this morning but about 9 Oclock broke a large casting in the power, sent a telegram to Ann Arbor for another, 40 ct. Orra and Wellie made bale ties this afternoon . . . got the casting they sent for yesterday paid $1.45 expressage . . . the men repaired the broken hay press by 9 A.M. worked the rest of the day did not quite finish here, left a little in the mow. Wellie took the press to the farm this evening. Paid McLain $4.00 . . . the men took the rest of the press to the farm set it up and baled this afternoon . . . the men worked at the hay until after noon when they broke the same casting that broke before. Orra ordered another by telegram . . . Jerry got the casting at the express office paid

$1.80 for expressage . . . Orra & Wellie put the new casting in the Baler this afternoon it is ready for work again[18] . . . the men baled hay all day, commenced on the last mow . . . the men finished baling hay this afternoon, they had 1831 bales altogether, paid McClain $6.90 for help- ing. . . . *15 May* Phol the hay buyer was here this morning. . . . *18 June* Mr McKee was here this morning, offered $15.00 pr ton for the hay.

Margaret's record reveals several interesting facts. The sales agent came personally to set up this equipment. His arrival on the evening of 19 March and departure the morning of 22 March, clearly suggests he spent two full days working with the men to get the equipment operating and boarded for three nights at the Gebbys. The fact that they had the equipment ten days before sending payment suggests that it would have been returned had it proven unsatisfactory. A power casting that broke twice before baling 100 tons and a tongue that the crew lengthened to increase leverage suggests the equipment still needed design improve- ments. But the fact that word of a broken casting could be telegraphed from Bellefontaine, Ohio, to Ann Arbor, Michigan, and a replacement received by rail express the following day is a marvel even by current standards with computer-managed parts inventory.

Margaret's reference to making bale ties is the only time in eleven years that she indicates helping with farm work in any way. When the press was working they hired an extra man, suggesting that it required at least four men to operate—perhaps one with the horses, two pitching hay into the press, and one tying finished bales. The only diary reference to quantity cites 130 bales as about six tons, suggesting bales of at least one hundred pounds. This probably means the 1,831 bales completed during the first year they owned the hay press represented nearly ninety tons of leftover loose hay in the barn mows. If so, the meadows in the crop rotation were undoubtedly included for soil conservation or emer- gency pasture in drought, since they were producing far more hay than the farm livestock needed for winter feed.

CLOVERSEED

Modern farmers might be surprised that this farm only made one cutting of hay from the meadow during the growing season. Some of this was no doubt related to the labor involved, but a key factor was that the second growth was allowed to mature for cloverseed. What was a cash crop for this farm is one now handled completely by seed production specialists.

27 September–15 October 1886: the men set up the reaper preparatory to cutting clover seed . . . cut cloverseed this afternoon . . . Jerry mowed cloverseed, broke his machine spring, got it mended 15 cts . . . Jerry mowed clover seed all day . . . The men husking corn in the morning, then hauled clover seed the rest of the day . . . the men finished hauling clover seed . . . Rained considerable this morning the men went out to cover the clover seed stacks with fodder . . . Jerry and Orra uncovered the clover stacks this morning, the clover hullers came about three Oclock, got supper for the thrashers who all went home at night . . . they finished hulling clover this evening had 23 bushels & 8 lbs besides the screenings

Cloverseed was stored over winter to sell for the best price at spring planting time. The pattern remained the same throughout the decade and it is clear that other farmers in this neighborhood were also raising clover for seed. By changing screens the same equipment could be used for threshing wheat and hulling clover, and those who threshed at the barn in November frequently combined both jobs. The Gebbys saved their own seed, broadcasting it with a handseeder as soon as the ground thawed in the spring. Their surplus was sold for cash.

14 March 1887: Jerry & Cal took the cloverseed to town had 18 bush 24 lbs. at $4 pr bu $73.60.

27–28 September 1889: the boys and Cal worked at the clover seed, hauled in six loads into the barns . . . the men finished hauling clover seed, had 12 loads put it in the east mow unloaded with the hay fork.[19] . . . 10–11 October the clover hullers came this P.M. hulled 7 loads, 7 bu, Jim & Orra Cook, David McLeary were here for supper, baked five pumpkin pies, four apple pies and cake . . . finished hulling clover at the farm about four Oclock, had nearly 22 bushels, the machine moved to C.C.Cooks.[20] . . . 11–15 November the thrashers came unexpectedly Jim & Orra Cook & Andy Wallace were here for dinner, did not work any Jerry looking up his hands, got a load of coal for the engine. Jim & Orra here tonight, Andy went home . . . Thrashed at the farm finished about two Oclock had 411 bush. weighed 418 at Coltons Mill, 16 men ate dinner 11 supper, hulled 9 bushels of cloverseed, Martha Ann & Anna Robeson helped get dinner[21] . . . finished hulling clover seed, had 24 bush. had 8 men for dinner . . . Cal & Orra took the cloverseed to Kerrs warehouse, cleaned and stored 36 bu. 28 lbs. kept four sacks at home for seed.

1 February 1890: Jerry sold the clover seed, 36 bu 28 lbs at $3.10 pr bu. = $113.05 . . . *17–20 March* the men expected to sow clover seed but it was too windy . . . the men sowed clover seed this morning untill it got too muddy to walk . . . Jerry, Orra & Cal finished sowing clover seed this morning.

WHEAT

Winter wheat was the primary grain crop on this farm, although enough oats were grown to feed the horses and to grind with corn for the family milk cows and any hogs about to be butchered. The Gebbys were using a reaper to cut grain in the 1880s but the field had to be opened by hand, cutting with a cradle scythe. It took two men and two teenage boys two weeks to harvest this farm's grain, binding it by hand, shocking it in the field, and later pitching it into wagons to carry it to the barn where it was stacked for threshing.

30 June–16 July 1886: Went for the Reaper to cut wheat tomorrow. Cradled some in the field here this eve . . . Commenced cutting wheat this morning at home did not get quite done. Jerry & Elmer worked the reaper, Cal & Orra shocked . . . Finished cutting at home this morning went to the farm to work. The wheat is badly down, tedious cutting, broke a cog, sent to Springfield for another wheel[22] . . . Cutting wheat at Cals, finished the piece they were at yesterday, $1.75 for binder wheel . . . cutting wheat on the farm got along very well, finished the field went to the field between orchard and barn . . . still very warm and dry, cut wheat on the farm, finished all but a stumpy piece next the barn . . . finished cutting wheat this forenoon . . . finished hauling wheat at home . . . hauling wheat at the farm, took in the field between the orchard and the barn and two loads in the other, fifteen loads . . . hauled wheat all day, thirteen loads . . . finished hauling wheat this afternoon . . . Jerry paid George Shawoor $9.75 for binder twine . . . Cal cradled the oats this afternoon

Before it reached the threshing machine every sheaf had already been moved by hand at least four times. This farm belonged to a thresh-

ing ring that exchanged labor, some threshing in the field in August and others like the Gebbys threshing at the barn about November after the moisture content of the grain had declined.

Jerry delegated threshing ring assignments to the hired man and oldest son, and this neighborhood apparently had a simple system of exchanging a day's labor. If a farm sent two men, they received two in return. Margaret helped cook dinner only at the Aikins and the Robesons, and they were the same ones who helped her in return.

12 August–11 September 1886: Cal helped Neers thrash . . . Cal helping Andy Keener thresh . . . Cal helped David Kaylor thresh this P.M. . . . Cal helped Abednego Detrick thresh . . . Cal and Orra helped McAras thrash this afternoon . . . Cal helped Jim Working thresh . . . Orra helping George [*Aikin*] thrash . . . Orra, Cal and I helped G.W.Aikins thrash . . . Cal at P. Dows thrashing. . . . *2–6 November* Jerry went to the election this afternoon saw his hands to thrash tomorrow, set the machine in the barn on the farm. got coffee and tea 56 cts, cheese 48 cts, baked bread and pies, busy all day . . . Thrashed at the farm today had 576 bushels of wheat 19 men eat dinner about 10 or 12 for supper, Martha Ann helped all day . . . Finished thrashing here at noon about 18 men ate dinner had 142 bush. of wheat and 20 of oats, stored 106 bush 15 lbs in the warehouse and 47 bush 25 lbs in the mill for flour[23] . . . Jerry, Orra and Cal put the machinery back in the dry and fixed the strawstack . . . paid John Marsh for hulling clover & Thrashing wheat $39.21.

A few years later when Margaret's nephew ran a threshing machine the Gebbys moved this task to the summer, and the whole operation sounded like a family reunion. Perhaps they were anxious to catch the highest possible price before quantities of newly harvested wheat were delivered to market.

15 August–2 September 1891: Wheat is selling for $1.00 . . . Jerry went to see Jim Cook about threshing, he could not promise to come for two weeks yet, we came past G.W.Aikins to report arrangements . . . the boys hauled wood for the thrashers this P.M. . . . Orra and Bob helped McAras thrash, helped Robesons thrash this P.M. Grandma and I helped get supper and wash the dishes . . . Orra & Elmer helped Aikins thrash. Fred Dillon helped Peter Dow thrash for Jerry paid him 50 cts. I helped cook at Aikins got home in time to milk . . . Elmer & Bob thrashing at G.W.Aikins, finished about 4 Oclock then went to our place thrashed 52 bu wheat, wheat damp not in good condition. thrashers here to night, got ½ bush. Sweet Potatoes $1.00 . . . they thrashed 655 bushels of wheat had 21 men here for dinner 18 for supper, Mary Aikin, Anna & Lizzie Robeson helped us cook. Joe Horn brought roast for dinner. I got 6¼ lbs of steak for supper, baked bread, pies &c. the thrashers all here to night . . . finished thrashing had altogether 1085 bush 250 here and at the farm 835, averaging 28 bu to the acre & here 23 bu. had 164 bu. of oats. finished about 4 Oclock. Mary Aikin and Anna Robeson helped cook. George got some beef for dinner. gave Jim Cook a check for threshing $42.32.

This steam-powered machine obviously burned wood and required a crew of about twenty men. Margaret must have taken pride in the meal she laid out for the threshing crew since she bought fresh beef and sweet potatoes to accompany the homegrown potatoes and chickens the family regularly ate this time of year. She did not take time to itemize in her diary, but she certainly had several kinds of pie for both dinner and supper.

The Gebbys were clearly pleased with their 1891 yield, as well they might be. The Ohio average was only 17.5 bushels per acre.[24] By the time they finished threshing, wheat prices had dropped and much of the crop was stored to wait for higher prices. It was a decision as disastrous as some made by current investors in grain futures on the Chicago Board of Trade. Grain prices had begun a four-year slide, and like many others the Gebbys finally gave up and sold near the bottom.[25]

4 November 1892: Orra finished hauling the wheat to the mill making a total of 1974 ½ bushels stored in Coltons mill, the crops of 91 & 92.

20 May 1895: Jerry went to town had the wheat in Coltons mill insured for $1500, had to pay $40 for it

25 April 1896: Jerry sold the wheat he had in the Colton mill, 2630 bushels at 55 cts pr bu $1707.23, some of it had been there since 1891.

But like farmers long before and long after, the Gebbys maintained a spirit of hope that times would get better and an obstinate determination to keep on simply because they did not know what else to do. There was no government intervention to protect them from prices below the cost of production.

21 September 1896: Orra & Jerry finished drilling wheat for 1896. They sowed 60 bu of wheat to 32 acres.

LIVESTOCK

CATTLE

A s a percentage of farm income, cattle were the major enterprise on the Gebby farm. They specialized in finishing steers for market by purchasing yearlings rather than maintaining a breeding herd. In the early years of Margaret's diaries Jerry was buying cattle locally a few at a time. Gradually he progressed to buying at local auctions, and eventually to buying and shipping in cattle from the western plains. In similar manner he changed from selling to local cattle buyers and eliminated the middlemen by shipping directly to stockyards at Buffalo or Chicago.

Buying steers locally was time-consuming business, driving miles to locate and bargain for them, and then herding them home a few at a time. Buying range cattle, however, involved a trip to Chicago and gambling on what would be coming to market, or trusting a commission agent in regard to quality and price. Shipping cattle directly to market was even more challenging: deciding when cattle had reached the best weight to sell, ordering rail cars, feeding cattle enroute, and timing the journey to get cattle to market with minimum shrinkage.

16 June 1886: John Sloan and Mr. Hankinson of Roundhead was here for dinner. Mr. Hankinson bought 18 head of Jerry's cattle for 5 cts pr lb to be taken between now and the first of August . . . 23 July Mr. Hankinson and John Sloan came this eve to stay all night and get the cattle in morning . . . 24 July got up before 4 Oclock got breakfast for the men started for the cattle before five Oclock, cattle weighed 1460, came to $1286 after deducting $25, shipped them at Huntsville on the

nine Oclock train . . . *16 August* Jerry went down the Ludlow road to see some cattle but they did not suit him . . . *18 August* Went to Mrs Bonners in Shelby county, started at half past six this morning got there about eleven, called several places to see cattle, started for home at four arrived at 20 min till nine called again to see cattle but did not get any. Elmer & George kept house . . . *23 August* Jerry and Orra went to Roundhead and other places to look at cattle but did not get any . . . *24 August* Jerry and Orra went to Andy Wallaces to see some cattle, too large, looked at some others of the Pattersons but did not get any, then went to Bridgemans saw some more but did not buy . . . *26 August* Jerry and Orra went beyond Walnut Grove to see cattle but did not succeed in buying any . . . *27 August* Jerry went to George and Cris Culps to look at cattle but did not succeed in getting any . . . *28 August* Jerry, Elmer, and Georgie went to Ezra Hubers to look at cattle but did not buy. Jerry saw Gourley Patterson on the street and bought two steers from him $84.00 . . . *30 August* Jerry, Cal & Orra went to Gourly Pattersons got two steers paid $84.00 weighed 2210, in the afternoon they went east & southeast got one from Whitehill for $42.00 took him to the farm this evening . . . *31 August* Jerry and Orra went to John Mays this morning bought 8 head of steers from May and 2 from Foust . . . *1 September* Jerry & the boys went for the cattle averaged 1007 lbs costing $363.48. This afternoon he bought two from Scott east of town paid $70.00 . . . *4 September* Jerry, Cal and the boys went to Scotts brought home two steers one weighed 1100 other 850 . . . *6 September* Jerry and Orra went to Fusons & Mathews to look at cattle but did not get any. Hen McKinnon called to sell some cattle . . . *22 September* Jerry went to Bridgemans this morning bought five head of steers for $3.75 pr hhd . . . *24 September* got up at 4 Oclock Jerry, Orra & Cal went to Bridgemans, got five head of steers, paid $208.12.

19 September 1887: Jerry went to W. Liberty this morning to try to sell the cattle did not succeed yet . . . *20 September* Cal & Jerry fed the cattle this morning, Alf Miller & Muzzy were out looking at them this morning did not make an offer, then John Enochs was out he offered $4.25 for 32 head . . . *4 October* Jerry went to town ordered stock cars . . . *7 October* Cal & Jerry hauled sawdust to bed cattle cars this morning . . . *8 October* Jerry, Orra & Cal bedded two cattle cars this forenoon after dinner they took the cattle away, loaded them and started about 4 Oclock . . . *11 October* Jerry and Orra got home at two Oclock last night. Jerry sold 30 head of cattle weighing 1453 lbs for $4.65 and 8 averaging 1440 for $4.00 received $2363.14.

9 July 1888: Jerry and Orra were out looking for cattle bought eight head from John March for three cents a pound then they went to the western part of the county spent 40 cts in Logansville for crackers cheese and bologna got home between four and five Oclock . . . *10 July* the men went to the Kaufman pasture for cattle bought from John March, they averaged 732½ lbs at 3 cts pr lb = $175.80, took them to the Miller pasture, came home and ringed 21 pigs and 4 old sows . . . *27 July* Jerry bought four steers from Andy Koons average 870 lbs at 3¼ = $113 . . . *28 July* Jerry and Orra were out hunting cattle bought seven head near Quincy for $200 . . . *9 August* Jerry & Orra were out looking for cattle again today they were at Bowers & Oders, Shicks and other places but did not succeed in getting any took dinner at John Coffetts, got home about five Oclock . . . *4 September* Jerry, Orra and Cal went to Frank Smiths on the Ludlow road got eight cattle they averaged 881 lbs at $3.30 pr hhd. $232.60

2–3 January 1889: Jerry, Orra and Cal went to Milt Wolfs to look at cattle, bought 21 head for $600, Orra stayed all night . . . Jerry and Cal went to Milt Wolfs for the cattle bought yesterday, got home about four Oclock, weighed them after getting home, they averaged 967 lbs . . . *7 November* Jerry went to Bellecentre stock sale, bought 14 head of cattle paid $393.82 for 13, $27 for one, brought them as far as John Grimes pasture . . . *5 December* Jerry & Orra were at the Bellecentre stock sale bought nine steers $242.09, average weight 962 lbs, left them at Andy Wallaces

28 October 1890: Jerry weighed the cattle one load (18 head) averaged 1525 lbs the other (16 head) averaged 1435 . . . *29 October* Jerry was at town this afternoon, ordered cars to ship the cattle. took Mr Gest of Mount Tabor to see them, he only offered $3.80 pr hhd, Jerry asked 4 . . . *30 October* Jerry ordered another car for cattle . . . *31 October* Orra hauled a load of straw this P.M. to bed cars. Jerry and John Riddle looked at the cattle thought one load good enough for the Chicago market, they expect to ship two loads of cattle to Buffalo tomorrow, one to Chicago Tuesday . . . *1 November* Orra and Elmer brought the cattle from the pasture to the stock yards this morning. Jerry and Cal brought one load of those at the farm Shipped them to Buffalo after two Oclock. Orra went with them. Billy Clingerman also shipped a load, Riddle failed to get cars for his . . . *4 November* Orra got home from Buffalo at 8 Oclock this A.M. one load weighed 1381 sold for 4.15 the other averaged 1248 lbs sold for 3.70. Jerry bedded the car, brought in the cattle this P.M. left for Chicago with Ed Patterson and one load of his cattle at 10 Oclock this evening our cattle ave 1525 lbs Pattersons 1680 lbs . . . *6 November* Received a message from Jerry, he sold the cattle for 4½ with light shrink . . . *8 November* Jerry came home from Chicago this forenoon, sold his cattle for 4.50 pr hhd, averaged 1474 lbs draft on N.Y. for $1148.20

17 November 1890: Jerry was at town ordered a car load of cattle from Wood Bros of Chicago, sent a draft on New York for eight hundred dollars . . . *23 November* Received a letter from Chicago stating that they had bought & would ship a car load of cattle last eve. are expected to arrive at 12.30 . . . *24 November* the cattle bought in Chicago arrived this morning a little after one oclock. Jerry and the boys brought them home put them in the barnyard till daylight, then took them to the farm, all muleys 24 in number, weighed them this P.M. the freight and bedding from C. home was $33.00 the total cost $832.66

5 March 1891: 2 deg below zero this A.M. Jerry & I went to Belle-centre stock sale. took dinner at Dr Phillips saw the new daughter a nice babe. Nannie and I called at Cal Murdocks, met Andy & Alice Koonts, Arch & Emma Murdock. a great many horses, colts and cattle, also sheep were there for sale, but not many wanting to buy. a great many people were there. we went in the sleigh, the sleighing in the morning was excellent, but it thawed some during the day

13 January 1893: Very cold weather, 8 below A.M., 11 below P.M. Orra and Bob hauled two loads of hay to Mack Dickenson, almost too cold to work. Jerry received a telegram from Buffalo that the prospects for Mondays Cattle market was good . . . *18 January* Jerry ordered two Hicks cattle cars for Friday . . . *19 January* Orra and Jerry went to the farm and weighed the cattle, they averaged 1320 lbs . . . *21 January* the men drove up the cattle this forenoon to the stock yards. could not get them loaded untill about 4 Oclock the trains were all behind time. they left about 5 this evening . . . *24 January* received the returns of the sale of those shipped to Buffalo Saturday, 20 head sold for 4.70, 6 for 5.10, 14 for 4.655 making an average of 4.75, weight 1235 lbs expenses were freight $69.16, yardage $4.00, Hay $18.12, commission $20.00 making $111.28, leaving for Draft $2236.03.

12–16 January 1894: Orra and Wellie weighed the cattle before shipping tomorrow. they averaged over 1400 lbs . . . Orra and Wellie brought a load of bedding and the cattle. they loaded the cattle for the 1-30 train but the train over an hour late. they shipped two loads to Williamson & Co Buffalo . . . got the return from the cattle. met a very bad market. 240 cars at Buffalo. they sold for 4 cts pr lb, after deducting expenses had only $1932.90.

30 March–4 April 1895: Jerry got two drafts on N.Y. one for $900 & the other $800, expects to leave for Chicago Monday at 1.30 A.M. . . . Jerry left home for Chicago at 1 A.M. but found that the 1-15

train would not make connection at Indianapolis, he came back home untill this evening 6-15 train, expects to arrive in Chicago in the morning . . . Jerry got home on the 3.55 train. he was delayed by a derailed car. had to wait in Indianapolis. he bought 60 head of cattle at 3.50, they averaged about 700 lbs. Total cost $1558.36 (including freight $55.00) . . . The men went to the yard found the cattle cars at the Shoots, unloaded them and took them to the farm fed them hay, they are very tired.

10 August 1896: Jerry ordered a car of western cattle from Wood Bros. Chicago, sent a Draft on N.Y. for $900 . . . 3 September Jerry received a telegram from Wood Bros Chicago this evening that they had bought & shipped him a car load of cattle . . . 5 September The men went to the Depot got the cattle from Chicago. they being range cattle they were very wild and hard to manage. one got separated from the rest became unmanagable. Wellie and Edgar Aikin followed it to keep it from injuring people. Jerry, George & Orra took the others to the farm then came back took Jersey with them found the Steer in a barnyard on the Blue Jacket road.[1] they got them home about noon. they are quiet and eating tonight. they cost $3.40 pr hhd $808 with commission & other expenses. the freight was $30.90 . . . 5 October Jerry took John Riddle to the farm to see the range cattle he bought a few weeks ago . . . 8 October Jerry & T. Cook went to the farm to see the Range cattle . . . 21 October G.W. & M.A. Aikin was here for dinner, he and Jerry went to see the Range steers.

Margaret's financial records are enlightening, but they do not pro-vide sufficient detail to compute the Gebbys' return on labor. The agri-cultural depression during this period is clearly reflected in the fluctua-tions of both purchase and sale prices, dropping 20 percent to 30 percent between 1886 and 1890, but there were seasonal variations and this farm was buying and selling at different times, perhaps seeking some advan-tage by avoiding saturated markets. Over the years the difference be-tween buying and selling prices was relatively stable, bringing about one cent per pound for roughly a year of feed and care on the Gebby farm.

Compared to a modern cattle-feeding operation the weight gain was slow and the finished product was heavy. The Gebby cattle were on pasture sorted by weight from about the first of May until the first of November. They wintered in the barn and barnyard on hay and were usually fed corn only their final eight to ten weeks. This farm tried to finish steers over 1,400 pounds before marketing them, and only if they got above 1,500 were they considered worthy of the best-priced market in Chicago.

The clearest track on a single group of cattle in Margaret's diary is the group of twenty-four muleys bought in November 1890 for $800. She does not cite weight but if the price were about $3.50 per hundred pounds they probably averaged about 800 pounds. When turned onto pasture in April they averaged 1,067, were 1,330 when brought in to feed in mid-September, 1,418 six weeks later, and approximately 1,500 when shipped to market in mid-December 1891. This means they gained nearly 300 pounds over five winter months with hay, another 250 to 300 on five months of pasture, and a final 250 on three months of hay and corn. They were purchased at an average $34.30 each and sold on average for $55.80 netting the Gebby farm $21.50 per steer.[2] Since these cattle were sold in Chicago they were above average and probably reflect a good return compared to the average for this eleven-year period. One must consider this profit in relation to the constant care that was required in a livestock operation.

16 June 1887: We went to the pasture to salt the cattle, suppose they have got out, could not find them . . . *17 June* Orra & Elmer went to the Miller pasture to look up the cattle found them in Coopers pasture, repaired the fence . . . *16 July* Jerry, Cal & the boys took the big cattle over to the Miller pasture 48 head

1 May 1888: the men separated the cattle this afternoon, took 19 head down to the pasture their average weight was 1082 lbs, kept 19 at home average weight 1285, turned them on pasture

26 April 1890: Jerry and the boys went to the farm separated the cattle weighed them, one load averaged 1134 took them to the pasture, rained on them on the road, they were very wet, turned the other load out on the farm, they averaged 1313

14 April 1891: Quite warm, rained several showers, grass growing. Jerry and Orra went to the farm took 19 cattle to the pasture they averaged 1032 lbs, took a load of hay with them . . . *23 April* they separated and weighed the cattle, took the horned cattle to the pasture they averaged about 1200 lbs. left the Muleys at the farm their average weight was 1067, think the scales were not in good order . . . *15 September* they weighed the muleys. they averaged 1330 lbs . . . *2 November* the men weighed the muleys, 18 averaged 1475 lbs, 6 averaged 1270 lbs . . . *7 November* the men brought the horned cattle from the pasture this morning turned them into the colt pasture to feed them corn. weighed them averaged 1425.

2 October 1893: Commenced feeding the cattle corn (40 head) this morning

28 November 1894: Orra & Jerry brought the cattle from the pasture, their average weight was 1125 lbs . . . *1 December* Orra and Wellie weighed the cattle at the farm their average weight was 1380 lbs, commenced feeding them corn this morning.

8 February 1895: Still very cold, 14 deg below zero this morning at 6 Oclock. Orra was at the farm this A.M. helped Wellie load the corn and cut the ice for the cattle. John Dickenson was arrested to day for cruelty to his stock keeping them without food and shelter . . . *20 April* Jerry and George separated and weighed the cattle 35 of them averaged 660 lbs took them to the pasture, 25 averaged 815 lbs left them at the farm . . . *5 August* Jerry was at the pasture seeing about the water, there is still enough on our side, but the Case land is dry. Jerry sent a card to Ruff Taylor telling him that his stock had no water.

HOGS

The swine operation on the Gebby farm was smaller but similar to the cattle enterprise. They did, however, own a few sows and farrowed some of the pigs they fed for market. Several farms in the vicinity obviously had similar operations and frequently cooperated in shipping hogs to market. For the most part Margaret records basic facts about buying and selling, weights, and prices. An interesting entry, which makes one anxious to know more, is her brief notation about a farm wife who owned a share of some pigs and would not sell.

26 April 1887: Jerry & Orra delivered the hogs this morning they averaged 224 lbs at 5.20 pr hhd $291 . . . *28 November* 8 deg above zero this morning. Jerry and Cal were buying pigs today got 6 from Lim Braden at 4¼ pr to be delivered Thursday, 11 from Firestone $4 a head for 10 $5.00 for one, 7 from Bennett Snapp $2.25 a head for six $7.00 for one and brought them home ($25.00), got home at sundown . . . *30 November* Cal went to Firestones for pigs, paid $45.00, they weighed 780 lbs, Snapps weighed 500 lbs . . . Jerry went to the farm this morning met Jim Braden with eight pigs weighed 740 lbs at 4¼ pr lb 31.45, Jerry & Orra went to Lipencotts, bought 11 pigs at $4.00 pr head weight 75 lbs, Jerry was at town bought 10 pigs from Cal Freer . . . *5 December* Jerry went to the scales to meet Callie Freer with 11 head of hogs 5 large and six small weight 1068 lbs 5 cts pr lb $53.40 . . . *14 December* Jerry and Cal went to Linharts & bought ten pigs at $4.00 a head, averaged 78 lbs

13 December 1888: Jerry and Cal took the hogs to town (22 head) this morning they averaged 223 lbs got a check on the bank $233.22.

29 January 1890: Jerry & Orra rode over the country looking for hogs bought 16 from Will Whitehead at $3.65 pr hhd. to be delivered next Monday . . . *3 February* Jerry was at the farm weighed Will White-heads pigs 1685 lbs (16 head) at 3.65 pr hhd $61.50, then went to Eli Koonts bought 7 head at 3.60 pr hhd to be delivered on Wednesday . . . *5 February* Frank Kunts brought 7 pigs weighed 620 lbs paid $3.60 = 22.32

18 November 1890: G.W. Aikin and Jerry decided to ship their hogs next Monday . . . *24 November* John Longfellow, G.W. Aikin and Jerry shipped their hogs this morning, Longfellows weighed 3755, Aikins weighed 8855, our weighed 5320 . . . *26 November* Received the bill of the hogs shipped on Monday 16 sold for 3.95, 120 lbs shrinkage 82 sold for 3.75 . . . *29 November* Jerry settled with John Longfellow and G.W. Aikin which left us 179.92

24 October 1892: Jerry was at Dennis Moores after pigs to buy. could not get any. called at Hudsons to see why he had not brought those he had promised. said his wife owned part of them and she would not sell . . . *31 October* the hogs averaged 223 lbs a gain of 2½ lbs pr day apiece . . . *25 November* the men hauled the hogs to the stock yards (20 head) their average weight was 271 at 5 cts pr lb. received $270.75

15 March 1893: the men delivered the hogs this forenoon. they averaged 206 & a fraction at 7.25 came to $284.92, number 19.

2 March 1894: Orra brought home five of the smallest hogs to feed them on slop.

16 September 1895: Orra and Wellie separated and weighed the hogs, brought home 25 to ready to drive to the stock yard for Shipment tomorrow, their average weight 223 . . . *17 September* Jerry & George drove the hogs to the stock yards this morning, shipped them with Ella Emery 16, G.W. Aikin 14, Frank Hamer 15. They all make over 17000 lbs, the capacity of the car was 16000 lbs. Jerry took out 6 of the smallest & drove them back to the farm . . . *19 September* G.E. Emery called and settled for the hogs shipped Tuesday. they sold in two lots, $4.50 & 4.60. Jerrys share amounted to $199.06

The Gebbys bought pigs at 75 to 100 pounds and tried to market them at about 225, evidently counting on a gain of 2 or more pounds per day. Hogs were selling above $5.00 per hundred early in these journals but dropped as low as $3.75 in 1890 and peaked at $7.25 in the spring of 1893. This strongly suggests that farmers cut their breeding stock during the agricultural depression and prices rebounded with consumer de-

mand. The Gebbys marketed about twenty hogs at a time two or three times a year, frequently cooperating with neighbors to make up a railroad car. This probably evened out their labor and provided as much protection as possible from price fluctuations.

The casual way in which pigs were transported from one farm to another probably shocks the owner of a modern swine operation who carefully maintains a clean environment as protection from bacterial and viral infections. Hog cholera did reach Logan County in 1891 and may account for some of the price fluctuations previously mentioned, but treatment for livestock disease, like human disease, was primitive by modern standards. Preventing infectious diseases by isolating the contagious animals was not yet common practice.

ANIMAL ACCIDENTS AND DISEASES

Various accidents were always ready to descend on the livestock and pets around any farm, and the Gebbys were no exception.

13 February 1888: Jerry went to the farm this morning found the straw stack had fallen down and killed one pig . . . *14 November* Jerry & Orra brought home the three sows and twenty pigs he bought from Mrs. Pash paid $65.00 for them, put them in the orchard, one of the sows died in about an hour, having choked on a chicken leg. I went to the farm for the men but she died some time before we got home, put her nine pigs in a pen by themselves.

18 January 1890: A colt kicked Shep in the mouth knocking out one tooth loosening two others . . . *17 April* Jerry mixed up a box of Rough on Rats took it to the machine house at the farm trying to kill the thousands of rats there. Jerry & Cal killed 25 in the cornfield this morning . . . *1 May* Shep ate some of the Rough on Rats in the machine house at the farm, made him quite sick . . . *5 May* Shep not any better . . . *6 May* Shep died last night

13 August 1894: the men brought the pigs home this afternoon from the farm, will feed them slop. they left the slop barrel open & drowned three chickens.

By the late nineteenth century, roaming dogs had become a real menace to the sheep-raising business, which had earlier been quite profitable in Ohio. Margaret's entries regarding her brother-in-law's prob-

lems probably explain why the Gebby enterprise no longer included sheep.[3]

    2 November 1892: Dogs were in G.W. Aikins sheep last night killed 9, worried 35.
    8 April 1893: Dogs were in G.W. Aikins sheep last night killed 6.

Routine chores like dehorning cattle that would today be done by a veterinarian were handled by traveling crews that had special equipment.

    13 February 1893: Orra and Jerry took Jersey and a calf to Dave Kaylors had them dehorned, Koogler Bros. were doing that kind of work in this neighborhood. he dehorned all of Longfellows, all of Kaylors at 10 cts pr head.

Like the housewives who turned to their "doctor book" to treat minor family illnesses, farmers employed a host of home remedies for minor livestock diseases. If the first failed, one can almost read between the lines and hear experienced neighbors suggesting another or another. The patient eventually got better or died depending on the severity of the ailment.

    15 January 1889: Jerry and Cal washed the Neer steers with buttermilk and coal oil to kill lice . . . *31 January* Jerry got 5 cts worth of sulphur, went to the farm this afternoon, put sulphur on the lousy steer . . . *12 February* Tobacco for a lousy steer 10 cts . . . *15 February* Jerry took some tobacco juice out and washed the lousy steer . . . *27 February* Jerry went to the farm this afternoon put tobacco juice on the lousy steer he being much better

Veterinarians were rare, but there were often physicians in rural areas who would treat animals as well as humans.[4] *Even with an important source of income like hogs and a fatal epidemic like cholera, these diaries make no mention of seeking medical help. It was no doubt too expensive for an animal that would net the farm no more than five dollars, and besides, once cholera entered a herd of swine there was little treatment medical science could provide.*[5]

    21 September 1891: Jerry was at the farm looking after the hogs, the cholera being on both sides of them. they are all right yet . . . *26 September* Bob dug some in the gravel pit for water for the hogs, found three that have the Cholera . . . *27 September* the men doctored cholera hogs this morning giving them coal oil . . . *30 September* Orra & Jerry gave the sick hogs some more coal oil this morning & evening, they are not any better . . . *3 October* found one hog dead and the rest of the sick no better . . . *5 October* Jerry & Orra was at the farm this morning attending the sick hogs, not any better . . . *16 October* two more hogs dead this morning . . . *22 October* Jerry was at the farm buried another hog making the eighth dead one. some more looking badly . . . *26 October* Jerry was at the farm this morning, another hog dead & more nearly so . . . *7 November* another hog was dead this morning making ten that have died . . . *23 November* Jerry & Orra went to the farm to look after the stock, they killed 11 little sick pigs, the old ones are well now . . . *25 November* Jerry went to the farm, more little pigs dead.

This one cholera attack clearly cost the Gebbys one hundred to two hundred dollars, perhaps nearly as much as the annual wages of the hired man, but it was one of the hazards of the farm business and Margaret never calculated or commented on the total economic loss.

The only animals on the farm valuable enough to require the services of a doctor were horses, and then only after home remedies failed.

8 November 1886: Cal came for Jerry to go to the farm to see Fan sick swollen legs cant walk well . . . *9 November* Cal came in about eleven Oclock saying that Fan needed attention they went for Dr Logan, he did not say what was the matter but ordered her legs bandaged, he was out today think her symptoms some better, says it is some disease of the muscles, an epidemic . . . *10 November* Jerry went to see Fan, found her some better, swelling subsiding, went to town saw the Dr. thought it not necessary to see her again . . . *13 November* Fan is slowly improving . . . *6 December* Jerry paid Dr. Logan for Doctoring Fan $4.50 . . . *9 December* brought Fan home got some alcohol 20 cts cayenne 5 cts for liniment to rub on her legs.

21 April 1889: Cal came for Jerry that Old Charley was sick, gave him soda late this evening. I took out some laudamin and Peppermint drops think it relieved him some. came home about nine Oclock. Jerry went back at eleven found him worse called for Dr. Logan who gave him medicine, took the Dr. home again went to bed at two Oclock

3 May 1890: Old Charley was sick this morning, drenched him with soda & laudrum, better[6] . . . *18 October* they brought the bay colt home from the pasture to doctor it for Spavin, it being lame. Jerry got a bottle of Kendals Spavin cure $1.00

17 March 1893: Bob said old Charlie was sick he had given him some medicine, the men went out gave him laudamun and soda, then whiskey and Cayenne pepper, then went back gave him some turpentine and laudamun but he is no better

HORSES

Horses were the most valuable animals on the farm, and the only ones besides Margaret's milk cows that were given individual names. The Gebby farm used multipurpose horses for the family carriage as well as farm work. They were broken to harness at 1,200 to 1,500 pounds and probably did not reach a ton full grown.[7] An experienced mare or gelding was preferred for the family buggy. When Margaret drove herself she usually preferred Charlie or Harry, who were both in the Gebbys' possession the entire period from 1886 to 1896.

During spring planting season all horses might be needed by the men in the field. The Gebbys had at least four horses in 1886 and twice that number by 1896, with two sons in the farming operation and larger equipment that often required a three-horse hitch.

Horse trading legends abound, but Jerry's transactions appear to be strictly utilitarian, with no emotional attachment to a fast or showy horse. Margaret's attention to detail provides intriguing diary notations such as a ten-cent lunch for her husband the same day he paid twenty-five cents to feed his horse.

This farm usually worked geldings, often buying an unbroken yearling for fifty dollars rather than paying double or triple that for a prime workhorse. Jerry and the hired man or one of the boys usually broke their own colts to harness by gradually working them with one of the experienced horses. Margaret's diaries never mention anyone riding a horse for pleasure, although workhorses were often accustomed to a boy riding bareback from barn to field. The horses on this farm were clearly work, not pleasure, animals.

2 February 1886: Jerry went to David Hartzlers and bought an old bay mare for $65 in the afternoon bought a sleigh from J.A. Harzler for $23.00 . . . *25 October* Jerry went to Wolfingers and traded the colt and $53.00 for a gray horse (Bill), got Fan shod 15 cts

2 March 1888: Jerry went out the Northwood pike and round through Huntsville looking for a work horse to buy, saw several but did not buy any . . . *3 March* Jerry went to Dave Stevensons and bought a black horse (Frank) paying $150 for him . . . *4 June* Jerry was at Huntsville this morning wanted to trade old Fan and colt to H. McKinnon for a buggy. Henry was here this P.M. saw Fan, did not trade . . . *28 September* Jerry took Fan to the shop had her shod improved her walking some . . . *29 September* Jerry traded old Fan to Marion Wilder for a cow and $15.

29 January 1889: Jerry went to Sicafoos this afternoon bought a colt for $50 . . . *30 January* Jerry fixed the stable for the colts. Went for the colt he bought from Sicafoos. Cal rode Harry and led the colt. Jerry was in the sleigh, paid $50 . . . *4 February* Jerry fixed the stable to keep Charlie from kicking the bay colt . . . *7 December* Jerry was at Hebe McCrackens looking at a colt, didn't buy, looked at several others, was at McKinnons to see a colt this P.M. didn't buy . . . *16 December* Jerry went to Jake Detwilers to see a colt, did not buy too high price ($100) . . . *17 December* the men went to Campbells bought a colt paid $50.50, brought it home this P.M., they bought one from McKinnon for $50 expects to deliver it tomorrow.

30 January 1890: Weighed the colts, Fan weighed 1255, Selem 1235 . . . *27 March* Jerry, Orra & Cal hitched up the bay colt with old Charley to the wagon came home then back to the farm, did very well for the first . . . *1 April* Jerry, Orra and Cal hitched up the bay colt with old Charley drove around on the pike awhile then hitched up Fan, they both did very well . . . *15 April* Jerry and Orra took the colts to the farm this morning then hitched up old Charley and Selin to the wagon drove down the pike then drove Fannie awhile . . . *2 May* Jerry went to the farm got the bay colt hitched him with old Charley to the wagon, went with Elmer to the pasture for brick, the colt pulled very well . . . *31 May* Cal rolled in the A.M. with Bill and Fan, the P.M. with Bill & Selina, they did very well . . . *4 June* Jerry & Lon drove Lons horse to town to show him to Jim Wonders, did not sell . . . *9 December* Bob and Orra brought the stock at the pasture home, weighed the colts Fan weighed 1500, Selim 1570, Barnum 1210, Dick 1010, Harrison 1345, Morton 1225.[8]

24 April 1891: Jerry was at town got a halter and a collar for Selim $2.00 . . . *27 April* Orra and Bob plowed at the farm, worked Selim this A.M. Jerry took him to Dr Logan had wolf teeth extracted, paid 25 cts . . . *28 April* Bought a set of Harness for Selim, $11.25.

23 October 1891: Jerry took Frank to town showed him for sale, but did not sell . . . *4 November* Jerry left for Springfield this morning, drove Harry and led Frank expecting to sell him at a horse sale tomorrow . . . *5 November* Jerry came home about six this eve sold Frank for

$110, paid $1.15 for supper, breakfast & lodging, $1.00 for the horses, 10 cts for lunch, 25 cts for Harry's dinner, got Harry shod 35 cts

26 March 1892: Orra and Bob hitched up Old Charlie and Dick to the wagon went around by the McColly bridge pike several miles and back home again, the harness & wagon frightened Dick very much at first but he got over it. this P.M. they put Barney with old Bill, drove them several miles, he jumped some but soon got used to the harness [*perhaps the two young men considered this job an adventure*] . . . *29 March* Orra and Bob plowing. Orra plows with little Charlie and Selim. Bob with Bill and Fan.

17 December 1892: some horse buyers were looking at Fan this morning but she did not suit them

7 June 1893: Orra and Bob plowed corn to day. Jerry was at the farm this forenoon helping them start, trying to break Dick to the single line.

27 June 1896: Jerry traded old Charley off for a bay horse of Pattersons paying them $30.00 and a load of hay.

PETS

Cats and dogs were an inevitable part of any farm scene but the infrequency of their mention in Margaret's diaries suggests they had little relevance to her life. Cats were creatures who lived in the barn, desirable primarily because they controlled rodents. Dogs were the boys' companions and were of some assistance in driving livestock. The children might enjoy kittens and puppies, but they never came into the house and were of little concern to Margaret. If cats and dogs ran away or died from illness or injury, they could easily be replaced by someone anxious to give a litter away. Cats and dogs did not contribute to the farm income and by implication were of little importance.

21 June 1890: Orra bought a Pup this eve[9]

3 June 1891: Orra went to Harry Harners got two pups one for himself the other for Lon Robeson . . . *24 October* George took a picture of Tom (cat) and one of Button (cow) neither of them very good

25 July 1892: Orra got a black pup this evening . . . *1 November* Orra finished his dog house put it in the southeast corner of the yard.

18 June 1894: Orra sheared the dog.

7 April 1896: The dog run away last night and has not gotten home yet, think he has gone home, wrote to Middleburg inquiring about him . . . *8 April* George got a note to day that his dog is at his old home in West Middleburg . . . *10 April* George over to Middleburg and brought his dog home will have to keep him tied . . . *22 April* George has not yet heard of his dog, saw his former owner in town but he knew nothing of him

HOME

HOUSEKEEPING AND FURNISHINGS

HOUSECLEANING

The most vivid stories of housework a century ago have often dealt with "spring-cleaning," that backbreaking labor our grand-mothers and great-grandmothers pursued with such moral vigor. Grime deposited by wood-burning stoves was scrubbed away, bedding that had been subjected to various illnesses and washed infrequently had to be aired in the sun, and carpets tracked by winter mud were taken outside to be beaten clean. A good housekeeper was captain of her ship during spring-cleaning. All available family labor was at her command, and extra help was often hired. The daily chores of milking cows, feeding chickens, and cooking meals went on as usual, and in the Gebby household spring-cleaning often extended several weeks. It included out-buildings such as the washhouse, summer kitchen, woodhouse, and coalhouse as well as various cellar rooms for the furnace and food storage.

13 April–12 May 1886: I churned and with Elmers help cleaned the two little rooms and back hall and stairs . . . Elmer and I cleaned Grandmas and the boys room today . . . Cleaned the north room up-stairs and the hall . . . Very pleasant and warm, 80 deg. in shade reported. Elmer & I cleaned the furnace room . . . Saw Francis Holt promised to help clean house next week . . . Took up carpets in sitting and Bed rooms . . . took up Dining room carpet washed the floor and woodwork, windows &c . . . Cleaned and finished papering the dining room, put the Sitting, Bed and dining room carpets down today . . . took up parlor and hall carpets finished cleaning them, paid

Francis Holt $3.00 for house cleaning . . . Cleaned the coal house and the woodhouse . . . got ½ gal. paint for the kitchen ceiling, 75 cts . . . I baked bread and pies and churned, painted the ceiling of kitchen . . . finished painting kitchen ceiling, all the old chairs and the sink . . . Elmer & I cleaned big cellar and wash house . . . Moved the stove to the wash house.

Certain routines occurred with regularity each spring and fall. Year after year the wood-burning stove was moved to the washhouse about the first of May and back into the house about the first of November. Hand-woven rag carpets were laid each winter and taken out to be beaten clean each spring, when they were replaced by summer matting. Blankets, quilts, and curtains were washed. Windows were washed before screens were put in each spring and in the fall when they were removed. Cellars were cleaned and whitewashed, and one or more of the wallpapered rooms was redone almost every year.

12–20 May 1887: Father & Mother came and helped Elmer and I clean the sitting & bedrooms . . . we cleaned the little cellar white washed the walls and scrubbed the floor, cleaned the burea and safe . . . moved the stove into the washhouse, put down the oil cloth in the kitchen.

13–14 May 1890: Elmer and I began cleaning the sitting and bed rooms got the carpets and beds out, soon rained so we had to bring them in again. Charlie and Lizzie Cook were here for dinner, left about three Oclock, we did not get much cleaning done . . . too wet to work in the ground, [*field work obviously took precedence over housework*] we finished the sitting and bed rooms also the parlor except the window shades.

16 May 1895: We starched the curtains and dried them nicely in a frame.

Since the Gebby household had no daughters, it seems likely that the sons helped more with housework than usual. Margaret clearly expected help with the heavy chores of seasonal cleaning even if it meant that one of the boys would be kept home from school. Some jobs such as moving the privy were considered men's work.

11 August 1887: Jerry and the boys moved the privy this morn. Elmer & I put up the lattice in front of it this forenoon . . . I fixed a walk to the privy.

16 May 1888: Elmer & I white washed and cleaned the cellars. Grandma cleaned the fruit and pantry cupboards, Jerry and George plowed [*cultivated for weeds*] the garden. . . . *25 October–3 November* borrowed Mothers wringer to wash bed clothes tomorrow . . . I washed five blankets and seven quilts today . . . Elmer and I took up the sitting room carpet and put down the rag carpet. Moved the stove into the house again.

13 August 1889: the boys and Cal hauling manure. Jerry helping with the house work. I am not well, a severe pain in my back and shoulder.

29 May 1890: Jerry & I put up the screen doors and windows. . . . *30 September* cleaned the boys room, swept, George washed the windows very nicely. . . . *22 November* Elmer & George helped clean the Dining room, put down the old rag carpet.

16 April 1891: Cleaned Elmers room and the north room and the hall upstairs, George stayed at home to help me clean house.

Teenage sons helping with the heavy work of seasonal cleaning was routine throughout these journals, but the entry for 13 August 1889 is the only reference to her husband helping with everyday housework. It obviously happened when she was not well, but perhaps it is remarkable that it happened at all.

HIRED HELP

Upper-class families in the latter part of the nineteenth century relied upon "mother's helpers" for child care, but readers are justified in questioning whether this would be typical for an Ohio farm family with a widowed mother-in-law in the household. Nevertheless, the 1880 census shows a hired girl living with the Gebby family when the boys were nine, four, and two years old.[1] It is not known how long the family had live-in help while the children were small, but from 1886 to 1892 the only regular household help came from a neighbor who received dirty laundry early each week and was paid one dollar when clean clothes and linens were picked up, often by one of the boys. Although commercial soap was available by this time, Margaret evidently preferred, for economic or aesthetic reasons, to make her own laundry soap each spring.[2]

7 January 1886 [Thursday]: Washing $1.00 . . . *14 January [Thursday]* Washing $1.00 . . . *20 January [Wednesday]* Washing $1.00 . . . *29 January [Friday]* Washing $1.00

8–21 November 1887: Very pleasant and very dry, the cistern dry,

Mrs Conn washed here today . . . Mrs Conn washed here today having no water at home.

8–11 May 1888: Jerry went to the farm brought home the iron kettle to make soap . . . Elmer and I washed the carriage this forenoon, made a kettle of soap.

17–19 April 1889: fixed up the kettle for making soap . . . made a kettle of soap this forenoon.

21–22 April 1891: Mrs Conn came over got the soap grease to make into soap . . . Mrs Conn got a barrel of ashes to make soap . . . *1 May* brought the soap home that Mrs Conn made on the shares

17–18 October 1892: Mrs Conns children have the Scarlet fever . . . I washed a two weeks washing, my first washing for several years, am tired.

By 1894 Margaret was fifty-nine, the neighbor who did laundry was in her fifties, grandma was becoming quite feeble, and the youngest Gebby son was graduating from high school and working on the farm full time. Some combination of these reasons, in conjunction with the annual burden of spring-cleaning, must have prompted a decision in the spring of 1894 that the Gebbys again needed full-time household help. Margaret clearly sought household help who would share work with her as an equal rather than as a subordinate. It took some time to work out a satisfactory arrangement.

13 April–4 June 1894: we called at Horns to get help for the housework, but the girls were all engaged . . . went to Marches to get some help but the girls were all engaged . . . I was looking for a girl to help work this week called at Cantwells then at Handrahens, then at John Hubers and at Butlers but without success. this P.M. went to Hammas then to Parkers in the McBeth addition and got it there . . . Adda Parker came this morning to help me . . . Adda & I repapered some in the kitchen . . . Adda & I cleaned the dining room put down matting . . . Adda washed, I churned then we cleaned the coal and wood house . . . Adda & I cleaned Elmers room also Georges . . . Adda & I cleaned the front, west & Orras rooms to day . . . I got lace curtains $7.00 . . . Paid Adda $3.00 . . . got some charcoal for ironing 3 cts, Adda ironed, I run off some lye to make soap, baked pies, planted some flower seed, gave Anna Robeson some cosmos . . . we made a kettle of soap today . . . Adda and I took up the parlor carpet cleaned it put up the new curtains . . . Adda & I cleaned the bedroom and the Hall to day . . . Adda washed, I made a kettle of soap. Adda gone to converts meeting . . . Adda and I cleaned the sitting room . . . Adda and I cleaned the kitchen today. Adda gone to Hammys to stay with a sick child. their babe died yesterday, I paid her $4.15, what is due her up to Tuesday . . . I churned, cleaned the closets in our bedroom, Adda blacked the stove . . . paid Adda $2.25 . . . Adda went to Bellecentre to day, her Mother is filling her place here.

It was not uncommon for young women to hire out temporarily to earn money for clothing or other special needs, and Adda appears to fit this pattern. By August Margaret had hired a neighbor who shared the family's Scottish heritage and attended the same church. As a forty-year-old spinster Nannie McAra settled into the household more like one of the family than a hired girl. The 1900 census shows that she was still filling this role well after these journals end. She was apparently paid ten dollars per month plus room and board.[3] She obviously worked six days per week and many hours per day just as the family did, but arrangements were clearly flexible enough to allow her to participate in personal activities on days of her choice.

17–31 August 1894: Nannie McAra came this afternoon to help me work . . . Nannie washed and churned . . . Nannie ironed, I put up two qts of Pears . . . Nannie and I canned 7 qts of pears, cleaned the crabs [*crabapples*] cooked them ready for making butter . . . Nannie was at G.W.Aikins visiting to day with her sister Maggie . . . Nannie was at Missionary meeting this afternoon.
7 February 1895: I melted snow and washed the woolen underwear, repaired socks, mittens &c. Nannie ironed, baked pies. . . . *26 April* Nannie and I washed a good sized washing of things, gathered up two quilts, 4 old blankets and a great many other things. . . . *26 November* Nannie and I dried the clothes over the registers
22 June 1896: Nannie washed. I did other things, churned, baked bread, picked the currants &c. . . . *8 May* Nannie and I cleaned her room to day, took up the carpet but it was so badly worn that we could not put it down again. I went to town got some matting $3.75.

This homemaker obviously wanted a hired girl who lived in the household as a social equal and worked in partnership on household chores. This was exactly the same relationship the husband and sons shared with the various hired men who worked on the farm. It is a relationship quite different from those frequently portrayed during the same time period between upper-class urban residents and their servants, but it may be quite typical of a middle-class rural society. It may reflect a midwestern spirit of democratic independence or the charitable equality

of a Christian home, but it was consistent for this family in both house-
work and farmwork.

PAINTING AND PAPERING

Although the Gebby house stood in the path of Bellefontaine's ex-
pansion and was demolished without a recorded floor plan, diary
descriptions of cleaning and decorating can be combined with knowl-
edge of similar homes to create a reasonably clear picture. The two-story
frame house was a substantial farm home, but it had no particular archi-
tectural distinction. The ground floor apparently had front and back
porches, a parlor, a family sitting room, dining room, kitchen, pantry,
and hall. Front and back stairs apparently led to four large and two
small bedrooms on the second floor. All of these rooms had plaster walls
and ceilings that were covered with wallpaper and finished with paper
borders rather than wooden mouldings. Margaret had the skill to hang
wallpaper and with one of her sons assisting frequently refurbished a
room or two during spring-cleaning.

In 1891 paperhangers were hired to redecorate the main rooms.
Prices noted in these diaries over several years suggest that better quality
paper was chosen for company rooms like the parlor and cheaper paper
was used in the kitchen and bedrooms. While patterns are not described
in the journals, selecting wallpaper was given enough thought to suggest
the decision was important. One sequence of entries makes the interest-
ing implication that after discussion with her husband, better quality
paper was bought for the dining room. Lavender and red paint for the
kitchen might have been Victorian fashion, but it certainly hints that by
modern standards this housewife favored bright colors.

9–16 May 1891: paid for 16 rolls of side wall paper 25 = $4.00, 10
rolls ceiling 25 = $2.50, 16 rolls ceiling 15 = $2.40, 16 yds Border 12½
= $3.25 total $12.15, engaged a man to come Monday to hang
it . . . Elliott and Hamilton papered the parlor not quite done . . . Jerry
and I were at town exchanged the paper bought for the dining room for
better, got new border for the sitting & bedrooms 50 yds at 12½ pr yd,
bill was $7.45, the men finished the bed and sitting rooms, and the
dining room nearly half done . . . Elliott and Hamilton finished papering this morning, paid them $12.00, 60 bolts at 20 cts pr bolt, sold
them 3¼ lbs of butter 59 cts. George & I cleaned the sitting and bed-

rooms, Elmer helped us with the dining room . . . We put down the sitting and bed room carpet, washed the parlor woodwork and windows, put down the carpet. George helped me all day, tired . . . George and I churned & worked at the house, George put down the dining room carpet we got nearly done arranging things.

11–13 May 1892: Went to town this P.M. got paper for Grandmas room, 12 bolts wall, 8 ceiling, and 21 yds of border at 10 cts pr yd, paper 15 cts pr bolt . . . George and I papered the walls of grandmas room to day except the border . . . George & I finished papering Grandmas room, put down the carpet, all finished, looks very nice.

28 May–3 June 1895: got some paper for the Kitchen, 12 bolts at 6¼ pr bolt, 20 yds of border at 5 cts pr yd, 1 qt of Lavender paint 40 cts . . . Orra painted the ceiling of the Kitchen for me, we are preparing to paper the kitchen tomorrow. I was at town got another qt of paint 40 cts, 5 cts worth of venitian red . . . Nannie papered some in the kitchen . . . George and I finished papering the kitchen

While sons usually painted interior woodwork, exterior painting was considered a major job to be done by professionals. It is interesting to note that once a decision was made to paint the house, barn, and windmill derrick at the same time, competitive bids were sought and separate crews were hired to paint the house and barn. This may be related to cost or skill, but they were working simultaneously in apparent harmony. Since the total cost was $100.46 it is easy to compute the percentage for materials at $42.16 and labor at $58.30. The journals suggest that two painters actually worked on the house at least part of eight days for $23.30 and five days on the roof, barn, and derrick for $35.00. Perhaps the latter required more ladders and was more dangerous. Paint ingredients were purchased separately and mixed on site.

17 May–5 June 1890: Saw some painters about painting the house. Walter Stamats came to see the house, offered to do the work for $23.30 . . . Walter Stamats was here this eve looking at the barn, Derrick and roof of the house, his bill was $44.08 . . . paid $2.95 for paint stuff, 20 cts hardware . . . saw Arch Murdock he agreed to do the painting for $35.00 and board himself. . . . *9–28 June* The painters came out mixed the paint, painted the west end of the house, Jerry got paint stuff 73 cts, tin caps for windows $1.03, bucket 10 cts . . . Stamats painted the west side of the parlor the rain spoiled it some . . . Stamats painted today. Arch Murdock and Joe Woodrow painted the Derrick and some on the barn . . . the painters were all here today . . . Jerry got 10 gal more oil and 100 lbs of Ironclad, paid for paint stuff $19.00 . . . the painters finished the barn this afternoon paid Arch Murdock $35.00 . . . Stamats and Fisher painting at the house . . . the painters finished the house to day paid him $23.30. Jerry went to town, settled some bills A.C. Wallace for paints $18.35

Readers can estimate the value of the buildings on this farm from notations about insurance on the family home, the tenant house, and the barns at both farms. If insurance was costing approximately $.75 per $100.00 coverage during this period, the houses and barns were evidently valued between $5,500.00 and $6,000.00, with $1,200.00 to $1,500.00 of that being the house where the family lived. Numerous small buildings at both locations were obviously not considered worth insuring.

5 January 1886: Insured house on the farm $4.00, value $300. . . . *2 December* Jerry went to town this afternoon got insurance on the house renewed $25.00.

26 April 1889: Increasing insurance on the house on the farm from $300 to $400 - 75cts.

17 July 1890: Jerry got the two houses and two barns insured, paid $43.75 for insuring.

QUILTS AND CARPETS

Margaret's journal never specifically describes her home, but over a period of years a fairly clear picture of its rooms and furnishings emerges. As one would expect, quilts, comforts, and rag carpets top the list of furnishing items that were made at home. Frequent use of plural pronouns in her diary suggests that her mother-in-law helped in these activities, and female relatives who dropped in to visit probably joined in these projects as they talked.

These diaries clearly reveal handwork was ready to be picked up individually in any spare moment or become the focus of a sociable exchange when relatives or neighbors called. It was a rare winter that did not find one or more quilt tops ready for the frame, and there is a rhythm in the physical labor of daily routines intermixed with quiet moments of needlework. Completing a quilt in the Gebby household usually took about a week in between other work. Readers sense not only the sociability of exchanging patterns and visiting while one's hands were busy, but the satisfaction of creative accomplishment with finished products.

1–7 February 1887: We cut and sewed carpet rags today . . . cut rags, 7 lbs . . . we cut rags all day, Krouses got the Quilting frames this morning. . . . *9–18 March* put a quilt in the frames and quilted some . . . I washed some this morning, then quilted the balance of the day . . . We quilted all day . . . finished the quilt this morning. . . . *1–9 September* Got 18 lbs carpet chain 23 cts . . . Took the rags to the carpet weavers . . . sewed carpet rags this forenoon, took them to the weavers . . . got the carpet, paid $3.60.⁴

15–21 February 1893: cut blocks for a quilt, stamped a few blocks . . . I was at Krouses to day began to outline a Quilt . . . churned, worked at the quilt, read some, received a letter from Elmer. . . . *6–7 December* I was at Mrs Dowells at the sewing circle they sewed carpet rags and made two comforts. I got 5 yds of cheese cloth for a table spread 33 cts . . . I took some red floss to Lib Beattys to work a table spread.

As children the boys shared a room, and probably a bed, but as teenagers each acquired his own small room. These diaries reveal that this family was using a wide variety of bedding simultaneously. They seemed to be replacing rope supports with steel coil "mattresses" topped by straw and feather ticks.⁵ The latter were certainly inexpensive for a farm family that had these materials available for annual renovation.

12 October 1888: Bought a pair of scarlet blankets at Bradburys $5.75.

5 September 1889: Orra fixed the small east room for his things.

18–22 April 1890: called at Fathers borrowed their wringer . . . I washed some bed clothes, six quilts, two blankets with other things . . . I washed 3 blankets, two quilts, 3 curtains and other things this forenoon. . . . *29 September–28 October* ordered a mattress made for Elmers bed at McMillans. I varnished the old single bedstead . . . McMillan & Co brought home a spring bed & mattress this evening, put it in the little room for Orra, $4.75 . . . sewed, pieced Georges feather bed . . . Grandma & I went to the farm filled Georges bed . . . made the cover for a comfort . . . put a comfort in the frame and knotted a few stitches . . . finished the comfort, put in another, the red cheese cloth

25 April 1891: I washed two bed ticks filled them with straw.

26 April 1892: George and I cleaned the west small room and fixed it up for him, he sleeps in it to night.

3 March 1893: changed the feathers in Grandmas bed. . . . *28–30 December* went to town, ordered a spring bed and mattress for Georges bed at Herman Horns, to be delivered tomorrow . . . Horn delivered the Bed springs, paid $5.00.

1 August 1895: washed a straw tick & filled it for Georges bed.

KITCHEN

It seems clear that the wind wheel and derrick were purchased primarily to provide water for farm livestock, but major improvements were soon made in the kitchen so that water for the house did not have to be pumped by hand. This relatively major remodeling project converted the porch with its hand pump into part of an enlarged kitchen with a water tank and creamer. The month-long project cost about eighty dollars plus much do-it-yourself labor from the Gebby family.[6] The finished product with indoor plumbing and more than thirty feet of oilcloth-covered work and eating space must have embodied the height of convenience among farm homes in this neighborhood in 1890.

17 October–9 November 1889: Jerry & I went to Jim Bradens to see their water tank in the kitchen, called at the home,[7] to see their water arrangement . . . Scott called to see about enlarging the kitchen . . . Jerry took down the lattice &c, Scotts hand Geo Woodside put up the studding & put on the siding . . . Orra & Cal dug and put down the well pipe past the first machine house door. Woodside finished the carpenter work of the kitchen. Jerry got lath, lime &c. Charlie Stillwell put on some lath this P.M. Baked bread, pies, churned[8] . . . Charlie Stillwell finished plastering this afternoon paid him $3.00,[9] Cal waited on him.[10] Orra worked all day at the ditch . . . ordered a water tank made of galvanized iron 24 in. high & 24 in. in diameter. Orra & Cal worked at the ditch . . . Orra and Cal finished the ditch to the foundation. Ordered a creamer . . . Jerry brought the creamer $37.50, Lyman came to set it up . . . the men worked at the water pipes, got the creamer pipe in & the inlet pipe. Barker brought the tank out will finish it in the morning. Geo Woodside put on the casings and got the tank box nearly done[11] . . . they finished the water works to day, Geo Woodside worked till noon, Barker was here about an hour. Works very well. Broke the shaft of the pump this evening . . . Jerry fixed the broken pump shaft, the wind wheel badly out of order. Jerry was at town paid Lesourd $7.85 for lumber, John Frey $16.63 for hardware, Tom Stillwell 86 for lime, telephoned to Bellecentre about the pump 25 . . . John Emery fixed the wind pump this morning . . . paid Dave Scott $4.45 for carpentry work . . . Anna and Lizzie Robeson helped me paper the kitchen today . . . Cal & Orra took up the pump[12] in the kitchen this morning . . . we were at town got oil cloth 12 yds at 75 cts pr yd $9.00 . . . Elmer & I put down the Oil cloth in the kitchen, then worked at making a kitchen table. Jerry bought four table legs 50 cts.

FURNACE AND STOVES

Although this house had a coal furnace in the cellar that was used in the coldest weather, the cookstove in the kitchen and wood-burning stoves in the parlor and sitting rooms furnished sufficient heat in autumn and spring. When diary entries note water freezing in the kitchen and begonias freezing in the sitting room, one has to suspect that there were many times when rooms were extremely cold by modern standards. Bedrooms upstairs were not heated until Margaret's mother-in-law was almost eighty and a stove was installed to heat her room.

13 December 1888: put a fire in the cellar. . . . *22 December* Cool, froze in the kitchen for the first time this winter

18 November 1891: Froze all the begonias last night in the sitting room. . . . *31 December* Jerry & I went to town got a stove for grandmas room $13.00. Moore came out helped set it up.

2 March 1893: Jerry got a new galvanized iron top for the kitchen chimney $3.00, the old one was rusted and burnt so as to be dangerous. . . . *25 September–2 October* Jerry was at town got lime 15c, Fine clay 15c, got some sand at the gravel bank to repair the sitting room grate . . . made a fire in the parlor, the sitting room grate smokes badly . . . Geo Hackinger came out this P.M. and repaired the sitting room grate paid him $2.50.

10 November 1894: We put a fire in the furnace this morning, could not keep warm with the grate.

Both wood and coal were used for fuel depending on the need for a quick fire or a hot, long-lasting fire. Wood was less expensive since it

was cut and split on the farm. Coal was purchased and hauled from town. Furnace and stoves for this large, poorly insulated house required a large supply of both. No thought was given to environmental pollution, and this family frequently settled for local soft coal at half the price even though it produced less heat and dirtier smoke than hard coal.

4–6 March 1886: Jerry hauled two loads of stove wood this P.M. . . . Orrie and Cal sawing stove wood today. Jerry hauled two loads home.

22 October 1887: Cal and Orra hauled coal four loads of Massillon coal and one of slack to take to the farm, paid for hard coal 4150 lbs $6 pr ton, $12.45, soft coal 15880 lbs $3.25 = $25.80.

12 September 1888: Jerry was at town this afternoon paid F.R. McLaughlin $54.00 for coal

15 November 1889: paid Harry Kaylor $4.20 for cutting 7 cords of wood.

10–11 October 1892: Jerry engaged the coal for winter at $3.00 pr ton . . . Bob and Jerry hauled 5 loads of coal 17,660 lbs paid $26.48.

2 February 1895: Wellie hauled two loads of wood here, one for the cellar and one for the wood house.

6 November 1896: Orra hauled three loads of wood home, Jerry brought home a load of furnace wood. Orra and George sawed down more trees for sawlogs.

The diaries do not reveal whether this house was constructed with a furnace shortly after the Civil War, but it seems likely it was added in a later remodeling. It certainly had central heating very early for an Ohio farmhouse since it needed replacing in 1894–95. Maintenance was either poorly understood or a low priority for its deteriorating condition seemed to catch everyone by surprise and resulted in the family being without a furnace during the coldest part of the winter.

28–29 December 1894: we had some trouble with the furnace to day, it smoked badly, suppose there is some crack about it . . . the men examined the furnace this morning, found it badly burned and rusted, some holes and cracks, do not consider it worth repairs. Jerry was at town this afternoon and ordered a new one of Cook Bros. the furnace itself to cost $100.

21–30 January 1895: Orra and Wellie took down the brick wall and tore down the furnace, dug away considerable dirt from around the furnace, did not get quite done . . . Wellie and Orra finished taking out the old furnace then they went to the depot brought out the new furnace . . . Orra and Wellie cemented the place to set the furnace to day . . . The men came out this afternoon, got the furnace partly set up . . . The men came out worked at the furnace a while . . . Cold, at zero this morning, not above 10 deg all day. The men worked at the furnace got all done but one pipe into the bedroom and the cold air pipe. put fire in it, but it made a very disagreeable smoke by the burning of a mixture put on the castings to keep them from rusting which will burn off . . . took down the stove, cleaned the sitting room[13] . . . Jim Cook and Lane finished the furnace this forenoon, attached the bedroom pipe[14] and put in a cold air pipe. Jerry and Orra filled up the walls around the pipes this afternoon. . . . *19 February* Jim Cook was here and put a damper in the cold air pipe. Jerry settled with him for the furnace $114.70.

YARD AND FLOWER GARDEN

This farmhouse was surrounded by a yard that was fenced to keep out chickens and livestock, and everyone in the family helped care for the yard and flower garden. Grass was mowed with a manual rotary mower that Margaret or Jerry operated as often as one of the boys. The flower bed was obviously a source of enjoyment, and Margaret frequently exchanged starts of plants with neighbors or potted tender plants in the fall and brought them inside to save over winter.

29 June 1888: Elmer, George and I cleaned the Berea [*limestone*] walks, mowed the yard, hoed in the garden, sodded in front of the east veranda, all tired.

2 May 1890: Elmer and I fixed the flower bed this forenoon, took oxalis bulbs to Uncle Johns. . . . *14 June* Aunt Hannah gave me some pansy sprouts. . . . *12 September* fixed the Oleander bucket and a hanging basket of bulbous Oxalis [*to bring inside*].

20 April 1891: Aunt Hannah was here this P.M. brought a yellow rose bush, got a pink rose here and some pinks. . . . *9 May* Jerry had lawn mower sharpened 50 cts. . . . *26 May* I dug up the flower bed sowed pink & pansy seed and nasturtiums, George and I strung the [*sweet*] peas this morning.

14 September 1892: filled the tub with oleander and other plants.

25 April 1896: Mattie & Nannie made a Sweet Pea bed & planted it for me. . . . *29 October* I raked the yard this forenoon, did not get done, was too tired. . . . *10 November* I wrapped Elmers rose bushes.

FOOD

ORCHARD AND GARDEN

Although Margaret's diaries rarely indicate the menu for a family meal, the Gebbys' diet can be deduced from notations regarding food production and preservation. Both were time-consuming and required the assistance of all family members. Except for baking, food preparation was so routine it was rarely mentioned.

Like many midwestern farm families, the Gebbys had an orchard, berry patch, grape arbor, and rhubarb patch that produced continuously from year to year. Size and variety can be estimated from occasional diary entries regarding replacements. This family had abundant apple, cherry, pear, and plum trees and a berry patch that included raspberries, blackberries, gooseberries, and strawberries. With some variety producing from May through October, fruit was obviously eaten fresh, but most fruit was baked into pies or preserved.

22–30 March 1886: Sent an order to William Bennett[1] for apple trees and Raspberry and Blackberry . . . Jerry plowed the lot for the trees and Raspberries and Blackberries . . . Received apple trees, Black and Raspberries from William Bennett this afternoon, freight 92 cts, fruit stock $6.81 . . . *15 April* helped Jerry set out the berry sprouts, Jerry and Elmer set out 18 apple trees, six yet to set out[2]

12–16 April 1887: Jerry and Elmer put up a new grape arbor all day . . . Set out 11 plum trees and two cherries.

12 April 1893: bought 6 May Cherry trees $1.00 . . . *31 October* Jerry and I went to Kinnys got 12 Grape roots, 2 Concords, 2 Niagara, 2

Wordens, 2 Wyomings, 2 Moors Early, 1 Cataba, and one Moyer, set them out in the Garden in a row, paid $1.65

27–28 March 1894: Orra pruned apple trees at the farm . . . Orra finished pruning the young orchard at the farm to day. Wellie picked & burned the brush, looks very nice.

7 March 1895: Orra bored a hole in each of the cherry trees filled the cavity with sulphur endeavoring to kill the black knot, burned all the diseased limbs he could find, trimmed the grapevine and some apple trees . . . *4–9 April* Jerry bought a Sprayer $3.00, we sprayed all the plum trees & some cherry and some apple trees and the Gooseberry bushes with London purple . . . Orra and Jerry sprinkled the Apple trees at the farm with London purple the worms are getting very bad on them

24 June 1896: George & Wellie set posts and wired them for the grape vines, tied the vines to the wires

Like nearly all nineteenth-century farm families, the Gebbys annually planted a garden, which provided practically all of their vegetables for the entire year. By modern standards both quantity and variety seem immense for a family of six. It is difficult to determine production, but the only fertilizer was a dressing of manure prior to plowing and chemical control of insects was minimal. Seeds were purchased locally but the family cut their own seed potatoes and bedding plants were frequently exchanged between neighbors. The family grew a few vegetables, like celery, that are rare in modern home gardens.[3] But most vegetable varieties were common ones that could be canned, pickled, or stored in the root cellar for winter use: potatoes, onions, cabbage, sweet corn, beans, peas, radishes, beets, parsnips, tomatoes, peppers, cucumbers, muskmelons, lettuce, and squash.

Like most farm families, the Gebbys considered potatoes a daily essential and they routinely planted at least an acre. Seed potatoes were usually planted in April with the goal of harvesting the first small new potatoes by July. By late September the crop was dug and the family counted on thirty to forty bushels to be stored in the cellar for winter use.

11 April 1889: We planted 12 rows of Beauty of Hebron potatoes and two of Early Rose.

19 April 1890: Jerry and Elmer took potatoes to the farm, harrowed and furrowed a corner in the big field, planted 21 rows

11–20 June 1889: Elmer plowed the potatoes made sweet potato rows, set out 100 sweet potato plants bought from Jim McCracken 25

cts . . . Jerry went to town got paris green for potato bugs 20 cts[4] . . . set out 29 pepper & 68 sweet potato plants

9 July 1892: Grandma and I was at the farm got some potatoes, left them in the basket in the buggy, went in the house and Bobs cow eat more than half of them

23 September 1887: finished digging potatoes had 17 bushels very poor yield . . . *28 October* J.E. McCracken brought us fifteen bushels of potatoes 90 cts pr bu

23–29 September 1892: The men were digging potatoes to day brought home about 40 bushels, about ⅔ done . . . Orra and George assorted the potatoes, put the largest (33 bushels) in the cellar

Gardening was a family enterprise with everyone from children to grandma involved in planting, weeding, and harvesting. Early garden could be planted a month before the last frost, about mid-April in north-western Ohio, and celery, beets, and turnips were usually the last items harvested, just before the ground froze in November.

26–28 April 1886: I planted Beets, Parsnips, Onions, Beans & Peas . . . Made garden this forenoon . . . Cleaning and mowing yard this A.M. planted some sweet corn in Briar patch; planted cucumber today . . . *10 May* Jerry got Tomato & Cabbage plants at J.E. Mc. 60 cts Set them out this eve. then plowed the potatoes . . . *21 May* planted beans in the cornfield . . . *26 May* Considerable frost this morning no serious damage done . . . *28 May* stuck the peas

11 April 1887: Jerry & Elmer plowed the garden then we all planted peas, beans, beets, parsnips, onions, lettuce & onion seeds . . . *19 April* Froze quite hard last night an inch or two of snow last night all melted off today . . . *27 April* had greens for dinner . . . *3 May* set out 52 tomato plants this eve

21 April 1888: Jerry and the boys plowed the garden and briar patch planted some potatoes among the berries made most of the garden, set out the onions, sowed lettuce, beets and parsnips, planted two rows of peas. Jerry got three paper of raddish seed 15 cts Grandma and Elmer planted some this evening . . . *26 April* planted a row of sweet corn in the garden, also some beans.

25 April 1895: I planted some onion sets and raddish seed, stopped the chickens out of the garden or tried to . . . *30 April* I planted sweet corn, beans, peas and cucumbers in the lot . . . *1 May* I spaded the flower bed in the garden, sowed some Cypress seed, verna, nasturtion and Sweet Peas.

12 May 1896: Jerry and I set out the Tomato plants, planted more sweet corn and more beans and Hubbard Squash. I fixed the flower beds set out Geraniums, Pinks &c

5 June 1895: George was at McCrackens got cabbage plants (60) Tomato plants (60) pepper plants (30) pd 80 cts

20 June 1892: thinned the beets, took some to Krouses and sent some to Conns

26 June 1894: We had two heavy rains this afternoon every thing is much refreshed. I replanted the cabbage again after the first rain, about five dozen making in all about 225.

27 June 1892: I hoed in the garden untill I was tired, baked a ginger cake this afternoon

20 July 1891: put Paris Green on the cabbage this morning

19 July 1886: Plowed the garden, prepared it for celery. Elmer & I went to J. McC. for plants but he had none, got 500 at Mrs Carsons 20 cts pr hundred, we planted 3 hundred, Cal got 2 hun.

7 July 1896: I fixed a trench to plant Celery . . . *14 July* I got 150 celery plants at Mrs Carsons 25 cts. I set out 126 here with 45 I set out yesterday makes 175. Jerry took some to the farm set them in a damp place in the prairie . . . *5 October* I worked at the celery banked up half of it, tied all the bunches so all can be easily bleached . . . *10 November* I dug the celery, Jerry & George carried it to the cellar, put it in boxes to bleach.

8–11 November 1886: Quite cool fear our celery is frozen . . . We dug the celery today not injured by the freeze, dug the beets & turnips . . . cleaned the cellar put away the beets, onions, roots &c

Readers accustomed to supermarkets with year-round abundance of fresh produce may find it difficult to comprehend the joy that must have accompanied the first harvest of the season, but it was undoubtedly important for Margaret frequently commented. One senses a competi- tion with nature and an endless quest for a better season.

19 April 1890: Baked bread and pies, baked our first pieplant pie [*rhubarb*] for 1890

8 June 1895: I picked a half gal of cherries made three pies, the first of the season

2 July 1891: had our first mess of peas and new potatoes for dinner

27 July 1891: had our first cabbage

1 August 1890: had our first mess of green corn

1 August 1894: had our first mess of roasting ears for supper

Not all of the Gebby food supply required cultivation. Nature

yielded the bounty of spring mushrooms, summer berries, and fall nuts. Collecting seems to have been a time of sociability as well as harvest.

10–13 May 1890: too wet to work in the ground, the boys went to the pasture, Orra hunting snipes (got one), Elmer looking for mushrooms . . . Elmer went with a party of six picnicked in J.Horns woods, Botany students looking for flowers . . . Orra gathered mushrooms for supper.

9 June 1888: The boys went to Ewing pond got a lot of water lilies

3 June 1891: Orra went to Ewings pond for lilies got one bud & a root

10 July 1890: picked a few Raspberries they are very inferior being too dry for them.

10 October 1891: George, Tommy & Charlie went to T. Cooks woods gathered 4 bushels of hickory nuts, did not get home till after dark.

8 September 1894: Orra and George was at Kaufmans woods gathering Hazelnuts, got a 2 bushel sack full.

CANNING AND PRESERVING

Much of the orchard and garden produce was preserved for year-round use. For items that could not be kept fresh in the root cellar this meant canning, pickling, or making jam and jelly. Fruit preserves were often referred to locally as "butter," a well-cooked product that contained mashed odd bits and pieces of fruit. In addition to the common apple butter, Margaret often made peach, grape, plum, strawberry, and quince butter. When farm work permitted, her husband and sons frequently did the harvesting while Margaret and her mother-in-law or the hired girl did the kitchen work. It was constant work throughout summer and fall, but the variety of the results was rewarding.

Neighbors sometimes exchanged surplus produce. Peaches were the only fruit the Gebby family never raised but regularly purchased.[5] Without a telephone to search out an available supply and determine when the fruit was ripe, the project of buying peaches could consume parts of several days.

6 June–6 July 1886: Too wet to plow corn. Jerry and Orra picked cherries this forenoon. Churned and canned 28 quarts of cherries did not get done till ten Oclock . . . Baked bread and pies and put up five qts of cherries . . . baked pies, canned six qts of cherries . . . baked six loaves bread, four cherry pies, canned three quarts of raspberries this forenoon . . . Picked berries all forenoon except getting dinner. Canned 3 qts of Raspberries and one of Gooseberries, picked cherries for pies tomorrow . . . picked raspberries enough to make three pies, baked four cherry pies.

14 June 1890: Elmer & George picked cherries this forenoon, canned 13 qts of sweet cherries, made ice cream, churned twice today, had strawberry shortcake for dinner.

16–22 June 1891: gathered 2 gal of strawberries, made a can of strawberry butter . . . the boys picked 9 gal of sweet cherries, 1 gal of strawberries . . . put up 15 qts of sweet cherries, made a cake, churned. the boys made ice cream . . . canned 3 cans of strawberries, 4 qts of white cherries, 19 qts of May cherries, tired . . . Elmer and George picked cherries this forenoon we put up 15 qts of cherries and some pickles

18–19 June 1896: Nannie and I finished cleaning the Gooseberries, baked brown and white bread, also a cake . . . we canned 16 qts of Gooseberries this forenoon

25 June 1888: Jerry and Elmer and George picked cherries this forenoon, we cleaned and canned twenty six qts got done about ten Oclock

4–5 June 1894: picked a gallon of Gooseberries, what the chickens left us . . . George took off the palings of the fence along the Cherry lot put them on again much closer together

2 July 1888: picked two gallons and a qt of gooseberries canned seven qts left a few for pies tomorrow . . . *9 July* picked two gallons of raspberries canned five qts.

10 July 1889: George and I picked four gal. of berries put up four qts gave Uncle Johns the balance had raspberry shortcake for dinner.

1 August 1892: put up 12 qts of pears, gave M.A. Aikin a bucket full.

20 August 1895: Orra and George got about a bushel of wild plums this afternoon, very nice, they are very abundant now where there are trees they are full.

22 August 1893: I bought a half a bushel of Plums from Mr Trout of Lewistown paid $1.50 put up 10 qt cans, made 1 qt butter, 8 qts jelly

3 September 1895: put up 5 cans of Bartlett pears, got a doz new tin can lids & a doz Rubbers[6]

5 September 1891: put up 20 qts of plums, made 5 pies

15 September 1886: put up 21 qts of Tomatoes this afternoon

17–28 September 1889: Jerry and I went to get some peaches. went to Phil Krouses he promised us a bushel next Saturday or Monday, then we went to Oliver Fawcetts near Zanesfield, got the promise of some next Monday, then we came to John Dickensons got a bushel $1.00, no one at home except Emma . . . Jerry went to Oliver Fawcetts near Zanesfield this morning for peaches but they were not ripe enough. Phil Krouse brought us a bushel at noon $1.50, canned six qts, baked bread, pies and a cake . . . Jerry went to Fawcetts got a bushel of peaches, also one for Cal $3.00 . . . put up ten cans of peaches six qts cling four of freestones

23 September 1886: Made catsup, stuffed 3 doz mangoes

25 September 1894: I walked to Boals got one doz of tin cans 45 cts sealing wax 4 cts filled the cans with tomatoes have now 24 qts.[7]

4 October 1894: Nannie & I gathered the ripe tomatoes & Peppers, pulled up some tomato vines hung them in the barn to ripen.

10 October 1890: made some tomato pickles

8–11 October 1888: made three qts of peach butter and three qts of grape butter, baked pies, cookies and biscuit, churned . . . we chopped tomatoes cabbage and celery for chow-chow . . . made 4½ gallons of mango pickles

7–8 October 1895: George picked the grapes and then a bushel of Plums. Jerry and I were at town got 6 jugs for the grape juice 60 cts, and a dozen cans for the plums 70 . . . Nannie & I canned 22 qts of Plums, made three and a half gallons of Grape wine, very nice[8]

21 October 1892: put up 4 qts of Quinces, made a gal. of butter, 4 glasses of jelly.

24 October 1890: I went to Fathers made three gallons of Kraut

Apples were a major crop that were stewed for the table and baked in pies from midsummer until late winter, but fall was the special season for apple butter and cider. Much was consumed as sweet cider, but some went into a barrel to become vinegar. The large copper kettles for making apple butter were shared among relatives and neighbors. During the season, the long process of boiling juice, peeling, and cooking apples was done as quickly as possible so the kettle could move on to another family. Apple butter probably appeared on the table for every meal, but the consumption of twenty to thirty gallons annually by a family of seven and their visitors requires real imagination!

25–26 August 1886: Jerry went to Sam Goods shop got the cider mill repaired paid $3.50 . . . Elmer painted the cider mill . . . *18–21 September* Gathered apples for cider[9] . . . Jerry left for the cider mill half past three got home before 11 Oclock [*A.M.*] *had four barrels of cider, I boiled two down into one, took the other two to Cals . . . finished peeling apples & made apple butter took it off about five Oclock P.M. . . . 6–7 October* I boiled down three barrels of cider, Elmer & I went to Cals got a buggy load of apples for filling applebutter pealed a tub full of cored apples this evening very busy all day . . . made 15 gal of apple butter in forenoon and 13 in afternoon pealed the apples for the last kettleful this morning, went to town got 12 apple butter crocks 8⅓ cts apiece $1.00

28 September–1 October 1888: The boys and Cal finished picking cider apples. Cal took them to Fosters mill this afternoon had 163 gal. we got 86 gal, Cal 77 paid 88 cts for grinding. Father brought his grapes here, ground and pressed them on the cider mill, made about eleven gal. of wine [*juice*] . . . Orra borrowed P. Dows kettle this morning then picked apples to make apple butter. We boiled down two barrels of cider into one, peeled the apples ready for making apple butter Monday . . . Elmer and I made apple butter, took off 17 gal about five Oclock

17–18 October 1889: Cal took a load of apples to Fosters made three barrels and 26 gal of cider . . . Jerry went to Cals got two sacks of sweet apples, Orra picked some apples here. I went to Georges got their apple butter kettle boiled down the cider, put in the apples at two Oclock, boiled till nine, had 17 gal. very nice.

27 September 1895: Orra & George got up at 4 Oclock this morning and began the apple butter, finished it about 11 Oclock. Wellie finished his this afternoon he had 24 gallons, we had 30 gallons.

2 November 1895: got an ounce of sallicillic acid to put in the cider to keep it sweet

10 June 1892: a hoop of the vinegar barrel burst off and all the vinegar run out.

Late in the nineteenth century much of urban America could depend upon the iceman for home delivery of block ice to preserve food during hot weather. But in the northwestern Ohio climate, rural families like the Gebbys relied on the centuries-old system of cutting ice from local lakes and ponds and packing it between layers of sawdust for storage in special ice houses. The results were the same, and Margaret's journals provide ample evidence of the family's fondness for ice cream.

7–8 March 1890: Mercury 8 above zero this morning, 20 this evening. Orra, Lon & Sam Robeson cut ice on Pashs pond this afternoon.

Cal hauled one load this eve packed it in the old house . . . Cal and Orra went to Anderson Neers got each a load of saw dust for packing the ice.

7–9 January 1891: Orra took the sawdust out of the ice house preparing to refill it . . . Orra and Bob cut three loads of ice in Pashs pond hauled one load, packed it in the ice house . . . Orra and Bob hauled and packed two more loads of ice this afternoon.

11 January 1892: Bob cut, hauled & put away three loads 156 blocks of ice to day.

29 January–1 February 1894: Orra and Wellie cutting ice on Silver Lake . . . George and Wellie hauled three loads of ice from Silver lake to day, did not get the last one packed. hauled all that was cut . . . George & Wellie packed the load of ice brought home last night then went to the lake to cut three more loads. Orra helped haul and pack three loads today, making six altogether . . . Orra carried in some sawdust, put some water on the ice for it to freeze it being somewhat porous.

3 January 1895: The men finished hauling ice to day, put seven loads in the ice house, very clear solid and lovely ice.

28 April–14 July 1890: made ice cream for supper . . . Had ice cream for supper, sent Orra Dillon a dish of it; Father and Mother called this afternoon, we made ice cream all enjoyed it very much . . . Jerry got ice cream freezer $2.00 . . . The boys made 1½ gallons of ice cream, some friends spent the evening with us, John Foster & sister, Maud Hiatt, Jim Cook, Sofa & Miss Anderson, Ed, Harry, Sallie & Mary Aikin, Lon, Sam & Lizzie Robeson, and Arthur McCracken, left at 12 Oclock . . . Father, Mother, Aunt Mattie and Anna Doan were here for dinner, had ice cream . . . very warm 93 in the shade, Sam Robeson got some ice this P.M.

12 July 1893: got a dozen Bannas 25 cts to put in ice cream, made it for supper.[10]

11 June 1894: had ice cream & iced tea for supper.

A practice that was certainly common only among farm families was the preservation of some eggs for winter months when hens quit laying. Margaret probably counted on these primarily for baking. The use of oats as a preservative may have been based more upon folklore and convenience than scientific fact, but the results were evidently satisfactory for this housewife continued the practice for years.

29 September 1888: put up some eggs in oats

7 November 1893: Baked bread, churned, went to the farm this afternoon got some oats to pack eggs for winter, husked some corn for meal, called at Wellies

13 November 1894: packed away 100 eggs.

MEAT AND BUTCHERING

One naturally expects that a livestock farm would produce meat for the family, but lack of refrigeration facilities in the nineteenth century meant that this farm family, which received its major income by feeding steers for market, rarely ate its own beef. When the Gebbys did eat their own beef or veal, it was an old milk cow or a dairy calf and they usually kept only a hindquarter for their own use.

27 November 1888: Jerry took a forequarter of beef to Conns (133 lbs) and one hind quarter to Shingles grocery in exchange for a barrel of sugar, beef came to $11.66 paid the balance in money $13.14. Mr Conn is to work for his $5.32. Cal got 37 lbs at 5 cts pr lb $1.85, sold beef hide for $2.88, making in all for the old cow 21.71

13 January 1890: got the roan calf slaughtered, sold half of it to the Home [*Children's Home*] a quarter to Cal = $7.50 . . . *10 March* Orra took the red calf to the slaughterhouse, about ten Oclock they got the beef took a hindquarter to the Home (70 lbs) one to Cals (55 lbs at 4 cts) one to Uncle Johns, kept the other hind qr.[11]

23 October 1894: Paid Fred Dillon 75 cts for slaughtering a calf. brought the meat home from the slaughterhouse, John Longfellow got one forequarter and G.W. Aikin the other. We cut the hind quarters gave the Robesons some, Wellie some and put the rest in sacks on ice in the cellar.

Pork, however, could be preserved in a variety of ways and the Gebby family diet included a great deal of meat from their own hogs, mostly smoked or as sausage. In classic nineteenth-century tradition, butchering was a cooperative event with family or neighbors. In the midst of butchering, however, it is worth noting that the workers ate chicken! These, too, were homegrown and appeared on the family table frequently in a variety of forms.

11 October 1888: Cal and Orra killed a pig this evening, dressed it hung it up in the smokehouse . . . *10 December* Grandma and I were at Cals helping to butcher. they slaughtered four hogs. Andy Koonts and Alice, John Neer, Billy Huber, Mrs Huber and Arch Murdock helped. we got home about four Oclock

12–13 December 1889: We butchered three hogs, Cal, Lon & Sam Robeson helping. Sallie Murdock helped me, finished all, had 75 lbs of sausage and 15 gal of lard . . . we cleaned the hogs feet, cooked three crocks of sausage.

27 December 1890: Uncle Johns brought their meat to the smoke-house to smoke

17–20 February 1894: Wellie brought a load of green hickory wood for smoking meat . . . Orra & Jerry hung our meat in the smoke house this afternoon

10–11 January 1895: Orra prepared for butchering tomorrow. was at the farm brought home two hogs to slaughter, one weighed 285 the other 265. Wellie brought the lard press, kettles, & other utensils . . . We butchered two hogs to day. Harry Aikin and Wellie helped. Aunt Hannah and M.A. Aikin helped us in the house. we stuffed nearly all the sausage, had 61 lbs.

3–4 December 1896: The men brought home two hogs to butcher tomorrow weight 335 lbs. We baked a hickory nut cake for tomorrow. George bought some sausage cases 24 cts. . . . Slaughtered two large hogs, Sam & Lon Robeson, Lizzie & Mattie helped. We had about 14 or 15 gallons of lard 77 lbs of Sausage, did not get all the sausage stuffed, the machine did not work well. killed and roasted two chickens for dinner . . . *16–18 December* Orra helped Aikins butcher to day. George & Jerry & I helped Robesons, they had three hogs, we got along nicely, got everything done . . . Sam Robeson and Harry Aikins helped Orra slaughter two hogs, they weighed about 250 lbs. Nannie and I helped, got all done nicely they had 48 lbs of sausage, stuffed it all.

13 April 1893: dressed a chicken made noodles for supper

16 August 1889: killed and dressed two spring chickens for dinner, had our first mess of tomatoes

10 November 1896: We dressed two chickens fried one boiled the other to make salad.

Because of the proximity of two sizable lakes, the Gebbys ate fish with some regularity. Fishing was obviously a sport for the Gebby men and their friends, but the fact that Margaret also bought fresh fish at the store indicates it was a popular food with this family. Both Orra and George enjoyed hunting as teenagers, but they rarely contributed significant game to the family table.

30 January 1886: Went to town in afternoon to Harners staid for supper. Harry brought two bushels of fish from reservoir caught in dip net by cutting the ice

21 February 1889: Jerry was at the farm this afternoon looking after things caught a fish in the creek brought it home in his pocket . . . *18 June* got an eight lb. fish this morning 45c

31 May 1890: Jerry got a kit of Mackerel $1.65

15 May 1894: Orra and George was at the reservoir fishing, caught 72 fish but they were small, brought home 16, got home about 3 P.M.

24 July 1895: Jerry and George were fishing at Ed Lemens lake, brought home 11 sunfish

30 November 1889: Jerry, Lon Robeson, Rev. S. Bennett, Berry Lesourd & Homer were hunting all day, went to Ed Lemens got 30 Rabbits & 16 Quails. Jerry brought home four Rabbits . . . had rabbit pie for dinner

12–13 December 1890: Jerry Orra, Lon & Sam Robeson went to Ed Lemens hunting, expected Berry Lesourd and Homer but they failed to materialize. took along 2 cans oysters, 25 cts crackers, got 19 Quail, brought home 4 . . . Baked quail pie for dinner

18 March 1892: Orra went duck hunting, shot six at the pond in the big woods at the farm. gave two of them to Uncle Johns. we cleaned the rest this eve.

10 November 1894: Orra and George was hunting to day got 12 Quails and two Rabbits. We baked pies, cleaned a chicken, 12 quails & two Rabbits

COOKING AND BAKING

Like most farm families the Gebbys had three hearty meals each day, referring to the main meal in midday as dinner and the evening meal as supper. The focus of cooking was to prepare a quantity of "wholesome" food. For the most part this meant skillet-fried meats and boiled vegetables, and Margaret rarely mentioned her menu. But baking was a source of pride, and in this area homemakers exchanged recipes and sought compliments in the manner of modern gourmet cooks.

Margaret kept her own yeast starter and regularly baked five or six loaves of bread twice a week.[12] She frequently baked cookies or made doughnuts, and when expecting company or carrying food to a family dinner, her pride and joy was a coconut or hickory nut cake. But the

regular family dessert for dinner and supper was pie. It appears to have been the standard against which a "good cook" was measured, and these diaries reflect real pride in the variety of pies served.

8 January 1886: Baked bread, cake, pies, Doughnuts &c busy all day preparing for company tomorrow . . . *31 May* Made yeast and baked bread and pies three cherry and two pieplant [*rhubarb*] . . . *16 October* Baked bread, pies and burnt a cake[13]

15 February 1887: Baked five loaves of brown bread and one of white, pies, cookies and ginger snaps . . . *30 July* Mercury 96 on the porch at noon, baked bread, pies & cookies canned two qts of pears.

28 April 1888: Churned, baked bread and pies two plum and two pie plant, the first of the season . . . *15 June* Baked bread and six pies, three cherry, the first of the season, and three gooseberry . . . *15 September* Churned baked bread and three plum pies and one peach pie, the first of the season.

11 April 1890: I baked a Jelly cake and two fruit cakes . . . *5 December* Baked four pumpkin and 4 Apple pies

3 July 1891: Baked 6 loaves of bread, 10 cherry pies, canned 9 qts of Gooseberries, bought a knife for peeling vegetables 25[14]

20 April 1894: Baked bread and an apple, a pie plant and an orange pie . . . *7 June* Baked 4 Lemon pies and one pie plant . . . *9 June* picked about 3 gallons of Cherries, made four pies

18 June 1896: Nannie and I finished cleaning the Gooseberries, baked brown and white bread, also a cake.

Considering the frequency and quantity of baking, it is not surprising that the Gebbys stocked basic ingredients in bulk. They produced their own fats, of course, in the form of lard and butter. The wheat that the farm produced was a cash crop, but the family evidently had an account at the mill and took flour about one hundred pounds at a time, not necessarily from their own crop. Sugar was ordered by the barrel every six to nine months from the general store, and other sweeteners such as maple syrup, honey, and molasses were bought directly from local producers as available.[15]

16 April 1886: Jerry went to the mill got 100 lbs flour . . . *5 August* Jerry went to mill, got 150 lbs of flour

13 March 1888: Jerry went to mill this afternoon, got all the flour coming to him there

8 February 1888: Bought a barrel of sugar from Boals 345 lbs at 7.75 pr (100) lb $26.73

22 December 1893: Jerry bought a barrel of Sugar at 5 cts pr lb $17.05

17 March 1896: ordered a barrel of sugar 342 lbs paid 5½ pr lb $19.03 . . . *5 November* Oscar McLaughlen sent out a barrel of sugar ordered yesterday 326 lbs at 4½ cts pr lb $14.76

4 March 1887: Jerry engaged ten gal. of maple syrup at 75 cts pr gal

24 July 1893: Jerry bought 7¾ lbs of honey from Sam Snapp $1.17

14 March 1894: Jerry paid Jim Cook $10.00 for 12 gal of Molasses (80 cts pr gal)

Like most farm wives who sold butter and eggs, Margaret confined her trade to one general store even though towns the size of Bellefontaine had several. In regular trips at least weekly, Margaret purchased spices, coffee and tea, and fruits from other climates such as lemons and bananas. The variety of foods available to this farm family by rail transportation is dramatized by the frequency with which they purchased fresh oysters. By this time food was available commercially in tin cans, and Margaret often supplemented her home-canned supply by buying apricots or peaches.

26 January 1888: Had 7 lbs 10 oz butter 1.52, got sugar $1.00 coffee 28 cts peaches 32 cts, apricots 19 cts, Oysters 70 cts . . . *2 June* Went to town this afternoon, had 22 lbs 14 oz of butter 12 cts pr lb, got coffee, tea, bluing, muslin, candy, fish $1.61, left a balance of $1.13 . . . *25 August* sold 15 lbs of butter this week $2.25 got corn starch, cinnamon, under vest, buttons, stocking $1.16, got a basket of peaches 50 cts

30 January 1890: I went to town had 10 lbs 5 oz of butter $1.55, 4 doz eggs 48, got raisins, coffee, muslin, yarn, B. powder &c . . . *8 February* Jerry & I were at town had 9-3 oz of butter $1.23 got raisins, currants, soap, tea, Eng. plum pudding, sugar $1.00

10 May 1892: Jerry got two doz bananas 24 cts . . . *20 September* Went to town this evening had 3-6 of butter, 75 cts got coffee, cheese, S. Potatoes, Sugar, coconut and Lemons $1.31

14 April 1893: We were in town this afternoon had 10-10 of butter, 7 doz eggs $3.19, 22 lbs of tallow at 4 cts pr lb 90 cts, got yarn, Buttons, thread, muslin, whitewash, brush, mustard, cheese, tea, coffee, ½ doz oranges $2.92 . . . *17 July* Jerry was at town, got Lemons (3 doz) $1.00

14 April 1894: Went to town had 14-14 of butter, 6 doz eggs $3.58, got rice, coffee, cheese, Lemons, Apricots, vinegar & raisins . . . *11 May* Grandma & I were at town had 9-2 of butter 11 doz eggs = $2.09 got matches, coffee, flavoring, Bananas, B. Powder, Pickles & Mustard

16 March 1895: Jerry and I were at town had 7-12 of butter and 5-6 of Eggs $1.08, got Crackers, Tapioca, can fruit, chocolate, Oranges 7 coffee

6 July 1896: I was at town, went with Mattie had 8½ of butter 7-6 of Eggs, got Coffee, Pearlin & Coconut

BUTTER AND EGG BUSINESS

———⋆⟨✳⟩⋆———

Farm wives making their Saturday trips to town with butter and eggs to be exchanged for goods at the general store have become a stereotype of nineteenth-century social history. Margaret's diaries confirm this image, but perhaps because the Gebbys lived closer to town than most farm families, such trips were made whenever time was available, produce was ready to be sold, or purchases were needed.

The real surprise of these journals is that butter and egg sales not only provided the "pin money," which history has attributed to farm wives, but were in fact a thriving home business that made a regular and significant contribution to household expenses.[1]

Throughout these diaries Margaret was usually milking three cows and taking care of chickens every morning and evening. This was probably what she needed to provide a steady supply for her household and to sell enough butter and eggs to buy routine household supplies. Of course production peaked in the spring after the cows calved, but it is astonishing to note that butter prices could fluctuate as much as 80 percent during a single year, from twelve to twenty-two cents per pound in 1888. Farm wives had no choice but to adjust their spending patterns to seasonal fluctuations for they were forced to accept what the market offered for their perishable commodities.

The Gebbys always traded at Boals store, perhaps because this family attended the same church. Margaret maintained an account with a small balance that the boys used when she sent them to the store for something, and she did feel free to "lift" a little credit when necessary. But Margaret's Calvinistic ethic usually caused her to match her pur-

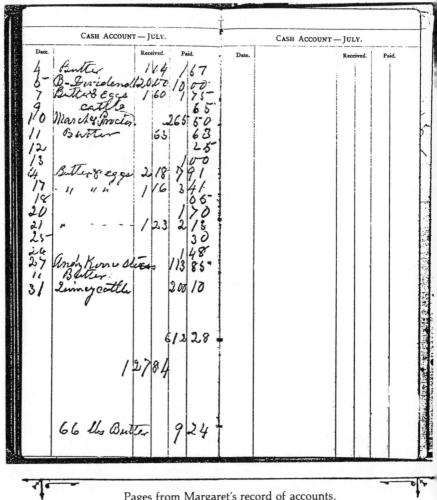

Pages from Margaret's record of accounts.

chases to the value of the produce she brought to sell. Precise control of purchases was somewhat easier when nothing was prepackaged and clerks measured everything to order. Farm wives sold what they had and bought as much as they needed and could afford. Today it is difficult to comprehend selling eleven pounds three ounces of butter or buying twenty-eight cents worth of coffee.

6 January 1886: Went to town had 15 lbs butter got some groceries and drygoods $2.05 cts. Paper collars 2 boxes 20 cts each . . . *8 March* Stormy, snowing but not very cold, went to town in afternoon got a calico dress and some groceries $1.95, had 12½ lbs of butter 15 cts pr lb. got milling, 150 lbs of flour, called at Mrs Wrights, Orries coat buttons 3 cts

17–18 November 1886: Caught three roosters and some hens to sell . . . Jerry took 18 hens and 3 roosters to the packing house got 4 cts [*per pound*] for hens & 2 cts for the roosters, in all $2.76

27 November 1886: traded with the rag peddler, got 4 tins 3 tumblers, glass dishes & bucket [*no money paid*]

5 January 1888: Grandma & I went to town had 11½ lbs of butter $2.10, got blue calico dress, tea, baking powder, peaches, oil cloth, braid for Grandma's dress &c $2.12 . . . *13 January* was at Boals store had 11 lbs 3 oz of butter $2.01 got table linen 2½ yds at 45 cts pr yd 6 yd toweling 2 yd at 11 ct, 4 yd at 10 cts pr yd, coffee 28 cts . . . *26 January* Had 7 lbs 10 oz butter $1.52, got sugar $1.00 coffee 28 cts peaches 32 cts, apricots 19 cts, Oysters 70 cts . . . *2 February* I began churning this morning before eight Oclock and churned till two, and still did not get butter . . . *3 February* worked at the churn two hours but still did not get butter . . . *9 February* churned but failed to get butter, quit milking Daisy . . . *27 February* quit milking Button this evening . . . *7 March* Susan fresh today . . . *21 March* I have a very bad cold, Orra milked for me this evening . . . *26 April* Daisy fresh . . . *12 May* Baked bread, pies and cookies, churned, went to town this afternoon, had 17 lbs of butter at 18 cts 9 doz eggs 89 cts = $3.06 got coffee, baking powder, corn-starch, beans, peaches, 2 cans apricots, scrim, lamp & chimney &c $2.95 Jerry got fish 63, Century 35, Harpers 10, Lemons 20, Bananas . . . *28 May* Put a hen in a coop, had four chickens, gave her five of another and twelve of another in all 21 . . . *2 June* Went to town this afternoon, had 22 lbs 14 oz of butter 12 cts pr lb, got coffee, tea, bluing, muslin, candy, fish $1.61, left a balance of $1.13 . . . *4 August* Baked bread and pies and apple dumplings for dinner, went to town had four lbs of butter 60 cts and 4 doz eggs 56 got a calico meat platter 60 cts. screen wire 35 cts rivets 25 cts took Mother a basket of pears . . . *25 August* sold 15 lbs of butter this week $2.25 got corn starch, cinnamon, under vest, buttons, stocking $1.16 . . . *13 September* churned this morning, went to town this afternoon had 12 lbs of butter, 3 doz eggs $2.25 got Elmer overalls, collars, copperas, cinnamon & pepper, mustard seed.

As a farm wife selling butter and eggs, Margaret represented labor and management, production and sales, long-range planner and chief of

daily operations. She kept meticulous daily and monthly accounts but did not record farm expenses and family expenses separately. It becomes challenging to separate household expenses for a specific year and attempt to conclude what portion of these expenses were met by butter and egg profits. In 1888, a representative year when this household contained husband and wife, three teenage boys, and an elderly mother-in-law, total cash expenses for family living appear to have been $615.51. Receipts of $130.41 from Margaret's dairy and poultry operation that year provided 21 percent of this total. That same year, a woman teaching full time in Logan County's one-room schools would have earned on average $182.[2] Arguments could be made that an old milk cow sold for beef should not be counted with the butter and egg income, and on the expense side arguments could be made against including $75 contributed to the minister's salary, $20 for a watch and chain for son Elmer, or $27 for Jerry's new suit and topcoat as "annual" family living expenses. Some readers might conclude that the butter and egg income actually contributed as much as 25 percent to 30 percent of the family's annual cash expenditures.[3]

Of course, the Gebbys kept what produce they needed for family use. Margaret's butter records for 1888 show that she sold 496 of the 612 pounds produced. At an average selling price of $0.18 per pound, the 116 pounds consumed would have cost the family $24.88 at the store. Between March and September Margaret sold eighty-three and a half dozen eggs, and the way she baked and cooked for family and company she must have used many more than that at home. The family often had chicken for dinner, drank buttermilk, ate cottage cheese, and used cream liberally when they made ice cream. It does not seem farfetched to assume that the cash value of the dairy and poultry products this family used at home exceeded the value of those sold. The church bazaar could count on Margaret to donate butter and cottage cheese, but when she sold to family or neighbors everyone carefully paid the price currently being paid at the general store. The business aspects of a farm wife's surplus butter and eggs were evidently recognized throughout the community.

26 February 1889: Went to town had 12 lbs 2 oz of butter, got crackers, beans, cinnamon, cloves, raisins, overalls, citron $1.88, left eight cans at the warehouse for molasses, took Mr Harner some butter milk, he is a great deal better . . . *20 September* Grandma & I went to town got coffee, sugar, Flower pot, three spools of thread, a box to pack eggs in for winter use, had 9 lbs 4 oz of butter, took Mrs Wright 50 cts worth of butter

4 January 1890: went to town this afternoon had 9 lbs 4 oz of butter $1.58, got tea, mustard, calico, buttons thread $1.58 . . . *14 June* Grandma and I went to town this afternoon, had 12.10 of butter 4.8 of eggs got ticking & cloves 28 cts, curtain chains 23 cts, window shades 71

8 April 1891: Went to town this P.M. had 4-10 of butter 92 cts, 5 doz eggs 65 cts, got crackers 25, coffee 30, Lemons 15, onion sets 25, & beans 25, 37 cts in money . . . *5 September* Went to town had 10-4 of butter 21 cts pr lb, got shirting & cinnamon, 98 cts, left $1.18 on the books for future use.

9 April 1892: Colder, the ground covered with snow this morning. Went to town had 8-6 of butter, 11 doz of eggs $2.87 got overalls, Lemons, sweet potatoes, mustard, tea &c. . . . *4 June* Martha Krouse [*neighbor*] got a lb of butter 12 cts, Lyman [*brother*] got 6 lbs 75 cts, Boals got 9-4 $1.13 cts, got 2 pr silk mitts 50 cts, 1 can apricots, 2 cans corn, Raddish seed, & Bananas 15 cts. . . . *18 June* were at town had 26½ lbs of butter, got muslin, batting, thread, flavoring, cheese, lamp chimneys, gasoline & Lemons $1.52

18 February 1893: The men not working too cold, everything covered with ice. Baked bread, pies and doughnuts. Went to town this P.M. had 10½ lbs of butter 20 cts pr lb got crackers, cheese, coffee, cinnamon, allspice, raisins, thread, dried beef and molasses $1.42 . . . *25 March* Went to town this afternoon. Boals got 15-4½ of butter ($3.36) got Apricots, Plums, corn, Beans, Raisins, coffee, braid, buttons, mustard, Oranges, & yarn $2.37, called at Fathers, he got 3 lbs of butter 66 cts, Mrs Parker 2¼ 50 cts . . . *5 May* We went to town this evening had 12-12 of butter & 5-6 of eggs $3.46, got cheese, coffee, mustard, matches, oranges, thread, overalls, 2 pr suspenders & pr towels $3.54

22 March 1894: Went to town this afternoon had 18-12 of butter 3 doz of eggs = 3.43 got lemons, oranges, ginger snaps, bannas, mustard, gingham & thread, pepper, & peaches & $1.20 in money, took 3 lbs of butter and 4 doz eggs to D.Dows for the Easter supper tomorrow evening.

Margaret managed the dairy and poultry operation, doing most of the labor as well as the decision making, but her diaries occasionally mention one of the boys helping with milking, feeding, churning, or gathering eggs. Chickens had free rein to search around the barnyard for their own food. Margaret usually intervened when it became time to set a hen to hatch a nest of eggs, but the chosen facilities were casual.

This "fend for yourself" poultry business was intended to produce meat as well as eggs, and Margaret did give some attention to improving her breeding stock. In her early diaries one envisions a haphazard collec-

tion of chickens and turkeys obtained by setting her own eggs or trading with neighbors, but during the 1890s the Gebbys developed a preference for White Leghorns and were trying to upgrade the flock. Desirable chickens were heavier than the lean broilers and fryers preferred today, so the Gebbys sought the largest rooster available. As a farm wife, Margaret could sell her tough old hens to market and select younger birds to provide roast chicken, chicken and dumplings, or chicken salad for the family.

10 April 1890: Set three hens, two in old house, one in the harness box in the machine house . . . 3 May Put a hen and 25 chickens in a coop

7 May 1891: Grandma and I were at Uncle Johns this P.M. exchanged a setting of eggs.

14 April 1892: Set a hen under a gooseberry bush, one between the houses, one in George's boat.

24 April 1893: Set a hen in the old house on the shelves, one in the calf stable manger, found one setting in the briar patch on 30 eggs.

18 October 1894: Caught some chickens that roosted on the trees put them in the chicken house . . . 7 December 1894: George took three old Roosters and four old hens to town this evening, the roosters weighed 15½ at 2 cts pr lb, the hens weighed 22 lbs at 5 cts pr lb, for all he got $1.41

25 February 1895: Jerry and I went to Gideon Zooks this P.M. bought two Roosters the larger weighed 8 lbs 2 oz the smaller 6-4, one was 75 cts the other 50 cts. We weighed our own tonight he weighed 7-1.

10 August 1896: I exchanged 2 sittings of Eggs with Mr George Ebrite, his were White Leghorns . . . 11 August Set a hen in the dog box and one in a box by the hogpen on white Leghorn eggs . . . 18 December A poultry man was here bought 30 hens 153½ lbs at 5½ cts pr lb $8.48

When it became necessary to replace a milk cow the Gebby choice was a Jersey, a breed that has almost disappeared from today's commercial dairy industry because of its comparatively low production and high butterfat content. But Margaret and her contemporaries prized butterfat production, a view twentieth-century consumers sensitized to the role of cholesterol in human health find hard to believe. Of course this family drank buttermilk rather than whole milk as a beverage, and cottage cheese was frequently served, but butter was used liberally in baking and cooking and no doubt spread on bread at every meal. It is worth noting that Margaret regularly weighed 120 pounds or less and lived to the age of eighty-five.

*Family milk cows calved annually to maintain maximum produc-
tion, but Margaret's moral code permitted no mention of a cow in heat
being taken for breeding. Since the Gebbys did not own a bull, it was
probably necessary for one of the men to take the cows to the neighbors
to be bred. Margaret was so matter of fact about many things readers
look in vain for any notation such as "Jerry took Daisy to Kaylors this
morning." Conception was unmentionable, but births were recorded.
Dairy calves were a nuisance, requiring care and consuming milk that
could otherwise be used by people. The Gebbys usually sold bull calves
immediately for veal, but when "Jersey" had twin heifers they became
such pets both were raised and one was given to the new daughter-in-law
for a family cow.*

26–28 May 1892: advertised for a good Jersey cow in the want
column of the Republican . . . Bought a Jersey heifer from Mrs Parker,
$23.00

27 January 1893: Daisy fresh last night sold the calf to Widner for
$1.00 took it away this evening . . . 11 February Jersey fresh this fore-
noon, calf was dead . . . 3 March Button fresh . . . 6 March Jerry saw
Wiedner Bros about buying the calf. This evening one of them came and
got it paid $1.00 . . . 17 April churned Jerseys milk of Saturday and
Sabbath got 2¼ lbs of butter . . . 10 May churned Jerseys milk for one
day got one lb of butter . . . 8 June Sold "Daisy" to Z.Dilly for $20.00

27 May 1895: Jersey was fresh today, has twin calves, little
beauties . . . 9 December A. Snoddy came and dehorned the calves,
Bonny & Pet, paid him 40 cents . . .

4 November 1896: George brought Pet home from the farm. She
weighed 655, Mattie's heifer weighted the same.

*Margaret acquired a creamer to store milk and separate the cream
when the kitchen was remodeled with a new water system in 1889, but
her diary does not describe her churn until 1893 when she bought a new
one. The choice of a Sidney churn seems justified as a labor-saving
device when she records getting butter in eighteen minutes.[4] The time
span between invention and adoption is particularly revealing in this
instance, when such a vital piece of equipment as an improved churn
only cost about the sum of two weeks' butter sales. The Gebbys brought
the churn home, set it up and used it, and paid for it only after Margaret
was satisfied with its performance. Since they enjoyed the same privilege
with new farm equipment, it must have been common practice in this
rural community, at least with established customers.*

16 June 1887: Jerry, Elmer & I set the milk tank this forenoon and the east spouting in the afternoon . . .

22 February 1893: Jerry & I went to town looked for a churn to suit us, we liked a Sidney churn quite well, ordered one . . . *27 February* Jerry got the churn I ordered last week . . . *28 February* Churned with my new churn, had nice butter but was a long time in churning, think I had the cream too cold . . . *1 March* Paid for the churn $4.50, churned again this morning in about 18 min.

The butter and egg business portrayed in Margaret's diaries was probably one she maintained for more than thirty years. The main observable difference between her operation and a modern homemaker who might operate a business such as a catering service from her home is that Margaret, like her sisters and neighbors who were doing the same thing, thought of herself strictly as a housewife. Her time commitment to the business, the percentage of family living income that she earned, and her decision-making responsibilities are remarkably similar to a twentieth-century woman operating a part-time business from home. The dramatic difference is society's concept about this type of economic contribution.[5] An even more startling revelation is the record throughout these diaries of paying one dollar per week to a neighbor woman for laundry, paying the hired man's wife to cut or sew a dress, hiring a young woman to help with spring-cleaning and a mother and son to hang wallpaper. In this neighborhood many "full-time" homemakers generated regular cash income. In the economic hierarchy the butter and egg business was usually conducted by upper-middle-class farm wives who had more than one family cow. Since this activity preceded any income tax law, checking accounts, or credit cards, it is almost impossible to trace this economic network accurately.[6]

CLOTHING

SEWING AND KNITTING

Margaret owned a sewing machine when her diary record began, and she and her mother-in-law very likely made most of the children's clothes when they were small. As teenagers, their need for work and school clothes was beginning to exceed her time, skills, and equipment. During these journals all women's clothing, both Margaret's and her mother-in-law's, was handmade either by themselves or a dressmaker, but most of the men's clothing, except underwear, was purchased ready-made.[1]

It is interesting to note that silk and corduroy were nearly equal in cost, but the latter was in less demand by home sewers and required a special order at the general store. It evidently took about two weeks to receive the special order for corduroy fabric and two days, interspersed with her regular housework, for Margaret to complete a pair of corduroy pants for her son.

16 February 1886: ordered Mr Boals to get some corduroy for Orries pants. got two shirts for Jerry $1.80 . . . *3–6 March* Bought 2¾ yds of Corduroy for Orries pants $2.90 . . . Cut Orries pants sewed some on them . . . finished Orries pants, broke two machine needles.

18 October 1886: I got 2¾ yds of silk to repair my dress & thread $3.19

When Margaret wrote of buying a dress, she meant that she purchased fabric to make a skirt and waist. Although ready-made skirts and waists were beginning to appear in cities, Margaret and her mother-in-

law were probably typical of their rural community in having wardrobes that were completely handmade. For everyday wear this was usually a calico dress that she made herself, using an old dress as a pattern to cut the new. It is not surprising, of course, that Margaret did most of her sewing in the winter when she had more time in the house, but even then it took a couple of weeks during spare moments around her regular work to complete a dress. These diaries confirm the standard image of nineteenth-century grandmothers sitting beside an overflowing sewing basket with a constant supply of mending and knitting for winter evenings or spare moments.

27–28 October 1887: I ripped my gray dress turned it wrong side out and sewed this P.M. . . . ripped up my old red calico to make aprons

21 December 1888: I worked the button holes in Grandmas basque, knit and mended underwear and darned mittens.

10 January–2 February 1891: Jerry, George & I went to town had 4-11 of butter got calico dress, ginger snaps, cheese = 94. Jerry got a pair of shoes $4.00, George $2.00 . . . finished my calico dress . . . made an apron of my old calico dress

8 November 1892: I was at Boals store got two skeins of yarn to knit George mittens

All of Margaret's clothes were eventually recycled. Everyday dresses became aprons and good dresses were remodeled or turned inside out for a fresh appearance. Since she evidently did this to be thrifty, it is obvious why she did this tedious work herself rather than hire a dressmaker. The mainstays of Margaret's wardrobe for church and special events were silk, cashmere, and wool flannel, materials found today only in high-quality garments.

5–21 April 1888: I got 2½ yds of Cashmere and a spool of thread to repair my dress . . . We were at Cals this afternoon borrowed her Delineator fixed my black cashmere dress . . . finished my cashmere skirt, Martha Krouse draped it for me.

17 January 1889: cut my old cashmere polonaise into a basque . . . *5 February* ripped up my old blue calico dress made two aprons

23 September 1891: I ripped up my green dress, want to get it turned and made over

18–19 April 1895: I worked at my old black dress, washed it and cut over the skirt. I was at town had 8 doz of eggs, got coal oil, oranges

82 cts, some velveteen and duck for my dress . . . sewed all day repairing my old cashmere.

Grandma may have helped with the mending and remodeling, but she was in her seventies when these journals began and her eyesight was probably becoming too weak for careful sewing. Margaret or a dressmaker made her dresses. For a "good" dress Margaret paid a dressmaker to cut and fit it from one of her patterns and then took the pieces home to sew together herself. For a special dress, it might take several weeks to complete this job, working it in around her regular work.

30 October–4 December 1886: We went to town Grandma got a dress $1.00 pr yd $8.60 left it at Mrs Campbells to get it cut . . . We went to town got Grandma a pair of calfskin shoes $1.50, paid Mrs Campbell $1.25 for cutting & fitting Grandma's dress . . . Commenced sewing on Grandma's dress this afternoon, shamed [*interlined*] and faced the skirt . . . I sewed at Grandma's dress this afternoon . . . Dressed a chicken for dinner, baked a cake pies & bread, sewed on Grandma's dress . . . fixed Grandma's dress . . . buttons for Grandma's dress 19 cts

Margaret was in her fifties and had no daughters to assist her during most of this period. She often relied on Sallie Murdock, the hired man's wife, for sewing help. Sallie Murdock was a young mother with small children and there is no way of knowing whether she was earning some cash for family luxuries such as Christmas presents or whether she regularly did sewing to supplement the family income. It was certainly one of the few sources of cash money that could be earned at home by a married woman with small children. It was also popular work among the spinsters of the community like Anna Robeson, Jerry's first cousin, who during the 1890s lived less than a half mile away.

Margaret's daily diaries rarely give sufficient details to follow the entire dressmaking process, but in one example of 1889 she clearly bought nine yards of wool flannel for a dress and paid $8.94 for the completed dress, $6.44 for materials and $2.50 for having it made. She never mentions remaking this particular dress so it seems likely that she was still wearing it when her diaries ended seven years later.

19 November–23 December 1889: Grandma & I went to town this P.M. she got a silk warp Henrietta dress $11.25, a flannel skirt $1.25. I got a green striped flannel (9 × 60) = 5.40, linings & thread $1.04 . . . I left my measure and dress with Sallie this morning . . . I went to Sallies had my dress fit . . . Sallie Murdock called this afternoon got the buttons for my dress . . . went to Sallie Murdocks got my dress, paid $2.50 for making it . . . George took Grandma's dress to Sallie Murdock this morning for making it, Grandma disappointed not going on account of Charlies sore foot[2] . . . took Grandma to Cals having her measure for her dress . . . Grandma went to Sallie Murdocks got her dress, paid $2.50

DRESSMAKERS AND MILLINERS

These journals make a clear distinction between neighbors or relatives (whose skills were evidently comparable to Margaret's own) who were paid to sew a dress together and professional dressmakers who were expected to take measurements, cut a pattern, and fit the garment to a live model. Dressmaking skills were learned through an apprenticeship and Margaret and her mother-in-law took advantage of cousin Anna Robeson's need for experience while learning the trade.

Although the Gebby women and Robeson women regularly exchanged work when cooking for threshers or making sausage at butchering, once Anna became a professional dressmaker Margaret never sought her help in cutting a dress without paying for it.

31 January 1890: I went with Anna & Lizzie Robeson to Mrs Thrifts, Anna engaged to sew and learn dress making with her about the first of April . . . *17 February* I took my cashmere dress to Anna to make over . . . *12 June* Anna took Grandmas measure to practice cutting with a model . . . *8–17 October* I bought a dress $8.39 . . . went to Uncle Johns this P.M., left my dress for Anna to make . . . I went to Uncle Johns this afternoon had my dress fitted . . . Anna called tried on my dress, fits very well.

4–18 July 1891: went to town got Grandma & I each a dress. Pongee 15 cts pr yd & trimming $2.55 . . . Anna Robeson got my dress to cut it this evening . . . Anna fitted my dress this evening . . . I am not well to day sewed some on my dress paid Anna 50 cts for cutting it . . . paid Anna 35 cts for cutting Grandmas dress . . . finished my dress this evening, sewed some on Grandmas

Margaret could afford to pay a dressmaker for an extra special dress, but she obviously watched her expenses closely. On one occasion she hired an expert to work with an expensive fabric, but her extended

family included nieces who were evidently pleased to earn some money sewing everyday dresses.

13 May–8 June 1893: Jerry and I went to town I got six yards of lace goods for a dress $12.00 . . . called at the dress makers Miss Chamberlin about making my dress but she was not at home . . . went to town left my dress for Miss Chamberlin to make and my hat at Miss Youngs to fix . . . I stopped at Miss Chamberlins left my measure [*had measurements taken*] to make my dress . . . I had my dress fitted this morning . . . got my dress, paid Miss Chamberlain $3.50 for making it.[3]

31 August–21 September 1894: got a gray dress, 50 cts pr yd, 7 yds with trimmings $6.67 . . . I was at G.W.Aikins this afternoon left my dress for Mary to make . . . Mary Aikin was here tried on my dress . . . Mary Aikin brought my dress home to day paid her for making it $2.00.

There was clearly a code even within the family about work that was exchanged and work that was paid. Margaret paid cousins and nieces who sewed for her or her mother-in-law, but she and her sisters occasionally spent a day at her mother's helping her sew. The same pattern began with her daughter-in-law after Orra married. Within the immediate family of mothers and daughters no money changed hands, but in the extended family of cousins, aunts, and nieces sewing services were paid rather than exchanged.

2–27 March 1896: Mattie and I was at town this afternoon, got a dress and trimming . . . I was at Orras all day, had my dress fitted. I hemmed a table cloth all round . . . Jerry and I were at the farm this morning tried on my dress. Mattie & I were at town this P.M. got trimmings &c $3.50

The new daughter-in-law was evidently a skilled seamstress and Margaret began confining herself more to finishing touches and the mending and remodeling chores. Mattie was even tackling millinery, a job Margaret had always paid to have done.

16–23 November 1889: I looked at bonnets in Mrs Lees, the Hicks sisters & Mrs Moore, agreed to send my bonnet in Monday for repairs . . . Grandma & I went to town got my bonnet done over $2.00

4 June 1890: Went to town, Grandma got a bonnet $3.00, I took a frame and some lace to Mrs Moores to get one made.

16 November 1895: Mattie and I was at the Milliner store. Got a bonnet frame, flowers, velvet &c. $1.90. Mattie made it for me very nicely.

MALE AND FEMALE WARDROBES

In the Gebby family everyone evidently got a new pair of shoes about once a year, and their service was extended by wearing rubber overshoes in muddy, snowy, or wet weather.

Margaret's outer garment in cold weather was always a shawl or wrap and her journals give the impression that she bought quality and expected these items to wear for many years. It is interesting to speculate whether it was a coincidence or whether there was a direct link between the fur wrap she bought in 1896 and the interest she received the same day on an agricultural society note her father had given her before his death. Perhaps she considered this a luxury purchase and the interest on this note her own personal money.

2 April 1886: Went to town this afternoon got Orra shoes $3.00 Grandma shoes 1.50 rubbers 25, Elmers shoes $1.90, my rubbers 25 cts.

16 March 1889: bought a black cashmere shawl $7.00 . . . *2 December* went with Anna & Lizzie to town got a plush wrap at Bradburys $25.00

6 October 1896: I was at town with Mattie got a fur wrap paid $25.00 for it. Elmer[4] got the interest on the Agricultural note to day $70.00

While all women's clothing was made at home or by a dressmaker, the men's everyday clothes and dress shirts were purchased ready-made and good suits were tailor-made. Prices of clothing for the boys increased steadily as they grew older. It seems to have been a tradition in the Gebby family, perhaps in this community, for a young man to receive his first tailor-made suit for high school graduation. About the same time the boys began choosing their own clothing rather than having their mother shop for or with them.

18 October 1886: Went to town this afternoon got Orra a suit of clothes $16.00, tie 50 cts, suspenders 25 cts, socks (2 pr) 84 cts. . . . *6 November* got George a suit of clothes $6.75, boots 2.25

8 November 1887: went to town got Orra a suit of clothes $17.00, pair of pants $3.00 Overcoat $10.00 . . . *19 November* We went to town got Elmer a suit of clothes $8.50, a hat $1.50 George a suit 6.50, Boots $2.50

16 May 1891: Elmer looking at cloth for a suit of clothes . . . *18 May* Elmer ordered a suit of clothing made $25.00 . . . *23 May* gave Elmer 27.00 for his outfit for the commencement, $3.50 shirts & collars . . . *26 May* Elmer got his suit ordered at Abes $27.00

17 June 1893: bought George a suit of clothes, a hat, cuffs, buttons & holders $11.25

10 October 1894: Orra got $15.00 to buy clothes, got an overcoat $9.50, a knit Jacket $1.25

8–25 May 1895: George ordered a suit of clothes for commencement this morning . . . George got his suit of clothes $25.00

As a farmer Jerry wore overalls for work,[5] so a good suit for Sunday lasted much longer than the boys' school clothes. It would appear that he bought three suits, one of which was tailor-made, during the eleven years covered by these diaries. Most trips to town were probably made in everyday clothes, but serving on the jury or meeting with the bank directors would call for his Sunday suit.

2 September 1886: Jerry was at town got a suit of clothes and a hat $22.00

16 November 1888: Jerry was at town got a pair of overalls 85 cts . . . *10 December* Jerry went to town got a suit of clothes, an overcoat, hat, suspenders and tie for $27.50 (at Parkers)

2 December 1889: Jerry bought 6 shirts 50 cts apiece $3.00

24 December 1894: Jerry got a suit of clothes Bartram made for him, paid him $20.00

HEALTH and HOME NURSING

———✦———

ACCIDENTS AND ILLNESS

Considering the dangers involved in working around machinery and livestock, the Gebby family was remarkably free of accidents during the years of Margaret's diaries. In addition to her own family and hired men, a variety of workmen from painters to carpenters and threshing crews worked on the farm without serious mishap or liability insurance.

22 June 1887: Cal mowed clover all day at the farm, cut his finger with the sickle severely

21 July 1888: finished hauling hay took in four loads the sack of stones fell on Orras hand mashing a finger severely.[1]

18 September 1889: I went to see G.W. Aikin who unfortunately got his leg broke about noon. Drs Cretcher and Dow dressed it

8 January 1890: George came home [from school] at noon was coasting on a sled ran against a fence rail, struck him on the cheek scratching it some . . . 22 June All attended church except me I did not go because a Bumble bee stung my foot and it swelled up so I could not wear my shoe[2]

18–19 March 1895: G.W. Aikin fell from the Grape Arbor this morning and broke a collar bone . . . went to see G.W. Aikin, he is very sore to day

17 December 1895: Jane Cook slipped on the ice and broke one bone of her wrist.

The nineteenth-century housewife was considered capable of han-

106

dling all types of routine illnesses. Since her father operated a pharmacy for several years and her brother studied medicine, Margaret probably had more information than most housewives about current remedies. She relied on her doctor book and a variety of patent medicines for sore throats, colds, upset stomachs, and diarrhea.[3]

5 February 1886: Jerry went to town this afternoon got some medicine for Elmer. Bitter wine of Iron $1.00 Carters little pills 25 cts. . . . *9 August* I am almost sick with a severe cold

21 January 1887: Jerry has a very severe headache this afternoon took a dose of salts . . . *24 January* My back hurts me considerable . . . *28 January* My back is still sore did not do much work today, Elmer went to town this eve got me a bottle of "Warners Safe Cure" 1.25 . . . *2 March* Jerry took severe attack of pluerisy, all my remedies failed, gave him a mustard vomit, relieved quickly, Lobina 10, Ispicack 20 cts . . . *23–28 May* Jerry sick all day, took a dose of pills this morning . . . Jerry some better but not very well . . . Jerry sick, saw Dr. Rutter and got some medicine 25 cts . . . Jerry took very sick last night Orra went for the Dr. injected some morphine into his side, relieved him soon, been better all day though in bed . . . Jerry better but not very well . . . Jerry improving

10 April 1888: Jerry went to see Dr. Rutter who says his stomach and liver are diseased gave him some medicine to act on his liver . . . *31 July* Grandma sick cholera morbus[4]

19–20 January 1889: Jerry not well. Orra got him some medicine Laudamin 10 cts, essence Peppermint 10 cts, those Morphine powders 25 cts . . . Jerry not well, dizzy headed not able to go to church. Orra, Elmer and I went to S.S. and to church . . . *26 August* Jerry was at town got me some extract of Dandelion 40 cts

10–11 July 1890: George quite sick this P.M. had a chill then a high fever with diarrhea. Elmer sick also . . . Jerry laid off at noon, not able to work. George considerable better, Elmer a little better

24 May 1891: Orra has neuralgia, not able to go to church . . . *7 December* Martha Krouse borrowed the Doctor Book this morning.

2 February 1892: Orra laid up with sore throat, put a piece of fat pork sprinkled with pepper and turpentine on it this evening.

30 December 1893: Jerry some better. I was at town got an ounce of Quinine 60 cts, capsules 15 cts

21 August 1894: I was at Uncle Johns, Julia and children were there. Sadie and Mary have the Hooping cough, sent them some Jaynes Expectorant . . . *26 October* I took six Calomel tablets to day, my cold is not much better.

12–13 March 1896: Jerry was at town this afternoon took the headache had to come right back home[5] . . . Jerry not very well to day was at home all day. I knit a mitten, baked bread, did many other things . . . 30–31 March I helped George lead the calf this morning then worked around in the yard. I am sick to night, the result of getting my feet wet this morning . . . I have been sick all day Elmer got some medicine of Dr Covington for me . . . 6 August I was to the Dr this morning got some medicine he said I had some neuralgic affection, paid him 50 cts

The inevitability with which people accepted diseases such as mumps and measles that have now largely been eliminated by vaccination or regular eruptions of typhoid fever from contaminated drinking water is a shocking reminder of medical progress. Childhood diseases such as mumps and measles usually ran their course and the services of a physician were not sought. The social custom of visiting the sick surely contributed to the spread of infectious diseases, but housewives like Margaret who nursed the ill seem to have acquired immunity to most. Home nursing must have been backbreaking labor in the days before running water and indoor toilets were common and washers and dryers were available for dirty bed linens. These journals show that one child often brought a contagious disease home from school. By the time siblings caught it and ran its course, mothers invariably had at least a month of nursing sick children.

4 April 1886: Orra has the mumps, he and Grandma staid at home today . . . 7 April Orras mumps not any better . . . 12 April Orra better of his mumps . . . 19 April Orra not well with return of mumps . . . 21 April Orra still quite unwell . . . 24 April George has the mumps, Orra better . . . 26 April Elmer came home with the mumps . . . 27 April Elmer sick with the mumps, George some better, Orra better . . . 29 April Elmer and George some better . . . 30 April George very sick last night and all day, Elmer some better . . . 1 May George quite sick but some better this eve. Elmer still better . . . 7 May Elmer not able to go to school, jaw swelled . . . 10 May went to G.W. Aikins seven of them sick with mumps
13 March 1887: George taking the measles . . . 14 March George not well not able to go to school . . . 16 March George quite sick, coughs very hard . . . 17 March George not any better think he has the measles coughs very hard . . . 19 March George not any better but the measles are pretty much out now . . . 21 March Elmer taking the measles, George not much better . . . 22 March George some better but

coughs very hard yet, Elmer coughs and some measles showing . . . *23 April* Father and Mother was here this afternoon, they were at G. Aikins, six of them have the measles. George some better but Orra and Elmer getting worse . . . *24 March* George getting better but Orra and Elmer are quite sick all day, measles coming out very well . . . *25 March* George still improving but Orra and Elmer not any better real sick all day . . . *26 March* Orra very sick and restless, the measles are out now very well. Elmer and George improving slowly . . . *29 March* the boys are improving slowly, cough quite hard . . . *3 April* The children about the same as yesterday not able to go to Sabbath School, the rest of us went to church . . . *6 April* The boys gaining slowly Orra has a very bad cough, Elmer able to be out a little, George can go to the field

31 July 1895: called to see Dow and Jennie Aikin, they both have Typhoid Malaria, Dow is quite sick . . . *2 August* Dow Aikin is seriously ill with Typhoid fever, no better yet . . . *7 August* Dow Aikin & Cathrine are better to day . . . *10 August* Dow Aikin and Cathrine are improving . . . *13 August* Dow Aikin is improving. they took Cathrine to the country this evening . . . *28 August* Jerry & I was at G.W. Aikins this eve. Cathrine is no better, very much reduced indeed . . . *2 September* Jerry & I were at G.W. Aikins this evening to see Cathrine, she is rather worse yesterday & to day, not much hope of recovery . . . *11 September* Cathrine seems to be improving slowly

Today the elderly and physically infirm are encouraged to receive annual flu shots, but a century ago the scourge of "la grippe" periodically visited almost every community. These diaries frequently mention persons affected, but perhaps the impact on housewives who served as home nurses can best be understood by excerpting one influenza season in some detail. The winter of 1890 brought a severe outbreak in Logan County, Ohio, and Margaret's eighty-two-year-old mother and seventy-seven-year-old mother-in-law were severely affected. Margaret's journal is a rich source for analyzing the extended family female network that coped with exhausting home nursing responsibilities for a period of confinement to bed, which is hard to comprehend by modern standards.

8 February 1890: called at Fathers found Mother quite sick with the la grippe, has been bad for several days . . . *9 February* Staid with Mother all day, she is much the same as yesterday . . . *10 February* we went to see Mother this evening, found her some better . . . *12 February* Ma is up at Grandmothers is going to stay all night[6] . . . *13 February* I sat up with Mother last night, rested tolerably well, not much change or perhaps a little better . . . *14 February* I sat up with Mother, she was very restless part of the time, some easier this morning . . . *15 February* I left Mother easier this morning, walked about half way home, met Jerry coming for me . . . *16 February* Mother is some better. George quite sick, Jerry saw Dr Swan thought the symptoms of Grippe, fever, headache, and terrible aching of the limbs, better this evening . . . *17 February* I went to sit up with Mother. Martha Ann went home to sleep. Jane staid with me . . . *18 February* Mother rested very well last night, think her some better. We got some sleep. Martha Ann came in this morning, George brought me home . . . *19 February* Ma is up at grandmas to stay all night[7] . . . *20 February* I came home after dinner, sat up with Mother all night, she was restless, but easier now. I helped M.A. change Mothers clothes and bed then wash them . . . *22 February* Mother about the same as yesterday. Grandma sick all night, Jerry got some medicine from Dr Wilson 50 cts not much change in her yet . . . *24 February* went to see Mother this afternoon found her about as she had been. Grandma still very sick, Anna stayed with her this afternoon. Mr & Mrs Harner, Mrs Barnett, Mrs Maxwell, Grandma Beatty called to see her . . . *25 February* changed Grandmas clothes and bed, washed but raining did not get the clothes dry. Dr Wilson was here this morning & evening, ordered some whiskey for Grandma, Jerry got ½ pt. Mrs Conn & Mrs Dillon called today. Aunt Hannah is sitting up to night . . . *26 February* saw Mother, she is still very weak but thought to be a little better. Aunt Hannah staid with Grandma last night she is very sick, probably some stronger . . . *27 February* Grandma not much change, very weak not suffering much pain. the Dr thinks her a little better. Anna & Lizzie was here last night . . . *28 February* Mother is a very little better. this being the last day of school George thought he was able to go. Grandma seems to be improving slowly, the Dr was here this afternoon . . . *1 March* Dr Wilson was here this afternoon says Grandma is improving, Aunt Hannah sat up last night . . . *3 March* Grandma still improving, Lizzie Robeson came to stay with Grandma while I went to town to see Mother, found her some better, but discouraged. Uncle John, Mrs Krouse and George Harner called to see Grandma to day. Dr Wilson here this eve. says Grandma is better will not come back unless necessary . . . *4 March* A March day. Snow, wind, sunshine, freezing and thawing. Mother still improving slowly. Grandma considerable better. G.W. Aikin, Rev. Hamilton called to see Grandma, also Mrs Leedom & Mrs J.D. McLaughlin, who came in a cast . . . *6 March* Grandma still improving slowly, sat up some to day . . . *9 March* I went to church (communion day), Jerry went this evening, George and I stayed with

Grandma, she is about as usual . . . *10 March* Martha Ann called this eve. Mother not much better, Grandma some better . . . *11 March* Stayed at Fathers all night, M.A. Aikin slept till about 3 Oclock, Mother getting very nervous. I stayed up till morning . . . *12 March* Rained all night everything soaking wet, walked home this morning through the rain . . . *13 March* awful muddy, I went to town had 5 lbs butter 20 cts pr lb got coffee, baking powder, peaches, dried apples, called at Fathers, Mother much as she has been, quite weak . . . *14 March* I sat up with Mother last night, think her better. Lyman was there untill after one Oclock . . . *17 March* I staid with Mother last night, left her some better this morning, got home as the rest were eating breakfast . . . *19 March* went to see Mother, she is about the same . . . *25 March* Mother much improved . . . *5 April* Mother much better . . . *10 April* Father and Mother called this afternoon, the first time for ten weeks . . . *10 May* Jerry paid Dr Wilson for treating Grandma $14.00

EYES, EARS, AND TEETH

The relative primitiveness of corrective prescriptions available for those who suffered from loss of hearing and eyesight a century ago is confirmed by these journals. Eyeglasses were purchased by trial and error at the store rather than from a physician's prescription.

25 September 1893: Father and I took dinner at Charley Cooks then went to a Mrs Herrons about her opinion of artificial Ear Drums. she is satisfied with hers

2 January 1886: Went to Cals to hunt my Spectacles Cal found them in the yard

29 September 1887: Got a pair of spectacles for Jerry $4.50 a present from Orra, Elmer & George.[8]

13 August 1888: got a pair of spectacles $5.00

6–7 July 1896: Exchanged my broken glasses for a new pair at Charlie Millers $6.50 . . . Elmer brought home my glasses paid $5.75 and my old ones. did not get new lens but will in a few days.

Treatment of tooth decay by routine extraction of adult teeth may shock modern readers, who often hold an unrealistic perception of nine-teenth-century medical capabilities.

22 December 1886: Elmer came home with the toothache, went to the Dentist, took gas $1.00 got it pulled.

29 July 1889: Orra had two teeth extracted paid $1.50

17 September 1892: Grandma got her new teeth $10.00[9]

21 August 1896: George got his two front teeth filled this forenoon, paid $1.50 apiece[10]

BIRTH AND DEATH

Births took place at home, of course, but in communities the size of Bellefontaine the availability of doctors had largely eliminated the practice of experienced neighborhood mothers serving as midwives. Presence at a delivery was now more likely limited to the mother, mother-in-law, or other close female relative. The only births Margaret mentions are in the hired men's households, where the event and the relationship evidently called for her presence.

2–4 August 1886: Went to Cals this eve. they had a son born about six Oclock . . . Went to Cals to see the new boy

28 February 1891: I was at Bobs last night and until about 10 Oclock this A.M. they have a daughter

Such brief factual entries about these births reflect no joy or pain. Perhaps this is Margaret's sense of what is permissible in a written diary that any member of her family might read. It may portray her Calvinistic acceptance of the inevitability of life and death, or perhaps it reflects a farm wife who lives daily with life and death in the animal world.

Margaret was fifty when these diaries began, and only the deaths of her infant son and Jerry's brother had previously touched her immediate family circle. But during these years death was drawing closer. Among neighbors and family she recorded deaths of infants and elderly, sudden and lingering, expected and unexpected. In an era when deaths occurred at home rather than in hospitals, her entries suggest that housewives who cared for the sick developed attitudes of acceptance more comparable to modern nurses than grieving relatives.

Within the customs of the time and community, one can glean subtle emotional distinctions, particularly in her record of the deaths of three neighbor boys, one from tuberculosis and the others in a boating accident. One was anticipated and the others a shock. Readers can al-

*most feel Margaret's unspoken realization that the latter could so easily
have been one of her sons.*

*Several of Margaret and Jerry's aunts and uncles died during this
period, and her diary entries reflect caring interaction with relatives but
express no deep grief for persons who had lived a full life.*

25 February 1889: Grandma and I went to John Dows funeral at two
Oclock this afternoon.[11] Mr Hamilton spoke from the words "be ye also
ready," very appropriate remarks, quite a good many there.

4 September 1891: Dr & Nannie Philipps babe was buried this afternoon[12]

26 February 1895: G.W. Aikin told us that one of E.E. Clelands
children (Jennetta) is dead with Whooping cough.[13]

6–18 September 1890: I called to see Orra Dillon he seems to be
getting weaker took him a glass of Jelly[14] . . . Euge Dillon wants us to go
to their house, Orra much worse . . . Jerry & I were at Dillons last
night. Orra Dillon died of consumption at 15 min past three this morning, we got home about half past six this morning. funeral Thursday at 2
Oclock. Jerry went to John Hubers for a girl for them. Cora came for to
day only . . . this afternoon all attended the funeral of Orra Dillon at 2
Oclock. Services by Rev. Hamilton. Remarks from Ps 46.1 "God is our
refuge and strength" a large funeral. Pall bearers Orra & Elmer, Ed and
Harry Aikin, Jesse Kaylor & Harry Eaton

4–7 June 1891: a party of six young men went to the reservoir
fishing Albert Dillon, Harry Whitehill, Ed Foot, Doc Huber, Frank Whitehill, & Homer McCracken, 3 in a boat. Homer was rowing ran on a
stump & upset the boat threw Albert & Harvey Whitehill out & both
were drowned. Mr & Mrs Dillon were dispatched for, being at Clyde,
came home on the 12 Oclock train, an awful shock to all. I stayed there
untill after they came home . . . the bodies of the drowned boys were
found. Albert Dillon at half past six and Harvey Whitehill some later,
brought the remains home at once. Whitehill was left at the undertakers,
Albert was brought home, a terrible blow to the family. Jerry, Grandma
and I was there this P.M. . . . was at the funeral of Albert Dillon at 2
Oclock Mr Hamilton officiated Mr Singley assisted. the largest funeral
ever in this neighborhood at least 175 vehicles, a great many walking.

22 February 1887: Called to see Uncle Robert who is sick with
Brights Disease he was some better but restless this P.M.[15] . . . *2 March*
Called to see Uncle Robert who is not any better is weak looks worse
than when I last saw him . . . *21 March* Called to see Uncle Robert he is
no better but still getting weaker . . . *23 April* Uncle Robert
failing . . . *29 April* Uncle Robert Dow died last night at seven

Oclock . . . *30 April* Uncle Robert was buried this P.M. at 2 Oclock, a large funeral

17–20 July 1896: I drove to the farm this evening to bring Jerry home. Uncle John Robeson dropped dead in the haymow about 5 P.M. Jerry & J.D.M. Kaylor & wife stayed till nearly midnight. Elmer was at Harry Harners & Ed Lemens notifying them of Uncle Johns death . . . Jerry & I went with Lon & Aunt Hannah to the cemetery looking for a lot, bought one in the Southwest part, paid $100.00 for it . . . David Robeson of Piqua was here for dinner came to attend the funeral of Uncle John Robeson at 2 P.M. Rev Hamilton & Rev Silas Bennett officiated, a great many people there. John and Clarissa Kitchen of Monroe, O. who with David Robeson are with us to night.

In little more than three years Margaret's mother, father, and mother-in-law died of "old age." Her diaries report actions and decisions during their final illnesses and reveal a great deal about family and community customs regarding death. The fact that Margaret's brother was a physician who was involved in the care of his parents is unusual, but the contrast with current practice where actions and decisions are often entirely in the hands of medical professionals is still dramatic.

5 February 1892: I stayed with Mother last night she is very feeble not any better . . . *10 February* I sat up with Mother last night she is getting weaker very helpless . . . *11 February* Mother much the same as she has been for several days. Jane Cook is staying there tonight . . . *15 February* Jerry, Orra & George were at church. I stayed with Mother during service, she is still getting weaker . . . *20 February* I stayed with Mother all night . . . *28 February* Orra & George were at church I stayed with Mother she is very low. stayed with her during evening service may not live till morning . . . *2 March* I sat up with Harry Aikin, Maggie Dow and Mrs Ward of Upper Sandusky watching Mother. she slept nearly all night was more rational this morning . . . *3 March* Tommy Cook and I sat up with Mother, she rested well . . . *4 March* Mother still growing weaker, unconscious part of the time . . . *5 March* Mother still very weak, lying in the same position we left her yesterday A.M. at three Oclock . . . *6 March* Mother died at 11.30 P.M. was failing since Friday Morning at 3 A.M. aged 83 years 7 months and 14 days[16] . . . *7 March* Jerry, T. Cook, G.W. Aikin and Lyman selected a casket for Mother price $75.00 . . . *8 March* bought gloves and vail 90 cts . . . *9 March* All attended Mothers funeral at 2 P.M. the remains were open to view from 10 till 2, then were taken to the church. Sermon by Rev. Hamilton Text Ps 116 - "Precious in the sight of the Lord is the death of his saints." the church was full. Pall bearers were John and Eddie Aikin, T.J. Cook, Sammie Dow, Orrie Gebby, Grandsons and Arthur McCracken great grandson. the friends were all there from De-graff also Dr & Nannie Phillipps . . . *10 March* called at Fathers he is lonely and weak . . . *4 April* I went to town this P.M. was at Fathers, he is better now. Lymans moved in with him to day . . . *6 April* Jane Cook, Martha Ann & Sallie and I were at Fathers dividing Mothers things . . . *7 June* Jerry and I went to town this afternoon met Jane Cook, M.A. Aikin with Father & Lyman selected a tombstone for Mothers grave price $150 . . . *11 June* went to the cemetery with Father

19 June 1894: Grandma, Jerry & I were at Charlie Cooks to day had a pleasant visit got home about 5 P.M. . . . *22 June* Grandma not well . . . *24 June* All at church except Grandma . . . *30 June* Dr Wilson was to see Grandma, left her some medicine, she is better today . . . *2 July* Dr Wilson was to see Grandma this P.M. she is some better . . . *5 July* Grandma is no better, seems to be growing weaker . . . *6 July* Grandma is about the same as yesterday, Dr Wilson was to see her to day, left her some powders . . . *7 July* John Harner, wife and two children were here for dinner. Aunt Hannah, Josie & Elsie Lemen & several others called to see Grandma this afternoon, she is not any bet-ter, rather weaker . . . *8 July* Grandma rather worse to day. I sat up with her untill two Oclock this morning, Jerry then got up to care for her . . . *9 July* Grandma getting worse all night and morning and untill she died about 2 Oclock this P.M. aged 81 years & six months, she was born Jan. 9 1813.[17] Quite a good many called this P.M. Sent a Telegram to John Kitchen, some letters to others . . . *10 July* We were at town this P.M. selected a casket for Grandma. Aunt Hannah, Lizzie & Josie Lemen was with us. I got Portiers (chenille) 6.50. Jerry was at the 7-50 train but John Kitchen did not come . . . *11 July* Uncle John & Aunt Clara Kitchen arrived on the 10-30 train were here for dinner. Mr. Hamilton spoke from the words "and the inhabitants shall not say I am sick & the people that dwell therein shall be forgiven inquiries." all of the relatives were here and a great many friends and neighbors, 35 vehicles, the Pall bearers were Orra & Elmer, George & Clarence Harner, Sam & Lon Robeson. She looked very natural, indeed. Jerry hired a Cab. John & Clara, George & Jerry & I went to the Cemetery in it, the Choir, Mrs Swan, Allie Fulton, Anna Dowell, Gil Hehenson rode in our carriage . . . *14 July* Jerry was at town paid Grandmas funeral expenses (Homer Horn) $98.00, Dr Wilson $5.00

13 August 1895: I called to see Father, he is not well, had a chill this morning . . . *14 August* Father is not any better, has fever all the time . . . *15 August* Father is not any better, his temperature is

103 . . . *16 August* saw Father this forenoon and again this evening, he is about the same as he has been, his temperature was 102 . . . *19 August* was to see Father, he is much the same. Elmer and Jim Cook are sitting up with him to night . . . *20 August* Father is much the same, George is staying there to night . . . *22 August* was to see Father this evening, he is not any better, the hiccoughs are no better . . . *23 August* we were called to see Father at noon. he was taken worse about 10 A.M. and died at a quarter till 4 P.M.[18] Funeral on Monday at 2.30 . . . *26 August* Rev Huston of Bellecentre conducted the services, Rev Hamilton read the 90 Psalm, Huston preached from Rev. 1-17-18. Dr Kalb made a few remarks, also Rev Havinghorst, a great many people there . . . *12 September* I was at Lymans this afternoon, expected to divide Fathers things but Jane could not be there, did not do any thing : . . *14 September* Met sister Jane & Martha Ann at Lymans, divided the things belonging to Father.

APPENDECTOMY

The most tragic illness in the Gebby family during the years covered by Margaret's journals occurred in 1896 when the oldest son Orra was stricken with appendicitis. Through her diary entries readers sense at least some of the desperation that confronted a family when the statistical odds for surgery in this rural community were nearly as poor as no treatment at all.

The three-month recovery period for a twenty-four-year-old man accustomed to the physical labor of daily farm work attests to the complications from delayed diagnosis and treatment as well as prolonged convalescence from the prevailing medical practice of confining surgical patients to bed.[19]

14 May 1896: Orra got sick this forenoon went to the Dr got medicine, something like colic . . . *15 May* Orra is still quite unwell, he was to see the Dr again this afternoon. he says he has Appendicitis . . . *16 May* I was to see Orra he is still quite sick. Dr Hamer was to see him this afternoon, pronounces his case Appendicitis . . . *17 May* All at church this morning, after dinner Jerry & I went to Orras he is very sick, vomited about 5 Oclock seemed better. we came home had been home but a short time untill Wellie came for the Dr. I went home with him he was very bad all night . . . *18 May* Dr Hamer assisted by Drs Pratt &

Heffner Successfully performed a surgical operation on Orra for Appendicitis this afternoon, over an hour at work. is very much prostrated and nervous[20] . . . *31 May* Orra is getting along as well as usual this morning. Elmer staid out there last night, Jerry & I went out here this morning and staid all day. Nannie and the boys went to church[21] . . . *6 June* I went to stay with Orra while Mattie went to town. he is improving nicely . . . *8 June* Jerry got Orra an Invalid chair at H.K. Horns expects to get into it tomorrow[22] . . . *11 June* I was at Orras this forenoon, he was in the reclining chair is improving nicely . . . *12 June* Orra still improving, was rolled into the dining room today . . . *15 June* Orra improving slowly, walked a few steps to day with the help of the Doctor and Mattie, is very weak . . . *22 June* Orra still improving was out of doors, walked part way round the house . . . *27 June* Jerry settled Orras Dr bill $193.00, Dr Pratts bill was $40.00, Dr Heffners $15.00 for assisting with the operation[23] . . . *8 July* Orra and Mattie was here a while this P.M.[24] We had a pleasant visit from Miss Maggie & Jessie McAra, Mary Dow, Sallie, Mary, Mabel & Cora Aikin, Anna & Lizzie Robeson and Myrtle McCracken, all here for dinner . . . *10 July* Orra, Mattie & I rode out to the big woods, he shot three red squirrels . . . *24 July* Orra and Mattie was here. they got some plums at her Mothers . . . *29 July* Jerry & I with Orra & Mattie, Lon, Anna, Julia and two children visited at Ed Lemens . . . *7 August* Jerry & Orra was at the farm repairing the hay loader and wagon bolster . . . *11 August* Orra is sick was at the Drs to night[25] . . . *12 August* Orra was to see the Dr again to night . . . *20 August* Orra working some tying galluses preparing for cutting corn soon . . . *29 August* Orra cut 13 shocks of corn this afternoon, some that is dry on gravel points, says it did not hurt him.

PARENTING

LAUNCHING CAREERS

*S*ince the Gebby sons were teenagers through much of the period covered by these diaries, the parenting responsibilities related heavily to launching them in work and homes of their own. The rights of passage from boyhood to manhood took some time in the Gebby household and were marked by specific events such as the gift of a watch and chain or the ordering of the first tailor-made suit. The Gebby boys each got a watch when they were about sixteen, but curiously it was not a birthday gift or even associated with any obvious special occasion.

14 May 1886: Orra's watch $16.00
28 April 1888: Jerry, Elmer & George were town this morning, got Elmer a watch $18.00 chain $2.00
27–31 July 1894: gave George a check for $30.00 for work . . . George paid for his watch & chain this evening $20.00

The transition from school to career was gradual and took a distinctly different course for each of the three sons. It was apparently taken for granted that the eldest would farm and this evidently suited him fine. From his early teens he missed many school days in both spring and fall to help with planting and harvesting. This probably put him in classes with younger students, and at eighteen he left high school without graduating, apparently with his parents' approval. But he regularly attended Farmers Institute programs designed to encourage progressive farming methods.[1]

118

16 April 1889: Orra and Cal plowed after feeding the cattle, Elmer & George at school

29 January 1891: Orra was at the Farmers Institute this P.M.

22–23 January 1894: Orra not working, he attended the Farmers Institute this afternoon was pleased with it . . . Orra was at the Farmers Institute this afternoon.

Both of the younger sons graduated from Bellefontaine High School, but there was evidently no discussion of either of them going to Monmouth College, the United Presbyterian school that many of their friends and relatives were attending. This must have been a decision based on their academic abilities and interests rather than the family financial situation. Elmer appeared to be mechanically inclined and evidently wanted to go into business, but this distressed his mother if it meant leaving the Bellefontaine area. After several changes of plans in study and work, he returned and became a cashier in the bank where his father was a director. Two years away from home evidently established his independence from the farm and everyone was apparently satisfied.

18–22 September 1891: some of Elmers friends spent the evening here. Arthur, Will and Minnie McCracken, Omer Armstrong, Sam Dow, Laura Dow & Belle Newell, Nellie Garwood, Clara Miller & Edna Hellings . . . got Elmer a trunk $3.00 . . . gave Elmer $2.00 to buy a pocket Bible . . . Elmer left on the afternoon train for Cleveland to enter the case school of applied sciences. gave him $125.00, $50 for tuition, $20 for allowance of breakage in the Laboratory, the rest for expenses. I would much rather he had remained at home. Jerry took his trunk to the Depot.

10 December 1891: Jerry was at town sent a draft on N.Y. to Elmer for $30.00 . . . *24 December* Elmer came home on the noon train which was a little behind time. he & Orra are gone to town . . . *30 December* Elmer went to Degraff on the noon train [*visiting relatives*] . . . *31 December* Ralph & Mary Aikin, Arthur & Tommy McCracken called to see Elmer, here for supper . . . *2 January 1892* Elmer left home to take the 8.20 train for Cleveland, Omar Armstrong to go with him, gave him $50.00 . . . *1 February* sent Elmer a draft for $75.00 . . . *31 March* Sent Elmer a $50.00 draft . . . *3 June* received the Case school commencement card and a letter from Elmer this afternoon[2] . . . *9 June* expect Elmer home to night, had ice cream for dinner and supper . . . *10 June* Elmer came home on the 8.30 train this morning. the class of 92 called this evening to see Elmer.

8 July 1892: Elmer up town this eve, expects to return to Cleveland tomorrow morning . . . *9 July* Elmer left on the 9.25 train for Cleveland to work in the office of Badgely an Architect. Jerry gave him $35.00[3]

8 September 1892: Jerry took Elmer to the Depot, he left for Cleveland on the 9–25 train. the train was half an hour late, Jerry gave him $115.00 . . . *14 October* received a letter from Elmer that he was to enter the Spencerian Commercial College of Cleveland yesterday afternoon, sent Elmer $40.00 . . . *22 December* Elmer came home about noon, the train was about 4 hours behind time . . . *9 January 1893:* Elmer left for Cleveland on the 9 P.M. train, gave him $30, sorry to have him go . . . *18 February–23 May* Sent Elmer a Draft for $30 . . . Sent Elmer a draft for $40.00 . . . Sent Elmer a draft for $50.00 . . . Sent Elmer $50.00 . . . *26 May* Elmer surprised us by coming home this forenoon . . . *29 May* Elmer left for Cleveland on the 1.30 train this morning working for the firm of Walsh & Upstill[4] . . . *5 June* made a pair of over sleeves for Elmer sent them to him this evening, postage 3 cts, received a letter from him this evening . . . *6 July* got a letter from Elmer, expects to be at home Friday night . . . *8 July* Elmer came home on the 12.10 train. George & I went to the Depot got his trunk . . . *10 July* washed Elmers shirts to bleach them . . . *4 November* Elmer received his diploma from the Spencerian College of Cleveland[5] . . . *15 November* Elmer was at the Bank to see about getting a position there . . . *17 November* Elmer was in the Bank this afternoon having received a note asking him to begin at once . . . *1 December* Elmer began working for wages to day in the Bank . . . *21 August 1894:* The Bank officers raised Elmers wages to $30.00 pr month.

George seemed to receive the least parental pressure and developed the least definite goals. He was working on the farm as these diaries conclude, but numerous entries suggest he had less interest and aptitude than his older brother. He had friends and cousins who were teaching and one wonders whether his mother was encouraging that option.[6]

16 July 1895: George finished repairing the old buggy, washed it clean, then washed the carriage . . . *18 July* George made a halter for the calf, repaired the wheelbarrow, and a lot of chores besides . . . *20 July* George took the marketing to town this afternoon, had 9 lbs of butter 10 doz of Eggs $2.68, got Coffee, cheese, Salt, Mustard, Starch and Lemons. $1.60 It was so hot I did not go to town . . . *29 July* George cut some corn for our cows this morning the pasture is dried up . . . *9 August* George was at the Teachers Institute to day and at their Concert to night . . . *10 August* George put in a new water barrel and slop barrel, was working at them all day . . . *3 September* George made a very nice Chicken pen to day.

4 December 1896: George drove to Tommy McCrackens School, took supper with him at his boarding place, got home about nine Oclock.

COURTSHIP

Margaret never wrote it in her diary, but readers can sense that she hoped her sons would marry within their own religious faith. Reading between the lines it is possible to see that she preferred second cousins for each of her two eldest sons. Kate Wolf and Pearl Doan were frequent overnight visitors in the Gebby home, participating in the social activities of the mixed groups of the neighborhood. Margaret seems pleased that Cousin Pearl was her eldest son's first girlfriend. But this son, who was in such harmony with his parents' wishes that he take over his father's farm, eventually found his own girl and not his parents' choice. By the time he was twenty-one Orra was spending regular evenings in Bellefontaine. When his parents went to a niece's funeral in 1894 Orra kept his mother's diary, and his reference to "hard times" implies he and his girlfriend had quarreled. Only twice is Mattie Eades mentioned as a guest in the Gebby home—first at Orra's twenty-first birthday party and then at a party about six months before their marriage. One suspects that the latter was something of an engagement party although Margaret's diary never refers to them as a couple until after their marriage.

14 February 1888: Orra received a valentine, mailed at Degraff
6 February 1889: Orra got Pearl Doans picture.
19–20 March 1891: had a pleasant visit from Kate Wolf, Pearl Doan, Mary Aikin, Sallie Aikin, and Anna and Lizzie Robeson. Orra and Harry Aikin, Pearl and Kate are gone to a party at T. Cooks this eve. . . . Rained nearly all night, the folks got home from the party at 3 Oclock this A.M. I took Pearl & Kate to Fathers were there for dinner.
28 February 1893: Orra gone up town took his guitar . . . *25 July* Orra gone to town this evening
11–13 September 1894: Nice day, cut corn, cut and tied 80 shocks in the field east of the house. Old folks gone to Eva Kitchens funeral, El

gone to a concert at Huntsville. Kid gone to town, to late to go any place myself . . . Nice day, threatening this eve, cut and tied 122 shocks of corn today. El gone to a blank out at John Horns. Hard times . . . Rained this A.M. Only cut 63 shocks to wet. Kid went to the show & to church, the dandy at home. Kid shot a squirrel this forenoon. times still hard.[7]

22 September 1894 [Saturday]: Orra and Elmer gone to town this evening.

22 February 1895: Nannie and I prepared for company to night. Orra got a pound of dates 10 cts and a pound of candy. we popped two large dishes full of popcorn. had a real pleasant call from Lizzie, Sam & Lon Robeson, Ed & Sallie Aikin, Walter and Mary Dow & Jessie McAra, Tommy & Myrtle McCracken, Jim Cook, Mattie Eades and Tellie Maxwell. They stayed until 12 Oclock

On the other hand, the son who had such difficulty in establishing a business career seems never to have considered any girl seriously except his second cousin Laura Dow. Margaret clearly approved, and Laura was frequently invited to the Gebby home. Elmer and Laura often went out as a couple rather than socializing with a group as Orra did, but they dated much longer and did not get married until ten years after Margaret began referring to them as a couple.[8]

26 June 1891: Elmer gone to Dunk Dows to meet some company of Lauras. . . . *31 July* Elmer & Laura Dow are calling at Uncle Johns this evening.

19 July 1893: Elmer gone to a social at Dunk Dows this evening . . . *22 July* Elmer gone to D. Dows to supper this evening . . . *4 August* Elmer wrote up Canby & Robesons books then he and Laura Dow visited at G.W. Aikins.

9 August 1894: Mrs Duncan Dow & daughter Laura called here this eve . . . *17 August* Elmer & Laura Dow are gone to Wallaces near Huntsville to night . . . *3 September* we had a very pleasant visit from Dunk Dow, wife and daughter Laura, they were here for supper.

24 August 1896: Elmer & Laura Dow called on Harry Aikin and wife this evening.

There is no evidence in Margaret's journals that George was paying any particular attention to girls through his teens and into his early twenties.

BUILDING A HOUSE FOR A SON
AND HIS BRIDE

———◆———◎❋◎———◆———

S hortly after Orra and his bride returned from their wedding trip
the Gebbys began building a new house for them on the farm less
than a mile west. Margaret records no discussion of plans for this
house, but it had obviously been agreed before the wedding that his
parents would pay for its construction. The operation began the first of
October, and the young couple spent their first night in their home four
months later. It was an interesting combination of do-it-yourself projects
and hired labor. By modern standards it seems to evolve almost casually,
but no one was dealing with labor unions or inspectors enforcing building codes or zoning regulations. The design was a standard two-story
frame house undoubtedly well known to local carpenters.

1–19 October 1895: Jerry borrowed the Township road scraper this
afternoon . . . Jerry & I was at Detricks looking at the plan of their
house . . . Dave Scot was here to see about building the house[1] . . . the
men began digging the cellar for Orras house at the farm by plowing and
scraping, got along very well . . . the men worked at the cellar, got all
out they could do with the horses . . . the men got nearly done digging
the cellar to day Orra, Wellie & McClain worked at it all day . . . Orra
& Wellie hauled stone for the cellar to day. Jerry was to see Will
Daughenbaugh this afternoon, found him at the Philadelphia church, he
is too busy to do our carpenter work . . . Jerry paid C. McLain $1.25
helping dig cellar . . . Orra & Wellie hauled stone from the gravel pit all

day. they borrowed a sand screen from J.E.McCracken . . . Orra &
Jerry got 29 bushels of lime at 15 cts pr bushel. Orra & Wellie hauled 4
loads of sand for the wall of the house . . . Orra & Wellie hauled sand
for the house to day, have hauled 10 loads . . . the men working at the
house. Chris Culp began laying the cellar wall this morning, got along
very well. Wellie tended him.[2] Orra dug a door way and hauled stone.
Jerry and George made window and door frames for the cellar.

*The Gebby farm contained a gravel pit, which provided stone and
sand for mixing concrete, and a woods, which provided oak and walnut
sawlogs for most of the necessary lumber.*

21 October–2 November 1895: Orra hauled three loads five logs to
the saw mill for joists and studding for the house. Jerry saw David Scott,
he wants $190 for the carpenter work on the house . . . Orra hauled a
load of logs to the mill and a load of joists home. George got a load of
lime. Jerry was at town looking after carpenters. Oscar Randall was here
to night wanting the plastering and flue building . . . Orra got one load
of lumber from the mill, the men working on the foundation. Jerry saw
Carpenter Robinson did not conclude the bargain. Cut and sewed carpet
rags for Mattie . . . Orra and Jerry cut eight saw logs to day . . . Orra
hauled logs. Christ Culp finished the foundation and cellar walls at
noon. Jerry settled with him gave him a check for $28.15. Sewed carpet
rags for Mattie . . . Orra hauled logs and lumber. Jerry engaged Robinson to do the carpenter work of the house for $182.00 . . . the men
hauled logs and sawed down trees. Jerry paid the B. [*Bellefontaine*] Lime
Co $9.65 . . . Drizzled some all day but did not rain any scarcely. Orra
& Wellie cut and hauled sawlogs to the mill. Jerry was at town saw some
men about working on the house . . . The men hauled all their lumber
home.[3] Paid the saw bill $34.55. Bought the bill of Hardware $55.00.

*The fact that the Gebbys did not shop for carpenters until after
beginning work on the cellar, and then bargained with three before
agreeing on the price and a time for the work to be done, says a great
deal about the number of local carpenters with house-building skills who
could be available on one weeks' notice.*

4–22 November 1895: the Carpenters (Robinson & hands) began
work on the house this morning. The men worked out there this forenoon, hauled brick this afternoon. Jerry engaged Oscar Randall to build
the chimneys at 15 cents pr foot . . . the carpenters raised the house to
day.[4] . . . George and Jerry got a load of siding, 1000 ft and shingles. the

carpenters working at the house . . . the carpenters are putting on the siding. Jerry got 72 lbs of lathing nails $3.60 . . . Randall began work on the chimneys at noon, got up to the square with the dining room chimney . . . Orra & Wellie hauled a load of brick and a load of shingles . . . Orra and Wellie hauled sand this afternoon, went to the planing mill for lumber but it was not ready for them. Jerry engaged Frank Detwiler to paint the house for $47.00 . . . Orra and Wellie hauled one load of lumber and sand. Paid Oscar Randall $10.50 for building three Flues . . . Orra & Wellie moved brick and hauled a load of flooring for the house. Jerry was looking after paints and oils. Paid McDonald for the brick (3000) . . . Orra and Wellie hauled flooring, shingles and moulding . . . Orra and Wellie hauled a load of lumber and lath. there were five carpenters at work to day on the house today. Jerry got outfit for an extra window in the west room upstairs paid $1.25 . . . Jerry and Orra was at town selected brackets for the gavel [*gable*] ends of the house.[5] Lesourd orders them from Columbus. they bought 15 gal of Linseed oil at 45 cts pr gal. 200 lbs of white lead at 6.10 pr hd, a butter bucket to mix paint 15 cts = $19.10 . . . The Carpenters finished all they can do at the house until the plastering is done. Frank Detwiler was priming the sash this afternoon. Jerry & I were at the farm. Orra was gathering up the pieces of lumber put them in the cellar. paid Robinson the carpenter $100.00 for his work.

25 November–6 December 1895: Orra and Wellie got the plasterers mortar boxes and other things. Oscar Randall and hand were lathing to day. Jerry was at town got cord for windows 50 cts. Orra got more lath and the brackets for gables . . . Jerry got hair for plastering $2.00[6] . . . the men are still lathing the house. Orra and Wellie brought the wagon in got an old stove from Joe Pine paid $2.25, they took out the old cook stove put them up to keep the plaster from freezing . . . Orra got some more lath, they are nearly done lathing have the mortar mixed in the cellar . . . Orra put sand in the cellar. the plasterers began plastering this morning, got upstairs nearly done, put two stoves up stairs keeping fire to night to prevent freezing . . . Orra & Wellie was working at the house, the plasters finished up stairs. Orra was at Randalls got a mortar box and an old stove to warm the house so the plaster will not freeze . . . Orra and Wellie hauled sand, got seven bushels of lime. the plasters at work. Orra gone to keep fire to prevent the plaster from freezing . . . the plasterers still at work at the house. Orra has to keep fire all day and part of the night . . . Orra still working around the house keeping up the fire in five stoves. the Plasterers finished the first coat this P.M. . . . paid Oscar Randall $30 for plastering.

Jerry was obviously performing the role of contractor and Orra and the hired man were doing all of the hauling and serving as helpers to the skilled workers doing the masonry and plastering.

11 December 1895: Jerry was at town paid Williamson & Lesourd $300.00 [*lumber*], Carr & Lawson $9.72 [*lime*], Robeson Bros. $4.00 [*Plaster of Paris*]. Mattie & I were in town . . . then drove out to the house it is drying very well.

17–28 December 1895: Orra working around the new house, two plasterers working to day . . . Orra and Wellie got a load of finishing lumber this afternoon. Randall was plastering this forenoon, finished down stairs . . . no one working at the house to day. Joe Randall died this P.M. the Bros. not working . . . Randalls were whitecoating at the house, did the front & back stairways . . . the Randalls finished the whitecoating the house to day, 869 yds. Orra has to go to the house about midnight to see to the fires.

13–28 January[7] 1896: the carpenters finished the house this evening the painters began varnishing to day . . . Jerry was at town settled with Robison the carpenter, paid him $82.00, settled with Williamson & Lesourd for lumber paid them $30.00, Cook Bros for spouting $16.88 . . . the painters worked in the house to day. I finished quilting Orras quilt today . . . the tinners put the caps above the windows & door, 20 cts apiece . . . the painters finished painting the first coat on the house this P.M.[8] Mattie and I was at town this afternoon looking after the house furnishings did not buy got prices &c . . . Jerry & I was at town got carpet for the sitting room Bedroom & vestibule of Orras house. ordered shades for the two large windows. got a set of dishes, 100 pieces, $7.00[9] . . . Jerry was at town got the window shades 15 at 45 cts apeice paid for some paints in all $9.87. I finished making the bedroom carpet . . . Orra and Wellie cleaned windows this afternoon, Jerry was at the farm this forenoon, saw the painters. they finished painting about noon. paid them $47.00 . . . Mattie and I cleaned the Sitting & Bedrooms and the Kitchen this forenoon, then she & Orra cleaned the Parlor & Hall and the upstairs windows . . . Orra & Mattie cleaned three rooms upstairs and the Dining room, put up six window shades. went to town to night and selected a cook stove. Nannie washed I churned. Jerry & I was at town bought a bedroom Suit, six chairs, a rocker & a stand, paid $35.00[10] . . . Orra got the cooking stove of Plummer this afternoon a very nice and useful outfit for $30.75,[11] he also got Matties furniture from her Mothers. they are staying at their new home to night.

It is interesting to note who selected and paid for furnishings and who did the cleaning prior to moving in. During the next couple of weeks as the young couple settled in Margaret made them a comforter and they each brought personal items from their own homes. Friends waited until they were settled before giving them a housewarming.

11 February 1896: Arthur McCracken called saying a crowd was going to surprise Orra & Mattie tomorrow evening. . . . *12 February* [*Wednesday*] Nannie washed, we baked a cake took it to Orras to night they were surprised by 21 of their friends Aikins, Robesons, McCrackens, Jim Cook, Orra & Clarence Longfellow, Jessie McAra & Mary Dow. had oysters.

Margaret's financial records give an interesting perspective on the costs of home construction in 1895.

Carpenters (83 man days)	$182.00
Stonemason (cellar)	28.15
Plasterer	60.00
Painter	47.00
Brickmason (chimney flues)	10.50
TOTAL LABOR COSTS	$327.65
Lumber, brick, paint, hardware, windows, shingles, spouting, plaster, etc.	
TOTAL MATERIAL COSTS	$676.76
TOTAL HOUSE COST	$1004.41
Carpets and rugs	$29.43
15 window shades & parlor curtains	10.45
Bedroom suite, 6 chairs, rocker & stand	35.00
Cooking stove	30.75
Dining table (12 ft. extension)	7.80
Set of dishes (100 pieces)	7.00
TOTAL FURNISHINGS PURCHASED	$126.25

While it seems generous for his parents to build and furnish this home, readers should remember that Orra had been working on the farm without regular wages for years. Margaret's diary implies that even before he quit school six years earlier he had been doing work equivalent to the hired man who was paid twenty dollars per month. Orra was being given an excellent opportunity to begin farming on his own, but he was paying for the privilege with his own labor.

It seems likely that farm materials from sawlogs to sand and gravel, as well as the labor the Gebby men and hired man provided, might have doubled the actual cost of this rather typical eight-room home had they all been purchased retail. Likewise, many of the furnishings were made by the young couple or their relatives. Margaret and Mattie made quilts, comforts, sheets, and pillowcases, but references to Orra digging "his" potatoes and Mattie bringing "her" fruit from her mother's indicate both had been preparing for their own home for months.

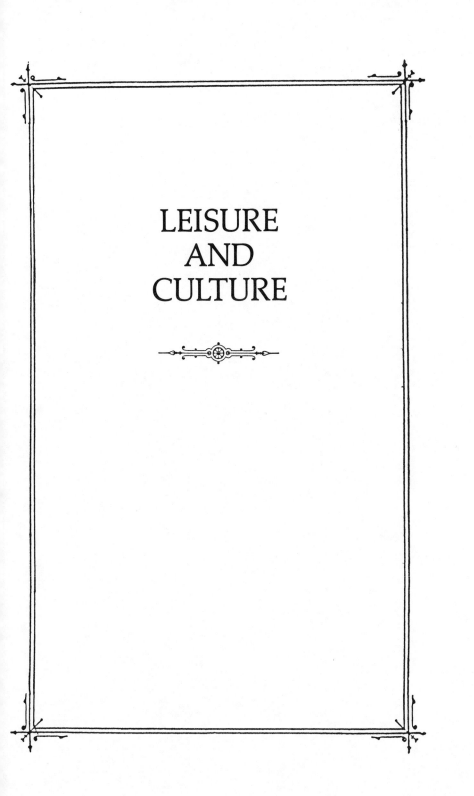

LEISURE
AND
CULTURE

LEISURE

The joyous experience of "calling" has certainly declined in the past century. Any modern reader who spent time with the Gebby diaries would receive two impressions that will not be as dramatic in this edited version. First, a population that did not have access to telephones called on others for business and personal reasons in a quantity which seems startling today. Second, the isolation of farm families emphasized in most historic accounts was an accurate reflection of the sparsely settled plains, but as these diaries attest there were also nineteenth-century farm families throughout the Midwest who routinely made and received several visits each day.[1]

These excerpts reveal a great deal about business and personal reasons for calling on others, the social network of the extended family, and the type of food or entertainment offered to unexpected visitors. The diaries also include numerous visits for pure pleasure after being confined by bad weather or hard work.

18 February 1886: Warmer and thawing went to J.M.Williamsons on a visit found no one at home, gone to Blairs to spend the day, came home got dinner, went to J.E. McCrackens and very pleasantly spent the afternoon. . . . *10 November* Went to George Aikins took some potato ball yeast.

28 April 1890: Grandma & I went to J.E. McCrackens saw the young daughter . . . *12 May* Martha Krouse brought over a curiosity, a full sized hard shelled egg within an egg.

17 June 1892: Father walked out here this afternoon brought some

131

radishes given him for us from Josie Lemen . . . *23 June* too wet to work in the ground and too threatening to cut hay. Jerry, Grandma and I with Uncle John & Aunt Hannah visited at C.C. Cooks to day.

4 March 1893: Martha Krouse brought an orange for us to see, it was 15 in. in circumference, the largest we ever saw. Frank Tannehill brought it from Florida.

7 March 1896: Orra & Mattie called this afternoon brought two owl eggs.

Although most calling in this community was spontaneous, Margaret's diaries record a few instances when she and other women made a series of calls that resemble those commonly described among urban upper-class women.

15 November 1889: Aunt Hannah, Grandma & I called at Mrs Wrights, was not at home. then we called at Mrs McBeths, spent a pleasant hour with her, stopped to see Lib Beatty who is still ill.

10 December 1890: went with Mrs Dillon to McDonalds, Conns, Horns, and to Millers had a pleasant call at each place.

7 August 1891: Aunt Hannah, Mrs Dillon, Grandma & I called on Mrs A.C. Wallace, Mr Hamiltons family and at Duncan Dows this afternoon . . . *13 August* Mrs Dillon called with her carriage took us with Aunt Hannah to Dave Kaylors, John Longfellows, Mr & Mrs McAras and to the childrens home had a pleasant call at each of these places. at the home they took us through the building. have 46 inmates in the home.

After the Gebbys installed a scale to weigh livestock at the farm, a frequent form of entertainment with visiting relatives was to ride around looking at the crops and livestock and stop by for everyone to be weighed. Such entries remind readers that these hard-working human paragons were relatively small persons by twentieth-century standards.

24 September 1888: Willie Davis and wife visited us today, went to the farm, got weighed Lib weighed 135, Grandma 97, Elmer 126, George 66, myself 116, rode around some, then to Andy Koones, then home.

14 August 1891: Jerry & I went to Degraff visited at Lyman Doans took dinner there, called at Joshs this P.M. were weighed in the Hardware store, Mary Doan weighed 93 lbs, Jerry 131, Bent Doan 134, Josh 148, I weighed 117½

19 July 1895: Uncle John, Aunt Hannah with Mr Joe Holmes visited us to day, were here for dinner, had a nice visit, all were weighed Uncle

John weighed 146½, Aunt Hannah 156½, Jerry 122, Nannie 104, and I weighed 114

Visits by invitation invariably included a meal, usually dinner at noon, which allowed time for a pleasant visit in the afternoon and a return home to do chores by five o'clock. One exception is a supper in town, which included only adult couples, but most visits included adults and youth together. These diaries never mention any instance that could be construed as baby-sitting.

3–4 December 1888: baked three plum pies and five apple pies and a cake, dressed a turkey and a chicken . . . Andy Moore and wife, Ed Lemen, wife and son, Charlie Cook, wife and children were here for dinner, had a very pleasant visit.

17 June 1890: Elmer took Grandma & I with Mrs McBeth & Mrs Armstrong to Mrs Wrights for dinner, met Mrs McKee, Mrs Kerr, Mrs McMillen, Mrs Lloyd, Mrs Jamison and Dr Grier. had a very pleasant visit. Elmer came for us about five Oclock[2]

9 January 1891: Jerry got one qt of oysters and crackers 65 cts, we had a very pleasant visit from Uncle John & family, C.C. Cook, Lizzie & Mary, John Harner, wife & baby and Mrs Longfellow, here for dinner

27 February 1894: Jerry and I were at Dunk Dows for supper with Hamilton & wife, Wallace & wife, Swans, McLaughlins, McCrackens, Dowells, Dows & Boals, 20 in all, had a pleasant time.

5 December 1896: I was at T. Cooks, dinner with Madames Wallace, McKee, McBeth, Bruner, Maxwell, Barnett, Fitchthorn, Aikin, McCracken, Jeffers, Cook, Antrim, Galer and Collins, and five children

Relatives were by far the most common excuse for visiting. When relatives from a distance arrived for overnight visits, they invariably made a round of calls throughout the neighborhood. The kinship connection might be as remote as the niece of grandma's sister-in-law, but it was enough excuse for a visit.

18 January 1889: baked bread and pies, roasted a piece of beef and two chickens preparing for company this eve. We had a very pleasant visit from Eva Kitchen, George Harner, Jim & Nannie Cook, Orra Cook and wife, Arthur McFadden and Sophia Cook they went away about 11 Oclock. Eva and George stayed all night.[3]

21 August 1891: Jim Dow & wife, Nelly & Harry visited us this P.M. and evening, had ice cream for supper

10 August 1893: Jennie Cleland and four daughters and her Mother visited us this afternoon[4] . . . *12 August* Joe Steddam, Julia, Sadie & Mary with Lizzie Robeson called this afternoon.[5]

28 December 1894: We had a pleasant visit from Wm Bennett wife & daughter Ellenear, James & Mrs Williams, Berry Lesourd, wife & Myran, Uncle John, Aunt Hannah and Lizzie[6]

19 September 1895: Anna and Lizzie Robeson, Nellie Patton, Nannie & I was at the farm to show Nellie how corn is cut with a sled. we called at the barn weighed ourselves, Nellie 129, Lizzie 104, Nannie 102, Anna 101, I weighed 110[7]

6 November 1896: Jane Cook and Mattie Dow called for me to go with them to G.W. Aikins for dinner. met Mrs John Aikin & children there, had a very pleasant visit.[8]

HUNTING AND FISHING

Hunting was a popular leisure activity among the men and boys of this neighborhood, but it was as clearly for sport as it is today. Any game brought to the family table was a bonus, but not one to be counted on regularly. Margaret's oldest and youngest sons seem to have been most fond of this activity and her diary entries often poke fun at their lack of success. Although a variety of small game and fowl was hunted, these diaries never mention deer, which are now common in that geographic area, probably evidence that the intensity of nineteenth-century farming had eliminated cover for large wildlife.

7–22 June 1888: Orra went hunting this forenoon got four squirrels . . . Orra hunting this forenoon got six squirrels

4 June 1889: Orra and Elmer hunting but didn't FIND

15–20 January 1890: Orra hunting wild geese without success . . . Orra was wild goose hunting this morning proved to be a wild goose chase, saw a good many after they saw . . . Orra again on a wild goose chase . . . Orra was on another wild goose chase, did not see any . . . *5 November* Orra got a Breech loading gun $18.00, an overcoat $14.00 . . . *17 November–13 December* Rained a great deal. Orra and Lon Robeson was hunting this forenoon. Orra got a Quail and a wetting . . . A beautiful day. Orra and Lon at Harry Harners hunting, got six Quail . . . Orra, Lon and Sam was hunting to day, got nine Quail and one rabbit . . . Orra brought 5 Quail home . . . Baked Quail pie for dinner

5–18 March 1892: Orra went out looking for a good place to set his decoys and to try his duck caller. decided on the lake as the best place, caller a grand success. called a duck clear across the lake . . . Orra went duck hunting, shot six at the pond in the big woods at the farm. gave two of them to Uncle Johns. we cleaned the rest this eve. . . . *10–19 November* the quail law expired to day Orra and George was hunting. Orra got five quails, George got one rabbit and one quail. A great many hunters out to day and a great deal of ammunition wasted . . . Orra and Lon was hunting this P.M. Orra shot six Lon four . . . Orra and George were hunting this afternoon Orra got 7 quail and George one . . . Orra was hunting got six Quail

8 March 1893: Orra went hunting this afternoon, got five ducks . . . *23 March* George did not go to school to day wanted to take a duck hunt, was out this forenoon but did not get any, shot one squirrel, forgot about it being illegal . . . *10 November* Orra and Elmer was quail hunting got 7. this the first day of lawful hunting for Quails, a great many hunters were out.

11 September 1895: George ordered a gun from Chicago $13.31.

3 April 1896: George & Lawrence Thrasher is gone to stay at his hunting camp to night so as to hunt Ducks early in the morning . . . *4 May* George and Lawrence Thrasher are coon hunting with Frank [*dog*] to night.

Fishing was also popular sport among the men and boys of this neighborhood, and it likewise contributed to family meals. Several nearby farms had small ponds or lakes, but for serious fishing trips perhaps two or three times a year they would head for the reservoir, an old glacial lake about ten miles from the Gebby farm that had been enlarged during Ohio's canal era.[9]

23 October 1886: Jerry, Cal & the boys went to the reservoir fishing started about half past five & got home about five this evening, caught nine catfish, two bass, nine ring fish, paid 15 cts for bait (minnies)

13 June 1888: Were at Ed Lemens, Jerry, Ed, George and Ira went to the lake, caught 15 fish. Ed 8, George 3, Ira 3, Jerry one.

23–31 May 1889: Went with Robesons, C.C. Cooks and George Harner to the reservoir fishing, altogether the men caught about a hundred fish, got supper at Charlies, got home about 9 Oclock, Orra brought home 13 fish, still cold this eve, paid 50c for the use of boats . . . Orra and Elmer replanted corn in the east middle field, the rest of us with Uncle Johns visited at Ed Lemens to day, the men went fishing caught about twenty small fish . . . Orra, Elmer and A.H. Robeson was at Shorts pond fishing got 36 minnows expecting to go to the reservoir tomorrow . . . *18 July* Very warm, too wet to work at the hay. Orra went to the Lake fishing this morning, did not get home till near 4 Oclock. Jerry & Sam went to see what kept him[10] . . . *29–30 August* Orra and Elmer got some minnows in Blue Jacket [*creek*] to fish at the reservoir tomorrow . . . Jerry and all the boys with Lon & Sam left for the reservoir about three Oclock this morning, had good success fishing untill it got warm got home about five Oclock.

    4–6 June 1890: sent a note to C.C. Cook that we intended going to the reservoir . . . Orra & Elmer caught some minnows expecting to go fishing at the reservoir tomorrow . . . We with Uncle John, Lon, Sam and Lizzie, Eddie & Harry Aikin and C.C. Cooks family were at the Reservoir to day got home about 6 Oclock, the fishing not good, too windy, paid 50c for boats.

    24 May 1894: We were at Ed Lemens to day. Jerry & Orra drove Charlie & the colt. Grandma & I drove Harry. the men were fishing on Eds lake but without success. we got home about 6 P.M.

    17 July 1895: Jerry and Mr Joe Holmes, Lon Robeson and Rev Hamilton was at Lake Ridge to day. caught a good number of fish but they were small did not bring them home.

                                    HOBBIES

    The oldest Gebby son apparently had a sincere interest in music and at least some ability. The diaries mention his playing a variety of string instruments from violin to bass viol to guitar. These seem to have been popular in this rural community more like band instruments might be among teenagers today. Diary entries frequently mention playing with others. Margaret seems somewhat detached, approving this musical interest but allowing her son to make his own decisions about buying instruments and taking lessons. One gets the impression, however, that his mother suspected there was a girl involved when he took his guitar to town.

    17 November 1886: Orra went to town got a violin string 5 cts & a book, the "Red Eagle" 35 cts . . . *25 December* Orra bought a violin case and an E string $1.50

    18 April 1887: Orra taking his music lesson . . . *25 April* Orra got an A violin string 15 cts . . . *28 May* Orra settled & paid L. Wright for his music lessons 2.45 . . . *1–2 August* Orra and Harry Aikin are gone this eve to Tommy Cooks to have some music on stringed instruments . . . got violin strings D.10c G.15c . . . *6 September* Orra gone to Tommy Cooks to an Orchestra meeting.

30 January 1888: Orra bought a violin at Dillons grocery this evening for $1.00 . . . *11 February* Orra gone to G.W. Aikins to fix Harry's fiddle for him . . . *20 June* Mrs Krouse and Martha over this evening to hear Orra play . . . *9 July* gave Orra 25 ct to buy violin strings . . . *28 September* Orra gone to Rolland Grays to play on the guitar . . . *20 November* Ed Fitchthorn and Earle Kitchen here this evening, discoursing sweet music with Orra on the violins and Organ . . . *7 December* Orra went to John Grays for instruction on his guitar.

11 June 1889: were serenaded about 4 Oclock this A.M. with delightful music on the Zither and Guitar by some unknown musicians . . . *25 October* Orra gone to Dunk Dows to play on the violin . . . *11 November* Orra gone taking guitar lesson from Mollie Jordan

31 March 1890: Orra gone to Warder Dowells, for a bass viol he bought of Jim Cook ($2.00) . . . *9 December* made a Guitar cover for Orra

20 February 1891: Orra gone to town with his guitar to play somewhere this eve . . . *24–25 February* Orra boxed his bass viol ready for shipment to Cleveland . . . Orra shipped his bass viol to Cleveland to be exchanged for some other instrument . . . *24 August* Orra & Ed Fitchthorn gone to Robesons to have music.

23 March 1892: Orra gone with his Guitar somewhere

Tax records show the Gebbys had an organ in their home but Margaret's diaries never mention who played it. It seems unlikely that such a luxury would have been idle, and if others played she would likely have noted it at some point. Perhaps she played but everyone took it for granted, and she did not write about it any more than she wrote about cooking breakfast or washing her hair or gathering eggs.

Neighborhood singing schools were popular in this time period and the middle Gebby son apparently had some interest or talent in vocal music.

11 February 1888: Elmer gone to the school house to a singing school taught by John Huber . . . *19 June* Elmer gone to singing school

18 March 1891: Elmer saw Mrs Acton about taking lessons in vocal music . . . *1 April* Elmer taking his music lessons this evening paid $2.00

Elmer was the most outgoing of the sons and he seems to have been casually involved with dramatics.

19–22 March 1889: The boys are rehearsal of Jeptha and his daughter . . . the boys gone to assist in an entertainment given by the high school at the Opera house.

14–20 November 1894: Elmer gone to a rehearsal of the Ben Hur pantomine . . . Elmer at the opera house taking part in a pantomine of Ben Hur, an entertainment given by the Kings daughters for the benefit of the poor.

The youngest son apparently had some interest in art and photography, and it was his mother who helped him develop photographs. One wonders when and why she had developed that skill, or whether she was simply reading whatever directions came with the materials and helping her son.

15–21 August 1890: George got a Camera from Perry Mason & Co, Express 40c . . . George working at his Photography . . . *8 September* We had a pleasant visit from Uncle John & Aunt Hannah, Julia & Joe Steddem & Sadie, Mr & Mrs A.R. Harner & Mrs Wright. they were here for dinner went home about 4 Oclock. Joe & George took the picture of the house and of the dog.[11]

7 July 1891: George got his Artist supplies paid 50c expenses[12] . . . *23 July* George & I took a picture of some flowers at the corner of the house, it developed nicely . . . *12 August* George sent Orra Cooke two of his pictures taken with the bicycle . . . *24–26 October* George took a picture of Tom [*cat*] and one of Button [*cow*] neither of them very good . . . I printed some pictures for George . . . *26 November* George took Orras & Sam Robesons pictures this evening.

WINTER FUN

Leisure activities varied with the season, but the traditional winter fun of coasting, skating, and sleighing seem to have been popular with the Gebby boys and their friends.

23 January 1886: Boys all skated this afternoon

21 January 1889: Elmer was skating on the pond with some other boys.

26 December 1890: Elmer went to town got a pair of shoes and skates.

28 December 1892: Elmer gone with a skating party this evening

30 December 1886: Orra and Sam Dow went to Tommy Cooks a sleighing.

27 January 1888: Elmer gone with his teacher and eighth department sleighing, very clear evening the moon shining brightly.

19–27 January 1893: Orra gone to prayer meeting this evening and then sleigh riding, which is very fine, could not be better . . . Orra is out sleighing this evening . . . Orra gone sleighing this evening

29–30 January 1894: Elmer out Sleighing, too stormy to be out . . . Elmer gone skating this evening

19 January 1891: after church Elmer with some others went to Kerr hill coasting.

9 February 1895: the boys are all at town tonight. they have rolled and sprinkled Sandusky Ave from Stanley Street to Detroit ready for coasting, a grand time is expected.

8 March 1887: Mary McCracken and children, Grandma, Elmer, George & I went to Tommy Cooks, the boys had a good time at the sugar camp gathering water and eating wax we got home about five oclock.[13]

12 March 1891: Elmer and George went to Tommy Cooks sugar camp this evening for a good time.

PICNICS AND SOCIABLES

The annual Sunday school picnic seems to have been a favorite for the Gebby family. Silver Lake, a popular recreation spot with its own railroad station, was only about a mile from the Gebby home.

31 August 1887: We were all at Sabbath school picnic at Silver lake. Quite a goodly number present had a very good dinner and an abundance of it. Had a very pleasant time the young people enjoyed boat riding very much.

20–22 June 1892: Orra and Elmer gone to the church to a meeting preparing for a S.S. picnic at Silver Lake on Wednesday . . . killed two chickens roasted one for supper and cooked the other for a S.S. picnic at the lake tomorrow . . . were at the lake at a picnic, quite a good many there, just got through eating dinner when the rain and wind commenced, all ran for the carriages and to the hotel.

There were many places to picnic and a variety of organizations, and Margaret was often preparing chicken.

8 June 1886: Went to the Indian Lake to a picnic. 86 eat dinner all seemed to enjoy themselves and everything went off very pleasantly, had a very nice dinner. . . . *25 September* Professors and Scholars picknicked at Silver Lake today[14]

31 August 1889: went to the Harvest home picnic at the fair grounds

16 August 1890: Jerry went to the Fair Grounds this being Grange picnic a great many in town

13–14 June 1892: roasted a chicken for Elmer to take to a picnic at Indian lake tomorrow . . . Elmer went with a crowd to Lake Ridge this morning, not home yet

13 June 1893: Elmer is gone to a picnic to the reservoir this being the annual picnic of the correspondents of the Bellefontaine Republican

12 August 1896: George gone to Lake Ridge to spend the day. Boats and everything is free to day to Bellefontaine people.

It was common for a variety of organizations to raise money through strawberry suppers, lawn fetes, and oyster suppers. Margaret usually contributed food and the family often attended.

7–10 July 1891: Jessie & Laura Dow was here this eve. soliciting for the lawn fete on Friday evening for the benefit of the O.Y.P. I promised a cake . . . the boys gone to a Lawn Fete in the Park given by the O.Y.P. of the U.P. church. Baked bread and a cake, attempted to bake a second cake for the lawn fete but failed entirely, forgot the baking powder.

16 June 1892: Strawberry Supper at the Grange hall this evening, quite a good many in attendance.

15–22 June 1893: having been appointed to solicit for a strawberry supper, I went to Robesons, McAras, P. Dows, & G.W. Aikins . . . A strawberry & Ice cream supper at Grange hall this eve.

5 November 1895: I took a gallon of milk to the Y.M.C.A. rooms for oyster supper.

Nineteenth-century summer fun also included some activities that

have not survived the passing of time—the circus parade, the "colored
camp meeting," and the militia drill.

2–22 August 1889: the boys gone to camp meeting this
eve . . . Elmer gone to colored camp meeting this evening

7 May 1890: George went to town saw the Shows parade then this
P.M. went to the show 25c, Orra and Elmer gone to the show this
evening[15]

22–23 August 1890: Elmer spread manure, then went to the lake to
see the militia. Jerry, Grandma, George & I with Sallie Murdock went to
the lake. saw the inspection of the soldiers . . . Orra plowed untill four
Oclock then went to the lake to see the regiment camping there on dress
parade. went with Aunt Hannah, Anna, Lizzie, Julie & Sadie to visit the
soldiers camp it was inspection day quite a good many people there.

22 July 1892: Orra gone to a concert at the campgrounds

CLUB MEETINGS AND PARTIES

*Beyond school and church, a number of community organizations
involved one or more of the Gebby family. All of the boys participated
regularly in the local literary society, reading papers or reciting poems.
With the exception of the Grange, which was the strongest rural organization in this time period, the other groups mentioned were urban and
involved Elmer after he began working as a bank clerk.*

19 January 1886: Attended literary with Mrs Dillon this eve. Orra
select reading "Mark Twain as a horse buyer." George recited "A little
boys first recitation" Critics say he did very well.

7 June 1888: Went with George & Elmer to the Granges also Mrs
Dillon and Mrs Houtz had a moderately pleasant time.[16] P.F. Kaylor
made the address of welcome, had music and literary exercises, got
home at half past eleven.

5 June 1894: Elmer gone to a meeting and entertainment given by
the Queen of the Kitchen club at Mrs Chandlers this evening . . . *20
December* Elmer gone to a Y.M.C.A. meeting in the parlor of the hotel
Ingalls to night.

4 February 1895: Elmer is gone to a meeting of the Good Citizenship
club at Amos Millers.

Parties were held for the same reasons common today, from holidays to visiting friends or relatives. From their midteens on, the Gebby sons socialized with friends independently of their parents, but group parties rather than couple dates were the norm.

7 February 1887: Elmer went to a taffy pulling at Harpers but came home at half past eight

3 December 1890: Elmer gone to Lymans to a party . . . *10 December* Elmer gone to a social at Mr Hamiltons . . . *29 December* Elmer gone to J.E. McCrackens to a party

13 February 1891: Elmer gone to a valentine party at Hellings . . . *27 February* Orra and Elmer gone to a social at Dunk Dows

8 April 1892: Orra is gone to G.W. Aikins a company is there in honor of Miss Becca Gustin of Piqua . . . *10 May* Orra gone to a social at James Rankins this evening . . . *16 May* Orra gone to a party at W.H. Neers

8 August 1893: Orra gone this evening to the Electric light celebration at Degraff.

6 July 1894: Elmer was at a lawn tennis party in Campbells grove this evening.

31 May 1895: I was at town got lace, gloves and handkerchief $2.79. George and I attended the alumni of Bellefontaine high school, quite a swell affair, a large crowd, a splendid house (at Levi Wisslers) all seemed to enjoy themselves, the banquet was grand, got home after 12 Oclock[17] . . . *27 December* Elmer & Tommy McCracken went to a Swell party at Parkers to night.

Neither these diaries nor contemporary newspapers provide much detail about entertainment for parties, but the Gebby's religion did not condone dancing. Margaret's entries for parties at the Gebby home suggest that they included games, music, and conversation. Refreshments were substantial and the hostess often borrowed silver and china. Parties often lasted until midnight, which seems late for farm boys going home by horse and buggy and getting up in time to do chores.

11 February 1887: I baked two cakes, six pies, Dow, Sallie, Mary, John, Eddie, Ralph & Harry Aikin, Lincoln, Anna & Lizzie Smith, Jimmy, Jessie & Sammie Dow spent the evening with us. Left about 12 Oclock had a very pleasant time. . . . *12 October* Quite a number of young people spent the evening here left about half past 12 . . . *7 December* A party of young people came this eve. had a candy pulling

Aikins, Cook, Kerr, Spellman, Jim Dow & Jessie, Effie McMillan, McKee, Jeffs, Herber &c

11 January 1889: Elsie Leman and Eva Kitchen are here tonight, there is going to be a party so I will reserve a space for what happens . . . every thing passed off very pleasantly. Jim Dow, Jessie, Mary McKee, Maud Hiall, two English girls, Harry Kerr, Dow, Ed, John & Mary Aikin spent the evening here

5–6 February 1890: Elmer entertained some of his school mates this eve. twenty in number, seemed to enjoy themselves very much, went away about 12 Oclock. Baked two cakes for the party bought a doz Oranges 40 cts Bananas 30 cts . . . washed 27 napkins took Aunt Hannahs silverware home

LEISURE AND READING

In spite of six-day work weeks and long hours, this farm family had moments of relaxation, particularly during the winter months. These times are probably underrepresented in diary entries simply because they were so mundane—playing ball or a game, knitting, reading.[18]

13–18 March 1886: Elmers ball bounced against the glass of sitting room door, broke . . . Got the glass put in sitting room door $1.25

2 February 1888: Bought Chambers cyclopedia at A.C. Wallace for $9.00 . . . *8 May* Orra and George playing old hundred . . . *1 June* Jim, Sam Dow and Harry Kerr are playing ball with the boys

9 February 1891: Harry McLaughlin was here borrowed a book from George (round the world in 80 days) left one, Mrs Custors work . . . *20 February* Baked bread, read the Spy

8 April 1892: A man was here this morning endeavoring to get up a biographical history of the county, we did not subscribe, price $15.00

8–10 February 1893: knit some this P.M., read the last of the Mohicans this evening . . . knit and read some to day, churned

26–29 January 1894: Father loaned George the "Paradise Lost" to read . . . Father presented Elmer with the "Prince of India" . . . *20 June* Orra and Elmer gone to a class social at Matt Abrahams. the literary exercises will be from Whittier. Arthur McCracken borrowed my copy of Whittier.

The most regular reading material in this family was their Bible, newspapers, and magazines. Bellefontaine, like many county seats in this period, had both Democratic and Republican newspapers, and the Gebbys subscribed to the semiweekly Republican. *They also received their monthly United Presbyterian paper and several farm journals. While the boys were growing up they regularly received the* Youth's Companion, *and* Harper's *was first purchased as a single issue and later by subscription.*

5 April 1887: Jerry was at town afternoon renewed subscription for Republican $1.50

2 February 1888: Renewed the subscription for the "Witness" 1.05 and "Youths Companion" $1.80 . . . *30 April* got a copy of Harpers Weekly 10 cts

13 April 1893: I signed for the Mayflower, a paper published by Lewis Childs, 25 cts . . . *22 April* Jerry subscribed for Harpers Weekly $4.00

These periodicals were often the source of art prints or literature that could not be purchased locally.

14 July 1890: got a picture from the "Companion Co" &c "Ice dainties"

4 February 1891: Jerry sent for the "Witness" with a book on natural history and a painting $3.35

LECTURES AND CONCERTS

Beyond newspapers and magazines this family's experience with the world came primarily from missionary programs at church and cultural programs at the Bellefontaine Opera House. Margaret seems to have gone to more of the former and her sons to more of the latter. Musical and theatrical entertainments were both local and imported, and an important part of every fall and winter was the lecture season.[19]

1 October 1888: The boys gone to the Queen of Fame this evening . . . *22 November* Orra gone to Opera house to entertainment by the Boston Stars . . . *21 December* Orra and Elmer gone to a concert at the opera house

8 February 1889: Orra and Elmer gone to a musical entertainment at the Opera House given by Mrs Acton some of the pupils of the school, and others for Mrs Actons benefit . . . *11 October* the boys gone to a concert by the Jubilee singers

3 January 1890: Orra gone to an entertainment at the Opera house given by the Waverly club for the benefit of the poor . . . *14 January* Elmer gone to a show of Uncle Toms Cabin . . . *12 March* Orra gone to a concert, Tom Wrights orchestra . . . *27 August* Orra to an entertainment (William Tell) at the Opera house

27 January 1891: Orra and Elmer gone to a concert given by the Lotus Glee Club . . . *3 February* Orra and Elmer gone to an entertainment at the G.A.R. Hall, music and literary . . . *18 February* Orra and Elmer gone to an entertainment at the Opera house given by the Bellefontaine Minstrels . . . *8 April* Orra and Elmer gone to a lecture at the Opera house by Rev Conway on the "Acres of Diamonds" the last of the season . . . *28 October* attended a lecture at the church by Mrs A.M. Nicol a retired missionary of Egypt, subject - Girls life in Egypt . . . *21 October* Orra gone to the first lecture of this seasons course.

12 January 1892: attended a lecture and Magic Lantern show of India by Emma Dean Anderson this evening a very good entertainment.

23 January 1893: Orra, George & I attended a recitation by Miss Spouts the eloqutionist. her performance was very good. a full house, tickets 40 cts . . . *25 January* Orra and George gone to a lecture at the Opera house this evening, by Geo W. Bain, Subject: Boys & Girls, nice and naughty . . . *22 March* Orra and George are gone to a lecture at the Opera house by Robert McIntire, subject "Buttoned up people," this is the last of the series.

28 February 1894: the boys are all gone to a concert at the opera house one of the lecture series . . . *24 April* All except Grandma and Adda was at an entertainment at the church given by Chauncey Murch a Missionary from Egypt. his Magic lantern views were very good. got home about 11 Oclock quite a full house . . . *12 October* The boys all gone to a lecture on Electricity by Prof DeMott, the first of the season given by the Star Lecture course . . . *26 December* The boys all gone to a concert at the Op. H one of the Star Lecture course.

7 January 1895: George and Elmer are to the opera house to hear the play of Hamlet by Walker Whiteside . . . *10 May* Elmer at an anti catholic lecture by Margaret Shepherd to night . . . *20 September* All attended the Concert given by the Knoxville glee club, very good . . . *11 November* Elmer gave Nannie and I his ticket to the lecture at the Opera house by Leland T. Powers an impersonation of the characters in David Copperfield.

22 January 1896: We all attended readings and music on the Harp &

Violin, by the Mrs. Laura Dainty & Co . . . *29 January* Elmer gone to the Opera house to an Oritorio of the creation given by many of the best singers of Bellefontaine . . . *27 March* We attended the Lecture of Robert McIntire, Sunnyside of Soldier Life, was good . . . *29 April* Elmer gone to an entertainment given by the C.E. of the Presbyterian Church, a reading of Midsummer nights dream by a Mrs Brice of Lima, O.

HOLIDAYS

R eaders may be startled to discover that 1 January was not a holiday a century ago. Stores, banks, and government offices were
open for business as usual.

1 January 1891 [Thursday]: A very wet day. Orra and George made
each a key for the P.O. but Georges did not open the lock.[1] Jerry was at
the farm this morning, everything all right, went to town this P.M. paid
the taxes $240.22, got bank div. $140. I swept and dusted the house all
over to day. Orra gone to prayer meeting this evening.

In this neighborhood there were no elaborate New Year's Eve parties. The Gebbys frequently, but not always, began the new year with a
large family dinner, sometimes with Margaret's parents and siblings,
sometimes with Jerry's cousins. This family had no regular pattern of
celebration, but extended family visits were frequent during December
and January. These celebrations were usually on a weekday since everyone went to church on Sunday. Dinner was at midday so everyone could
do their morning and evening chores. Most family dinners included
three generations, but it was rare for every member of the household to
leave home at the same time.

1 January 1886: All at G.W.Aikins, T & J Cook, Charley & Lizzie,
James McCrackens family, Lymans family & Father & Mother & the
Smith family were there also, altogether 44 persons.
31 December 1886–1 January 1887: Harry Harner was here inviting

us to a New Years dinner tomorrow . . . Grandma, Jerry and I went to Harry Harners for dinner today, A.R. Harner and wife, John Harner & wife & son, Ed Lemens family, John S. Horn & daughter & Clarence Harner, in all 19. Boys at home rigged up the old sleigh hitched up Charlie to it had some fun. . . . *5–6 January* Baked two cakes and nine pies dressed two chickens, mother came & helped. Jerry went to town got coal oil $1.00 Oysters 60 cts . . . Father, Mother, Lyman, Mattie, Nellie, Harry and Jane & Nannie Cook, Charlie, Lizzie & Homer Cook, Joshua & Lottie Doan, Milton, Anna & Kate Wolf, G.W. Martha Ann, John, Sallie, Mary, Mabel & Harry Aikin were here for dinner. with ourselves also J.E., Mary & Charlie McCracken, in all 32.

The last New Year's entry in these diaries shows the second Gebby son, who was by then working as a Bellefontaine bank clerk, had adopted a social custom more common in town than country.

31 December 1896: Elmer making new years calls.

DECORATION DAY

During the 1880s and 1890s, Decoration Day was an important holiday, but it focused almost exclusively on Civil War soldiers. Since the Gebby family had no personal casualties closer than first cousins, and no Civil War veterans in the immediate family, the holiday does not seem to have held extraordinary significance.

30 May 1888: This afternoon we went to the cemetery being decoration day a great many present Rev. Albritten the orator of the day, got home after five Oclock.
30 May 1891: went to town a while this forenoon it being decoration day. drove to & through the cemetery, the soldiers graves all decorated and many others.
30 May 1892: Decoration day, we did not go, too busy.
30 May 1893: Quite a good many people in town to day it being decoration day. after the graves were decorated, Rev. Whitlock made an address of an hour and a quarter long in the Opera house during the rain.
30 May 1895: this being Decoration day a great many people in town. Elmer was at home, a legal holiday.

FOURTH OF JULY

Comparison between local newspapers and these diaries suggests that Fourth of July celebrations were more significant to town people who had a holiday from work than to farmers in the midst of hay and wheat harvest. It also appears that fireworks were more important to the average person than patriotism and political speeches. Perhaps this reflects the fact that they happened during the evening when they were more accessible to farm families, but they were certainly the main attraction for teenage boys.

4 July 1888: the boys all went to town to see the fireworks this evening, the rest of us went to the pasture salted the cattle, stopped in town a while saw the fireworks, got home after nine Oclock.

4 July 1890: "The Glorious Fourth" the men with Conn & Tannehill worked at the wheat, finished cutting west of the railroad track and some east of it, shocked up what was cut yesterday. a great many celebrated the day at the lake swimming race, a tub race and other things. Fire works up town this eve, Elmer gone[2]

3 July 1891: George got some fire crackers.

4 July 1892: Elmer is gone on the wheel to a Lawn fete at Huntsville this evening. Orra and George up town celebrating the fourth by a display of sky Rockets.

4 July 1894: The glorious fourth. The men finished cutting wheat here before noon, cut at the farm this afternoon. Elmer helped this forenoon, he was at town this P.M. Arthur McCracken came home with him for supper. they all went to town tonight to see the fireworks. they had several races a bicycle race, a barrel race, wheel barrow race and a good many foolish things.[3]

4 July 1895: Laura Dow was here for dinner to day. This is the glorious fourth, the town was almost deserted to day, are making an attempt at fireworks to night.[4]

THANKSGIVING

Perhaps no nineteenth-century holiday image lingers more strongly than "over the river and through the woods, to grandmother's house we go." These diaries reveal clearly that individual families were quite dif-

*ferent and everyone did not celebrate Thanksgiving at grandmother's.
Some years the Gebby family had a very traditional celebration, and
other times they seemed to ignore this holiday completely.*[5]

25 November 1886: Went to Fathers for dinner Jerry and the
children & Grandma went to church. Grandma took dinner at J.M.Wil-
liamsons the rest of us at Fathers with G.W. Aikins, T. Cooks, Lymans,
C.C. Cooks & James McCrackens & George Harners in all 39.[6]

24 November 1887: Orra was hunting, came home about three
Oclock, got a squirrel and a rabbit, the rest at home all day, Father &
Mother were here for dinner (had a stuffed hen) sewed on my dress.

19 November 1888: Thanksgiving day, cool and cloudy. Orra and
Elmer went with Orra and Fred Dillon and Ed Foote hunting but got
nothing. Jerry went to Ben Yoders to see some pigs but did not get any.
Grandma, George and I went to church, services being in our church,
the house was very full.

28 November 1889: Thanksgiving, the boys with the Aikin boys
was hunting, got two Rabbits, ate turkey at Aikins for dinner. Jerry,
George & I went to church services in the M.E. church, quite a large &
attentive audience. Rev. Hamilton preached Text "In all things give
thanks," a splendid sermon.

27 November 1890: Thanksgiving services in the Lutheran church
sermon by Mr Kalb we did not attend. Orra, Elmer, Sam, Lon and Harry
Aikin were hunting this forenoon, got five Quail, gave them to Harry.
the boys pulled turnips this P.M. We dug the celery this morning, fried
up two gals of sausage in cakes packed the rest in crocks.

26 November 1891: Thanksgiving services at the Presbyterian
church. We did not attend. Orra, Lon & Sam Robeson, Jesse Kaylor and
Andy Koonts were hunting this forenoon, they got 5 Rabbits and a
Quail.[7]

24 November 1892: Thanksgiving. Orra was hunting this forenoon,
this afternoon he and Jerry weighed the hogs, 20 head weighed 5415,
averaged 275 lbs, delivered 7, hauled them in the wagon. Grandma and
Eva K. attended church services.[8] I was not able to go, George sick this
evening.

29–30 November 1893: I baked bread, pies & a hickory nut cake,
roasted a rabbit for supper, dressed two chickens for Thanksgiving tomorrow . . . Thanksgiving day. Orra and Lon Robeson was hunting this
forenoon, George and Lawrence Thrasher were hunting all day but not
successful. Elmer was at church. Rev. Hull of the Lutheran church
preached services in the M.E. Church. We roasted two chickens for

dinner. I was at G.W. Aikins this afternoon, Grandma at Uncle Johns, Jerry and Elmer at the pasture.[9]

28–29 November 1894: Wellie [*hired man*] and family went to Stokes township this evening to spend Thanksgiving. We dressed a chicken, made six pies and a cake . . . Thanksgiving services in the Lutheran church by Rev Thompson rector of the Episcopal church, we were not there. Orra hunted a while got 5 quails then went to G.W. Aikins for dinner. George and Lawrence Thrasher were hunting too. George got sick about 2 P.M. got home about 4 P.M. has pleurisy, some better now. Elmer went to Degraff [*visiting cousins*] at 12.30 expected to come home on the 8.30. C.C.Cook and family visited us to day. Nannie [*hired girl*] was at Peter Dows for dinner.

27–28 November 1895: Wellie got Maud [*carriage horse*] to go to his fathers tomorrow to a family reunion . . . Nannie was at home to a Thanksgiving dinner. Elmer at home this being a holiday. Orra and Mattie were gathering hickory nuts this afternoon got about a half a bushel. baked a cake and four pies. all the boys are gone to prayer meeting.

26 November 1896: Thanksgiving. Orra & Mattie was at church and then went to Mrs Eads to a Thanksgiving dinner. George and Lawrence Thrasher were hunting. Jerry & Elmer was at the farm to see the stock. Nannie took dinner at Mrs Nelsons. I sewed some.

Diary entries suggest this family struggled with the decision to have Thanksgiving dinner with his relatives or her relatives and never established a tradition of their own. Margaret seems to reflect a sense of duty regarding union church services, mentioning them even when the family did not attend. The young men established a tradition of going hunting on Thanksgiving Day, which appears remarkably similar to the current practice of watching televised football games.

CHRISTMAS

This family's most important holiday was Christmas. Celebrations always extended over several days with various relatives and always included participation in the Christmas Eve celebration at church.[10] The only gifts mentioned are small items that were usually purchased the day before, and the only decorations were evidently the Christmas tree for the Sunday school.

25–29 December 1886: All went to J.E.McCrackens to a Turkey dinner had a very pleasant time. T. Cooks family, all of G.W. Aikins family, C.C. Cooks family, Dunk Dows family, Jerry Gebbys family, Lymans & Mattie, Father and Mother 32 in all . . . Went to Johnny Harners today to a Turkey dinner. Rev Bigley wife & daughter, John Huston & wife, Mr. Norton & wife, Dr Elliott & wife, Mr Huston wife & daughter, C.C. Cooks family, Mrs Newman, Mrs Longfellow and our-selves in all 28 persons were there, had a very pleasant time, got home about five Oclock[11] . . . Went to G.W. Aikins for dinner, the Smith family, Tommy Cooks family, C.C. Cooks family, Lymans family, Winnie Doan, and ourselves in all 49 had a very pleasant time.

18–25 December 1889: Orra looked through the woods for a Christmas tree . . . Mr Hamilton [*minister*] came here went to the woods with Jerry and Orra looking for a suitable Christmas tree . . . got Grandma gloves, handkerchief, socks, $2.01 Jerry bought a Chatterbox and a Diary $1.75 . . . Orra, Elmer & John Aikin got the Christmas tree for the church. Orra helped decorate it this afternoon . . . [*Christmas Eve*] we went to town this afternoon took some presents for the Christmas tree. all went this evening had a very pleasant time the trees were beautifully decorated and some handsome presents were distributed, all seemed pleased. got home before ten Oclock . . . [*Christmas Day*] Elmer was at the entertainment at the Lutheran Church. Orra was at J.E. Mc-Crackens. Grandma, Jerry, George & I was at Mr Harners with Harry, Kate & Paul Harner, had a very pleasant time.

24 December 1890: Grandma & I were at town had 5-4 butter 84 c, got peaches, cheese, Almonds and stocking yarn 94 cts, at P.O. got a Christmas present for Orra, a package for George, bought George a knife 25, a handkerchief apiece for Orra & Elmer $1.00, put the presents on the Oleander[12]

24 December 1891: I went to town got umbrella $2.00, slippers $1.25, Knife 10, tidy 25, handkerchief 50.

24 December 1892: got Elmer a Toilet set & a collar & cuff box, Orra shaving mug & brush. The boys and I attended the Christmas entertainment at the church it consisted of singing and recitations and distribution of presents. got home at about half past 8.

23 December 1893: the boys made me a nice Christmas present of an Alarm Clock.[13]

24 December 1894: George was at the church this forenoon helping with the Christmas tree. We all attended the Christmas exercises at the church to night, a great many presents were received and the children were happy.

Christmas Eve was always celebrated at the church and Christmas Day was usually confined to the immediate family. Celebrations with extended family on both sides tended to come between Christmas and New Year's or in early January, but by 1896 the family was including their daughter-in-law, a widowed aunt, and some single cousins in the family circle. This entry is interesting evidence of Margaret's acceptance that her oldest son had set up his own home and was no longer considered one of the immediate family, who were evidently present but not named individually.

24–25 December 1896: We killed and dressed a turkey he weighed 8 lbs net, baked a cake. A Christmas entertainment at the church to night for the children, a program is prepared each one is to bring a pound of something to give to the poor . . . Orra, Mattie, Aunt Hannah, Lon, Sam, Anna & Lizzie helped us eat our Turkey at dinner had a very pleasant time.

MISCELLANEOUS CELEBRATIONS

The nineteenth century celebrated far fewer legal holidays than the twentieth, but these diaries give an interesting glimpse of local response to some special events.

30 April 1889: There was a union service in the Presbyterian church this being the centennial of Washingtons first inauguration as the first President of the U.S.

21 October 1892: George at home this P.M. this being the 400th anniversary the schools had exercises in the Opera house this forenoon.[14]

21 February 1894: Orra & Elmer are gone to class meeting at Mrs McKees. this being the evening before Washingtons birthday they intend celebrating it in a small way. Grant McMillen represents G.W., Mary McKee Mrs Washington, Effie McMillen Nellie Custus, Elmer the Marquis DeLafayette. I fixed a vest for him with gay colors & ruffles put lace around his coat sleeves, &c.[15]

CELEBRATIONS

BIRTHDAYS

Although nineteenth-century families celebrated fewer holidays than their twentieth-century counterparts, this family had more personal celebrations that involved a network of aunts, uncles, and cousins than many families do today. Extended families often lived nearby, but distance was measured by horse-and-buggy drives. The morning after the entry below Margaret recorded the temperature at twelve degrees below zero. It is obvious that traveling several miles with horse and sleigh in bitter cold and snowy weather did not interfere with a social occasion as much as driving across town by car in similar weather might today.

9 January 1886: Very stormy, snowing and blowing, very cold. Grandmas birthday [72nd] Ed Lemens family, Harry & Clarence Harner, Father and Mother, Lyman & Mattie, G.W. Aikins family, Mrs Wright & Jennie & J.E. McCrackens family were here in all 26. Mismores hotel burned this afternoon. Snow six or eight inches deep.

When the Gebby children were small, birthdays were evidently marked with a small present, usually homemade.

11–18 January 1886: Jerry went to town this afternoon, got red yarn 17 cts . . . Knit Georges mittens . . . Georges Birthday, Eight years old today.

The only birthday that rated a party was the twenty-first—a son's legal maturity.

11 January 1892: This being Orras 21st birthday some of his friends called and surprised him. John, Ed, Harry, Sallie, Mary & Mable Aikin, Lon, Anna & Lizzie Robeson, Jesse Kaylor, Mattie Eades, Tillie Maxwell, Jessie & Sam Dow. Robesons baked one cake Aikins the other, we got candy $1.20, oranges, 5 doz $1.00.

26 December 1893: Elmer was working again to day, is improving some [*from illness*]. Martha Ann Aikin & Jessie Dow helped me bake four cakes. this being Elmers 21 birthday about 30 of his young friends surprised him by calling on him. had a very pleasant evening, they left after 12 Oclock.

For Margaret and her husband birthdays were just another day, mentioned casually if at all.

14 April 1891: I cleaned the back stairway, baked bread, sewed. My 56 birthday.

As grandparents got older, however, their birthdays became annual occasions for a family celebration. The emphasis was always on eating and visiting rather than presents.

4 November 1892: Jerry, George and I took dinner at Fathers it being his 84 birthday. M.A.Aikin, Sallie, Mary, Mabel, John Dow & wife and Orra Cook were there, 20 in all. Jane Cook was sick.

9 January 1893: Elmer and Jerry was at town got two qts of Oysters and 25 cts worth of crackers 95 cts, this being Grandmas 80 birthday Ed Lemens family and Harry Harners family and Clarence Harner surprised her by visiting her. they were all here for dinner, had a pleasant visit. . . . *4 November* Jerry and I was at Fathers for dinner this being his 85 birthday the children and some of the Grandchildren took dinner with him, had a pleasant time.

3 November 1894 [Saturday]: Jerry, Elmer & I took dinner at Lymans with the Cook family had a nice time, tomorrow being Fathers 86 birthday we visited to day instead.

WEDDINGS

Many people have an image of nineteenth-century weddings that resembles the traditional bride and groom figures on a wedding cake.

These diaries, however, record a variety of large and small, formal and informal, religious and civil ceremonies, which is remarkably similar to current practice.

27 March–6 April 1888: Orra Cook and Eva C. Jeffers are to be married at 8 Oclock this evening . . . Winnie Doan came here this evening going to the reception. All went to Orra Cooks reception this evening, somewhere in the neighborhood of fifty were present, all seemed to enjoy themselves, the culinary department was all that could be desired, got home between one and two Oclock this morning. Winnie came back with us.[1]

25 December 1889–1 January 1890: Orra & Elmer received the wedding cards of Nannie Cook for New Years night . . . bought a clock for a wedding present for Nannie Cook who expects to be married on New Years evening $7.75 . . . all attended the wedding of Dr. W.H. Philipp and Nannie J. Cook at T. Cooks this eve at 7 Oclock. 83 persons ate supper. they received quite a number of nice and valuable presents.[2] Rev Hamilton assisted by Rev Currie of Huntsville performed the ceremony. got home about one Oclock Anna and Lizzie Robeson stayed with Grandma.[3]

14–23 May 1891: Received the wedding card of Herdman & Wright this evening . . . bought a rug for a wedding present for Jennie Wright $4.00 . . . Jerry, Grandma & I attended the wedding of Jennie Wright and W.G. Herdman of Omaha, quite a good many there, got home at midnight . . . called at Mrs Wrights got our spoons & forks from the wedding

24 September–5 October 1895: We all received an invitation to the marriage of Miss Mary E. Porter and Rev Samuel Victor Kyle Oct 8 1895 . . . I went with Aunt Hannah & Anna and bought a wedding present for Miss Mary Porter of Xenia. we got a Table cloth & napkins $6.12, I paid one half $3.06 . . . Elmer left on the 6-5 train to night for Xenia to attend the wedding of S.V. Kyle & Mary E. Porter tomorrow evening.

6–7 February 1896: Harry Aikin was married to night at 7.30 to Cora McCormick . . . Elmer, George & Nannie are at G.W.Aikins attending a reception for Harry & his wife. . . .

29 October Eddie Cantwell brought his bride, Katie Gallagher, from Pittsburg to day, the boys gave them a belling this evening.

Despite the obvious variety, two patterns are distinctly different from the twentieth-century norm. Practically all of the weddings and receptions referred to, whether large or small, were held in the home of

the bride, and close relatives loaned silver and china. Margaret never refers to anything resembling the bridal showers so common today, and parents of the groom seem to play minor roles in the festivities. Perhaps this explains the stark simplicity of her diary entry, quoted in its entirety, the day of her own son's wedding.

18 September 1895 [*Wednesday*]: Another very warm day. Wellie, George & Orra cut corn this forenoon. Wellie & George this P.M. Nannie ironed I did the other work. Orra and Mattie Eades were married at 8.30 to night, took the Knickerbocker at 10 for Cleveland and other points.[4] Jerry gave him $150.00 for travelling expenses. he bought two 1000 mile tickets. they cost $20.00 apiece. they are good for a year. cooked tomatoes to make catsup. sewed this P.M. finished my shirtwaist. baked bread.

This entry leaves readers wondering whether the groom's family even attended the wedding ceremony, but the Bellefontaine Republican's announcement would imply they did. "Sept. 18th 8:30 P.M. at the residence of the brides mother on East Columbus Avenue, Mr. Orra Gebby and Miss Mattie L. Eades. The ceremony was performed by the Rev. Geo W. Hamilton in the presence of relatives and the happy couple left the same evening for Cleveland and Put-in-Bay."

Martha Eades' father, a Civil War veteran, died when she was a small child, and her mother's modest home undoubtedly kept this wedding small. Margaret never mentioned inviting Mrs Eades to her home or being invited to hers, either before or after this wedding. It is a silence that suggests, fairly or not, that she was not enthusiastic about her eldest son's marriage. On their return the newly married couple lived with the Gebbys during the four months their house was being built, but many nights the bride returned to her mother's home in town.

24–26 September 1895: Orra and Mattie came home on the 6-35 train this eve. Elmer met them at the Depot . . . Orra & Mattie took dinner & supper in town . . . Orra took Mattie home this evening.

ANNIVERSARIES

Throughout these diaries wedding anniversaries were a favorite occasion for family get-togethers, and the pattern in this community was a "surprise" dinner brought in by relatives and friends. Like weddings, these celebrations called for presents from the guests.

25–26 May 1886: Baked a cake to take to a surprise at Charlie Cooks their fifth anniversary . . . Went to C.C.Cooks their fifth anniversary, about 55 eat dinner which was very nice, presents were a ratan rocking chair, a comb case, a waitor, 70 cts for anniversary.[5]

6 June 1892: I went with Aunt Hannah and Emma McAra to select a present for the 20th anniversary of Mr & Mrs I.L.Fellow, got a dozen pie plates $3.75, Mrs Dillon gave me a 1.00 as she could not attend on account of Ralphs sickness. Jerry & I were at the anniversary, quite a good many there, had a very pleasant time indeed, got home about 12 P.M.

11–13 December 1894: I was at G.W.Aikins this afternoon helping prepare for their 40th anniversary. Jane Cook and Ethel Aikin was there . . . Jerry, Orra and I attended the fortieth wedding anniversary of G.W. and M.A. Aikin to day. there were 68 persons there ate dinner. Mrs. Mary Neal, Mrs Eliza McMillan and the Misses Montgomery from Guernsey County, E.E.Cleland and children of Union Co and Ralph Aikin of Xenia were among the guests . . . Sallie Aikin and Miss Montgomery called brought my dishes home.

Certain milestone anniversaries were celebrated, just as they are today, but when Margaret and Jerry's friends thought they were honoring their twentieth anniversary it must have been a real surprise for it was actually their twenty-first![6]

30 September 1889: Jerry met the well digger at the train, they drove down about 20 feet broke the pipe four or five feet below the ground have not succeeded in getting it out. We were much surprised indeed by some friends calling on us telling us this was our 21 anniversary, 101 ate dinner, T. Cooks, J.E. McCrackens, Orra Cook & Mrs Jeffers, Belle Wallace, G.W. Aikins children, Mrs Maxwell & daughter, Mr Barnetes, Mrs Wright & Daughter & children, Dr Reed wife & mother, O.M. McLaughlin & family, Mrs Finly, M.L. & children, Mrs McBeth, Ferguson Ewing, Patterson, Wright, Robesons, Lemens, Harners.

It sounds as though the men were busy digging a well and no one was expecting company. Of course unannounced visits were much more common before telephones came into homes, but it strains the imagination of a modern reader to visualize a house able to accommodate 101 persons for dinner on the spur of the moment even though the guests brought the food potluck-style.

Major celebrations involved as much preplanning by relatives as they do today, but the chief difference was the lack of a party house to accommodate the crowd or caterers to prepare the food.

1–7 June 1889: Saw Martha Ann and Lyman arranged to go to Fathers next Friday celebrating their sixtieth anniversary . . . went to J.E. McCrackens to see about the anniversary dinner . . . Baked bread, pies and a cake, killed and cooked two chickens . . . We were all at Fathers for dinner being celebrated as their 60th anniversary of their marriage, tomorrow is the day but on account of meeting [*church*] we met to day the invited guests were Aunt Mattie and her family, Dunk Dows family, Sim Dows family and Sallie Dow and Effie, Also Peter Dows family, Jennie Cleland and two children also A.C. Wallace & wife & Miss Hawthorne all the children and Grandchildren were there except Jim & Orra Cook. 75 eat dinner.

Margaret's distinction between immediate family and extended family is interesting since practically everyone attending this celebration was related. The planning was obviously done by the couple's four living children and the oldest granddaughter who was married and living in Bellefontaine. Grandchildren living at home or married and living in the Bellefontaine area were part of the immediate family, but married grandchildren who had moved away were considered invited guests.[7]

COUNTY FAIR

T he most festive time of the year for this farm family was the week
of the county fair, which in Logan County occurred the first of
October. In eleven years Margaret never missed attending at least
two or three days, and the price of a family ticket was consistently one
dollar. This was a favorite time for relatives to come visiting and the
Gebby house was usually filled. It must have been an especially social
occasion among teenagers and young adults.

28 September–1 October 1886: J.W.Kitchen came today with 5
sheep to take to the fair[1] . . . went to the fair this afternoon [*Wednesday*] not a great many there. Sammy and Lizzie Robeson came this eve.[2]
J.W. Kitchen came home with us. Fair tickets $1.00 . . . All went to the
fair quite a crowd there, took dinner at the dining hall (Jerry & I,
Grandma, George, Lizzie) paid $1.65 had a very good dinner, got a pair
of overshoes 40 cts, went to see the battle of Gettysburg (Lizzie,
Grandma, Jerry & I) 40 cts . . . Quite cool and windy all day all went to
the fair had a very unpleasant time

5–6 October 1887: Winnie Doan and Kate Wolf came this
evening[3] . . . A.H. Robeson came on the morning train here tonight.

4 October 1888: All went to the fair . . . George Harner here
tonight.

4 October 1889: All went to the fair . . . Kate Wolf came home with
us.

5 October 1892: All went to the fair . . . John Kitchen came home
with us.

Year after year the Gebby family viewed farm equipment and livestock shows, garden and home arts exhibits, saw entertainment spectac-
ulars, shopped the commercial exhibits, and socialized with neighbors.
Exhibits were put in place on Tuesday and workers in the dining hall
might be involved until everything was dismantled on Saturday, but the
fair really ran Wednesday through Friday with the largest attendance on
Friday.

Margaret never mentions exhibiting any household goods nor the
men exhibiting any livestock. Whatever the reason, it seems likely that
the Gebbys were observers rather than participants, at least until Orra
married and Mattie began exhibiting. Margaret's journal strongly suggests she and her relatives were critical observers rather than casual
browsers.

2 October 1890: All were at the fair, a great many people there.
display very good vegetables very good for this season and hall very
fine. Floral good, horses splendid, also sheep and hogs, cattle not as
good as other years. parade of premium horses was very fine indeed.

1 October 1891: All went to the fair got home about 5 Oclock the
exhibiting was good but not up to some of the former fairs. In the art,
floral & vegetable halls the display was very fine, the stock and machinery departments were not so well displayed. the race was about as usual,
they have improved the track, it is much wider and better.

5 October 1893: the fair is not nearly so good as usual, a falling off
in all most everything.

23 September 1896: Mattie was here got some Crab Apples to make
some jelly for exhibition at the Fair.

Weather obviously affected both fair attendance and attitude about
its quality, with cold and rainy weather doing far more damage than dry
and dusty. Local newspapers speculated that the 1893 county fair suffered from the number of Logan County people, like the Gebbys, who
attended the Chicago World's Fair and found their own anticlimactic.

Although farm and household exhibits and the sociability of relatives and neighbors were obviously the county fair highlights, Margaret
was impressed enough to record some of the more spectacular entertainment attractions.

2 October 1889: The balloon ascension and parachute decension
was a success, the man came down again not far from where he went up,
he ascended about three thousand feet.

1 October 1891: The Kenady Bros. had their trained horses, one

man would ride with a foot on each horse, once they rode with a chair on their saddles and had a foot on each chair the horses going at full speed.

Margaret normally packed dinner for the family, bought hot water to make coffee, and the family ate picnic-style with any visiting relatives who happened to be attending. Some of this was no doubt frugality, some sociability, and perhaps some belief that home cooking was better. One wonders whether there was a specific location, almost as clearly defined as the family's church pew, where relatives tied their horses and met to share their picnic dinner.

5 October 1888: All went to the fair. rained last night laying the dust nicely, some warmer and calm, got a qt of boiling water at the dining hall for our coffee 10 cts, more people on the grounds than yesterday.

3 October 1889: All went to the fair, a very large attendance, display very good. Orra got his dinner at the dining hall his report not flattering.

3 October 1890: all attended the fair today. we took our dinner with us, the day was delightful, bought 1 qt of boiling water 5 cts.

Local groups evidently took turns operating the dining hall as a money-making project. When the United Presbyterians were involved in 1887 and again in 1896, Margaret and the boys ate in the dining hall, helped with the work before and during the fair, and probably saw less than usual of the exhibits.

12 September 1896: Went to town and to church this P.M. there was a congregational meeting with regard to running the Dining hall at the fair grounds . . . *22 September* I prepared Chow, Chow for the Dining Hall at the fair, will finish it in the morning . . . *25 September* fixed the old cook stove for the Dining Hall at the fair, got two new rods 20 cts put them in, stopped all the cracks with fire clay . . . *26 September* George took a load of wood to the Dining Hall at the fairgrounds this afternoon . . . *29 September* Nannie and I cleaned four hens to take to the Dining Hall tomorrow, baked bread & churned . . . *30 September* the Fair Grounds are almost complete failure on account of the rain, a few United Presbyterians were at the Dining Hall furnishing meals to what few are there. The Agricultural board decided that if it was still raining in the A.M. they would postpone the fair indefinitely . . . *1 October* Did not rain since about 8 Oclock last night. The Agricultural Society decided to go on with the Fair. George, Nannie and I were at the

Dining Hall this afternoon, took out some eatables. Elmer is there tonight . . . *2 October* Nannie and George was at the Dining Hall & Lunch Stand all day. George & Elmer there to night. Jerry was at the fair this afternoon, it is far below the usual standard. I was not well could not go to day . . . *3 October* went to the fair helped with the dinner and dish washing quite a good many ate dinner. did not hear how much money they took in, one Lunch stand took in $50.00 the other $20.00

The Gebbys often bought some small items at the commercial exhibits. It was almost an annual tradition for Margaret to buy flower bulbs and Jerry to buy buggy whips. The year Jerry bought the reaper-mower at the farm equipment exhibit was a notable exception.

3 October 1888: Went to the fair, the display is very fine but too cold to be pleasant. I got a vail 70 cts

3 October 1889: Jerry bought a Champion Reaper and Mower for $170 to be paid in about one year.

1–3 October 1890: Jerry bought three whips for 50 cts . . . bought 22 cts worth of hyacinth bulbs.

7 October 1892: It looked so much like rain we came home about 3 P.M. George bought a pair of Guinea Pigs, paid $1.00

5 October 1894: Jerry bought from a wagon two pair suspenders 25 cts, 4 whips 50 cts, one half doz pencils 10 cts. We got 2 qts boiling water for coffee 10 cts, bulbs 30 cts

4 October 1895: got some bulbs 40 cts, suspenders 25 cts, spoons 15 cts, whips $1.00

The fair was certainly the biggest annual event in Logan County, but these diaries seem relatively objective about its ups and downs. For Margaret it was an educational and a social event, not a competition. If the Gebbys had raised purebred cattle, sheep, hogs, or horses Margaret's record would very likely have viewed the fair more competitively.

4 October 1889: All went to the Fair, a great many people there, said to be 25,000 but that is somewhat exaggerated, the show was very good, a great many premiums awarded.[4]

5 October 1893: The fair is not nearly so good as usual, a falling off in all most everything.

EXCURSIONS

This farm family never took a vacation, but they had considerable flexibility to take off any day when work permitted to visit relatives or to go hunting and fishing. Of course they did the chores such as feeding the chickens and milking the cows before they left and timed their visits to be home by five o'clock to do it all over again. The Gebbys did take excursions of three to five days to visit relatives or see sights. By modern standards, passenger trains were convenient and affordable. They also offered the young and the old an independence that automobiles do not provide.

The entry below seems routine until one computes the ages and realizes that Margaret's mother was then seventy-nine and her aunt Martha Doan was seventy-seven. They were obviously visiting their older sister Jane Smithson, still living near their childhood home north of Marietta, Ohio.

23 September 1887: Mother and Aunt Mattie left for Duck Creek this morning.

Margaret's extended family network offered secure knowledge that relatives would be welcome anytime, even though they were unexpected arrivals or a cousin they had never met.

24–26 December 1894: Elmer went to Indianapolis to spend Christmas . . . Elmer came home on the 8.30 train from Indianapolis, visited Robert Campbells had a nice time.[1]

8 September 1896: Jerry & I left at 9-30 this morning for Monroe Station, arrived there after 12, as no one knew we were coming, there was none to meet us. a young man being there to meet a sister who did not come we paid him 50 cts to take us to Jerome Robesons. We were warmly received and got dinner, then Mrs Robeson took us to John Kitchens. they were much surprised to see us.[2]

Passenger trains competed for business by offering excursions at special rates much as airlines do today. Many people combined business and pleasure, and one of Margaret's entries makes it difficult to tell whether the art exhibit or the binder had priority. It is a surprising glimpse of cultural interest on the part of a midwestern farmer.

25 March 1886: Jerry went to Springfield with the excursion to the art exhibition and to get some repairs for his binder and spring harrow[3] . . . binder repairs $1.75, harrow $1.50, traveling $1.00 Admitt 25 cts, catalogue 5 cts, dinner 25 cts = $4.80.

In the period covered by these diaries two nationally noted exhibitions were held in the Midwest: the Northwest Territory Centennial Exposition in Cincinnati and the Chicago World's Fair. The Gebby family attended both, but the omissions in Margaret's diaries are as frustrating as the descriptions are interesting.

25 August–1 September 1888: went to John Hubers got Cora to come and stay with Grandma next week . . . Cora Huber came to stay with Grandma untill we come back from Cincinnati. Orra took us to the train (11-40). Charlie and Lizzie [*Cook*] and children were on the train . . . Arrived at Cincinnati between six and seven Oclock, stopped at the Indiana house engaged breakfast, supper, lodging and breakfast $1.50 pr day, not a very inviting breakfast, arrived at the Exposition about eight Oclock, went through all the buildings, staid untill evening very tired and sleepy. Charlie and Elmer took in the fall of Babylon they were much pleased with it[4] . . . went to the Zoological Gardens, went on the cable cars, had to walk some distance, saw about all the animals which seemed to be in good condition,[5] everything is very nice, got very tired went back to the city, took dinner at the restaurant 15 cts apiece, took the train for Monroe at 3.22 got there about 4.00 John Kitchen waiting for us, Jerry not well, staid at Kitchens all night . . . all went to Lebanon fair. Eva sick had to go to the dining hall and lie down.[6] Met Mr Bigger and two daughters, Mr & Mrs Steddam and Etta Robeson, a good many people there but rather a slim fair, went back to Kitchens,

Eva quite sick all day . . . John Kitchen and C.C.Cook out looking at sheep. Jerry, George and I went to visit Mr & Mrs Ayers, took dinner with them had a very pleasant visit, then went to Monroe station at 4.15 Oclock found the rest waiting, arrived home at eight Oclock . . . Cora Huber went home this forenoon, paid her $1.50. Expenses to Cincinnati $30.40.

Farm families were used to getting up early and putting in long days, but this group obviously wore themselves out seeing the entire Centennial Exposition in one day and visiting the Cincinnati zoo the next morning. It is frustrating that so little is recorded about the sights, but combining this trip with a visit to the Warren County Fair and a visit with cousins reinforces an impression that the extended family network was the first priority of social activity.

This excursion may have been Margaret and Jerry's first since their marriage twenty years before. Farm families had to have someone to do the regular chores of caring for livestock. This family left the seventeen-year-old son and the hired man in charge and hired a neighbor to help Grandma with the housework.

Family travel in shifts seems to have been common, partly to handle the work at home, but also because young adults preferred the company of their own friends. This is especially evident in Margaret's record of the Gebby family trip to the Chicago World's Fair.

25 July 1893: Elmer left on the 7.20 train this morning to attend the Worlds Fair at Chicago, $50.00 . . . *2 August* Elmer came home from Chicago on the 8.15 train this evening left C at 8.30 this morning.

16 August 1893: I sent a letter to Mrs Hartzler of Chicago for accommodations at her house while at the Worlds Fair . . . *19 August* Received a letter from Mrs Hartzler saying her rooms would be all occupied. Elmer wrote asking for rooms the 5 of September . . . *24 August* Ed Lemens was here this afternoon to know when we intend to start to the Worlds Fair . . . *26 August* met Josie & Elsie Lemen in town Elsie wants us to go to Chicago on Wednesday, we expect to go Tuesday. Wired to W. Hartzler if we could get accommodations at their house, 40 cts . . . *27 August* Received a telegram from Chicago that we could get accommodations at Hartzlers[7]

6 September 1893: got home this morning at 3 Oclock, walked home [*from Bellefontaine depot*], left Chicago at 9 A.M. arrived in Indianapolis too late for the eastern train, met a terrible jam, caused by an encampment of the G.A.R. the trip to the World fair cost us about $22 apiece ($66.90)

25 September 1893: Orra left for the Worlds Fair this morning, gave him $35.00 . . . *26 September* Eddie & Harry Aikins left for Chicago this morning . . . *30 September* Orra came home this afternoon, left Chicago at 11 P.M.

9 October 1893: A very large excursion train left here for the worlds fair this eve[8]

Readers can justifiably feel cheated that Margaret's diaries make no mention of sights and impressions! Fifteen-year-old George traveled with his parents, but each of the older boys went with some of their friends and cousins. News reports were full of the fair's dangers from pickpockets and con artists. It says a great deal about the parents' confidence in the boys' ability to handle the enticements of a big city celebration without supervision.

This was the most dramatic event in the area during this time and one must speculate why Margaret includes no descriptions. Does it reflect a parochialism on the part of this farm wife or could she have been too busy and tired to keep her journal? Considering her regular work schedule and the hours the family spent on the train during this trip, the latter seems unlikely. One is left feeling that the world beyond Margaret's farm home was visited but little valued. Perhaps the women's building with its model kitchen and the electric building with its irons, refrigerator, and washing machine were too far beyond Margaret's world. Strasser has speculated on what it must have been like for housewives to view these wonders and return to cooking on wood and coal stoves and to houses without plumbing. Perhaps it is too tempting to view Margaret's blank diary as her testimony.[9]

COMMUNITY

SCHOOL

The Gebby boys began their education at Blue Jacket School, a one-room grammar school about a mile from their home, which conducted a fall term of approximately twenty weeks and a spring term of about twelve weeks.[1] After completing this course of study the Gebbys paid tuition for all three sons to attend high school in Bellefontaine, where Elmer graduated in 1891 and George in 1895. Orra quit in 1889 to devote himself full time to farming, apparently with his parents' blessing.

Margaret faithfully attended closing exercises each term and her diary reflects more than a casual interest in the quality of teaching provided. Local school directors were men, but Margaret and a neighbor made regular evaluation visits at the local school and were directly involved in the selection of a teacher.

Even in this family with a school-teaching heritage, however, farm work had priority over studies. Sons were expected to stay home from school to help with harvest and planting. This was particularly true for the oldest son, who consistently attended fewer days than his brothers and undoubtedly found it impossible to keep up with town students when he regularly started high school classes about six weeks late and left six or eight weeks early.

Modern readers will note that students were responsible for purchasing their own textbooks and school supplies, and competence testing was used to determine placement in an appropriate course of study. Both of these issues are currently discussed by school districts concerned with the cost and quality of public education.

1 November 1886: Cal & Orra husked corn today, Jerry hauled wood and corn, Elmer and George started to school. Mr. Detwiler teaching . . . *24 November* Orra went to the union school was assigned to the ninth department (Miss Durkee) expects to start next Monday . . . *29 November* Orra got a Geography, Grammer & an Algebra $4.00 . . . *21 December* Orra was examined in Physical Geography today . . . *22 December* Orra was examined in Grammar this forenoon . . . *12 January 1887:* Orras tuition $6.00. Orra gone to G.W. Aikins for instruction in Algebra . . . *17 March* Baked a cake for dinner tomorrow at the school house it being the last day of school . . . *18 March* I went with Mrs Dillon to the school house this being the last day of school, had an abundance of and a very good dinner, the exercises were very good, the house was well filled . . . *11 April* School began today . . . *7 May* The boys ordered from Perry Mason & Co. a telescope $2.50 + 15 + 10 . . . *1 July* Went to a picnic at the school this being the last day of school

11 November 1887: Orra went to town saw Whit got blank books, science of Government, Philosophy $3.25² . . . *14 November* Orra started to school this morning . . . *1 December* gave Orra $4.50 to pay his & Elmers tuition for Nov. & Dec . . . *31 January 1888:* Paid $3.50 for Orra and Elmers tuition . . . *29 February* Elmers tuition $1.50 Orras for half month $1.00 . . . *2 March* the last day of school [*Blue Jacket*] quite a number of visitors present . . . *16 March* Orra brought his books home this evening, is not going to school again if the weather is suitable to work.

3 October 1888: Elmer went to see Whitworth about starting to school next week . . . *8 October* Elmer started to school this morning in the ninth Miss Durkee teacher, Georges school began this morning Maggie Beatty teacher. Elmers tuition for October $1.10 . . . *23 November* Orra went to see Whitworth about going to school, expects to start Monday morning . . . *26 November* Orra started to school he is in the high school department, gave Orra five dollars to get his school supplies . . . *1 February 1889:* Mrs Dillon and I visited the school this afternoon very well satisfied with their progress. After recess they spelled, then had literary exercises . . . *1 March* Mrs Dillon and I visited the school this afternoon, this being the last day of school had a few literary exercises.

30 January 1890: Miss Wray of Degraff applied for our school³ . . . *1 February* the Directors agreed to decide on a teacher next Saturday. I wrote to Maggie Beatty if she would accept it⁴ . . . *5 March* Mr Parker left the keys to the school house and the register here this P.M. . . . *10 March* Orra took the schoolhouse keys and Register to the

Schoolhouse this morning, George was at school this being the first day of the Spring term . . . *29 May* Elmer went to the Opera house with the graduating class this P.M. Orra and Elmer gone to the commencement this eve. Georges school closed to day.

6 October 1890: George started to school this morning Pat Chamberlain teacher, got an arithmetic 50 cts, ink 5, paper 5 . . . *14 October* George took the crazy fan to school for the purpose of decoration . . . *27 February 1891:* George and I were at an entertainment at the school house this eve this being the last day of school there were a good many recitations, some music and a Dialog by George, Harry Dillon and Henry Horn. the house was full. got home about half past nine . . . *16 May* Elmer looking at cloth for a suit of clothes . . . *18 May* Elmer ordered a suit of clothing made $25.00, he got his program for commencement, sent one to W.L. Davis . . . *23 May* gave Elmer $27.00 for his outfit for the commencement, $3.50 shirts & collars . . . *24 May* heard Rev Weston preach at the Lutheran Church the Bachelaureate to the Graduating class of the B.H.S. Text Glorify God with your bodies. Gird up the loins of your minds . . . *26 May* Elmer got his suit ordered at Abes $27.00 . . . *27 May* Elsie Lemen brought one of her paintings as a graduating present for Elmer . . . *28 May* All attended the commencement exercises this evening, the graduates, Edna Batch, May Lemen, Nannie Chandler, Bertie Rife, Inez Rathmel, Beth Defries, Martha Ritcheson, Tempa McCracken, Olive Horn, Alice Parker, Elmer Gebby, Thomas Moore & James Guthrie, got home 11 Oclock . . . Elmer gone to a reception given to the seniors given by the juniors at Clara Millers this eve

5 September 1891: George & Harry Dillon went to see Mr Whitworth about going to school . . . *7 September* George & Harry Dillon started to school in town, in the ninth department. George got books 72 cts . . . *26 October* Harry Dillon & George are getting their lesson. George studying his arithmetic lesson . . . *24 November* George was examined in Physiology to day . . . *2 February 1892:* George's tuition for Feb. $1.50 . . . *3 February* got George a school suit $10.50 . . . *25 February* George studying his Grammar expects to be examined on it tomorrow. was examined in Arithmetic to day got 85 . . . *26 February* George was examined in Algebra got 81 . . . *17 March* helped George work partial payments this evening . . . *23 March* George at school today examined in Physiology grade 95

8 September 1893: George was to see Whitworth about school next Monday . . . *3 November* Jerry was at town got the amount of School tax he pays in to the corporation school fund $5.22, sent it to Whitworth in payment of Georges tuition[5] . . . *18 January 1894:* Georges tuition

$1.50 . . . *30 March* George was examined in Political economy, got 96 . . . *29 May* George was examined in Geometry got 88

8 October 1894: George started to school to day, got a book $1.25, gave him $5.00 to get others . . . *3 May 1895:* George with Fred McLaughlin, Frank McCracken, Ralph Dodds and Harry Huffman left for Xenia on the 9.40 train to attend an Oratorical contest . . . *24 May* George was examined in Grammar and Arithmetic . . . *29 May* We all attended the commencement exercises of the B.H.S. there were 13 gradu- ates Ivy Gray, Isaac McArdle, Adelene Kunke, Ethel Hockett, Belle Wal- lace, Carrie Rausenberger, Effiebelle Miller, Fred McLaughlin, Harry Hoffman, Brad Hiatt, Frank McCracken, Earl Finch and George Gebby

With the Bellefontaine High School drawing students from a popu- lation considerably larger than the four thousand persons who lived within the city limits, graduating classes of thirteen members reflect the economic privilege associated with this accomplishment. In requiring families to pay tuition and students to defer economic independence, it was comparable to a modern family making a commitment to provide college education.

RELIGION

SUNDAY SERVICES

The Gebbys were members of the Bellefontaine United Presbyterian Church, a direct descendant of the Scottish Covenanter and Seceder faiths, more strict in its theology than the Presbyterian Church U.S.A. with which it later merged. Margaret's journals make no mention of daily Bible reading or family prayers, but this was probably so routine it rated no mention in her diary. The family observed Sunday as a day of rest and never did unnecessary work even though hay might be lying in the field and Sunday the only sunny day all week. Margaret often records Saturday work in preparation for the Sabbath rest.

6 September 1890 [Saturday]: too wet to drill, the men fed the cattle, cut feed for Sabbath
20 August 1892 [Saturday]: Dressed a chicken for tomorrow
4 August 1894 [Saturday]: killed & dressed a chicken for dinner tomorrow

Only illness or severe weather kept Gebby family members from their regular routine of attending Sunday school and Sunday morning and evening worship services. Margaret usually noted the sermon text in her journal and often made comments when she felt it was particularly inspirational.

3 January 1886: boys went to Sabbath school [evidently walked] we did not go could not take Harry, had distemper. Very dark and rainy. . . . 10 October Went to church and Sabbath School. George was

174

not very well, did not go. Morning text, "yea rather blessed are they that hear the word of God and keep it." The evening text 1 John 1.9 "If we confess our sins he is faithful and just to forgive us of our sin and to cleanse us from all unrightousness."

9 June 1889: Rev. Kyle preached Sol. Song 5.18 "This is my beloved and this is my friend" a splendid discourse.

5 January 1890: Went to Sabbath School and church, Rev. Hamilton text Mathew 10.16 "Behold I send you forth as sheep among wolves, be ye therefore wise as serpents and harmless as doves." Theme, the demands of the age upon the church. Raining quite hard, Orra and Elmer gone to church [*evening*] and young peoples meeting.

13 March 1892: Dr Moorehead preached a splendid sermon. Text Isa 55.10 & 11 For as the rain cometh down from heaven and returneth not thither, but watereth the earth, and maketh it bring forth and bud, that it may give seed to the sower and bread to the eater: So shall my word be that goeth forth out of my mouth: it shall not return unto me void, but it shall accomplish that which I please, and it shall prosper in the thing whereto I sent it.

16 April 1893: attended S.S. and church. Mr Hamiltons text Ech 4.9 & 10 Two are better than one because they have a good reward for their labor for if one fall, the one will lift up his fellow: but woe to him that is alone when he falleth, for he hath not another to help him up.

21 January 1894: A lovely evening, bright moonlight night. the boys & I were at church, the Text Genesis 4.9 "Am I my brothers keeper."

Religious holidays such as Easter and Christmas nearly always meant the family attended special services as well as regular Sabbath services. Communion Sundays were always preceded by special Friday night and Saturday services of consecration and often included infant baptisms and admission of new members.

27–29 September 1894: attended church this evening, Rev. Currie of Huntsville preached Text 1 Kings 20.40 "And as the servant was busy here & there he was gone" a good sermon . . . this afternoon we all went to church. Rev. J.E. Currie preached from Romans 1-16 "I am not ashamed of the Gospel of Christ" a good sermon. Ed Fultons babe was baptized (Sarah Elizabeth) . . . Attended communion service this morning. Rev. Currys Text 1 Cor 11-26 "This is my body broken for you."

5 April 1896: A beautiful day, all at church, this being Easter, the subject was the Resurrection.

*Given the strict origins of the United Presbyterian Church, the Geb-
bys were unusually ecumenical in their attendance when their own
minister was absent. Family members attended a variety of other
churches, apparently believing that any religious service was better than
none at all.*

  18 July 1886: Mr. Williamson at Silver Creek today, the children
went to Sabbath School, George came home, Orra went to the Methodist church, Elmer to the Covenanters[1]

  29 May 1887: Went to Sabbath School. Attended the Covenanter
church. Annie Robeson was with us Clarence and George Harner were
here for dinner. Annie went home with George in the afternoon. The
boys went to the Methodist church in the evening.

  1 April 1888: George and Jerry not well and being no services at the
United Presbyterian church no one went to Sabbath School except Orra
& Elmer. Orra went to the Presbyterian church and Elmer to the
Lutheran, in the evening Elmer was at the Methodist and Orra at the
Baptist.

  16 June 1889: Mr Hamilton assisting Mr Kyle at Springfield. Orra &
Elmer went to the Lutheran. Jerry at the Methodist, they had confirma-
tion services there admitted quite a number. George & I was at the
Presbyterian.

  11 August 1895: Mr Hamilton being absent taking a vacation, we
had no services in our church, nor in either of the other churches except
the Episcopalian. George was there, none of the rest of us were at
church. Rev Hull, Rev Havinghorst & Dr Kalb are all away on a vacation.

  16 August 1896: All at church to day Mr Hamilton exchanged
pulpits with Rev Sargent of the Baptist church who preached from
Romans 5-4.

*One senses considerable freedom for all family members, particu-
larly the boys, to explore other church services, but Margaret's Presbyterian background drew a line at Episcopalian ritual. Once during these
journals she was drawn by neighborly friendship to attend a Catholic
funeral and that elicited her only recorded comment of outright religious
prejudice.*

  19 May 1892: The remains of Mikey Cantwell arrived on the 11-30
train, I was there a while . . . *20 May* attended the funeral of Mikey
Cantwell at the Catholic church at 10 A.M. Father Conway went

through a great deal of ceremony in latin, had very good music both vocal and instrumental. after he was through with the flummerys he preached a sermon in English

PRAYER MEETINGS AND REVIVALS

The Protestant churches of Bellefontaine usually held united prayer services each winter and Margaret strongly encouraged her boys to attend. These were clearly an annual time for church members to reaffirm their faith, but in later years they assumed quite a revival aspect by bringing in an evangelist to actively seek new converts.

2 January 1888: Union prayer meeting in our church this afternoon, service also this evening, all went except Orra he has a cold. a goodly number of our own members out Subject "Prayer for the out pouring of the spirit upon the church and upon Christian workers . . . *3 January* Grandma, George, Orra & I went to prayer meeting this eve Subject, "Consecration to the service of the Master" . . . *4 January* Orra gone to prayer meeting this evening . . . *5 January* Elmer gone to prayer meeting, too dark for the rest . . . *6 January* Orra gone to prayer meeting

13 January 1890: Services this week none of us attended this evening, hope such will not be again.[2]

6 January 1895: there is a union service at the M.E. Church this being the first of the week of prayer . . . *9 January* We were at Union Prayer meeting to night Dr Keen an evangelist conducted the meeting which consisted of song service, a short exhortation on Judges 1-15 "Give me a blessing," than an invitation to the alter. a good many went up to the altar . . . *19 January* Orra & Elmer gone to Revival services for the men only tonight. Dr Keen had service for the women this afternoon . . . *20 January* The boys are gone to the M.E. Church to Union revival services, tonight is the last of the union meetings. Dr Keen goes away tomorrow . . . *3 February* U.P. Church 19, M.E. Church 50, Presbyterian 10, Lutheran 11, Christian 7 = 97[3]

The United Presbyterian Church accepted new members at any time by profession of faith and baptism or by a letter transferring membership from another congregation. Despite its strict theology new members were welcome from other denominations as well as from other geo-

United Presbyterian Church pictured in the centennial publication in 1931. The church was built in 1886. The Gebbys were active members of this congregation.

graphic areas. Margaret's diary often noted new members but never those leaving the church, a one-sided awareness that would still be common among most congregations.

19 January 1890: Nine united with the church to day, from the R.P. church, David Fulton and wife, Alice & Frankie & Mrs Lizzie (Elliot) Dowell, by profession Mrs Huffer & her children Libbie, Mamie & Sammie.

10 December 1893: were at church . . . Mrs N.A. Wallace gave in a certificate from the church of Los Angeles, Cal. Miss Mary Fulton from Bellecentre cong. Miss Minnie Fulton from the M.E. church of Bellefontaine

BUILDING FUND, PLEDGES, AND LADIES AID

From its formation in 1858 as a merger of the Associate Presbyterian and Associate-Reformed Presbyterian (A.R.P.) congregations, the Bellefontaine United Presbyterian Church worshiped in the remodeled former A.R.P. building, a 75 × 36-foot frame structure. During 1886 the congregation, by then grown to some two hundred persons, built a substantial brick church for eleven thousand dollars and furnished it except for an organ for two thousand dollars.[4] Margaret's journal provides a behind-the-scenes view of this accomplishment.

1 May 1886: Gave a check to the building committee of the new church for $500.00 . . . *13 December* Went to Mrs N.A. Wallaces met the committee to select a carpet for the church selected one then went to Bennetts to look at samples for making cushions for the pews then to Dunk Dows office to see samples of cushion of Damask

3 March 1887: Went to sew on the church carpet, did not commence sewing until after two Oclock, got along very well after getting started they said that eighteen women were there, a great many came in to see the church, got home about 5 Oclock got dinner at Fathers . . . *4 March* I went to sew on the church carpet in morning Grandma came this P.M. about 25 ladies were sewing we finished the auditorium carpet this evening, had quite a number of visitors today[5] . . . *5 March* We went to work again on the church carpet made carpet for the schoolrooms downstairs, will not sew any more until the Carpenters are done . . . *8 April* [*Good Friday*] We went to church dedication services. Mr Moorehead preached father read a history of the congregation & towns after which they tried to raise money to pay the indebtedness got four fifties, 3 25s, 4 10s besides the collection . . . *10 April* Went to Sabbath School in the old church, went to the new church which was crowded. In the evening the house was more than full, Dr. Carson preached from Ye will not come unto me that ye might. Raised a little over $15.00 leaving a debt of about $700 . . . *14 April* Went to town and church this afternoon selected a seat [*family pew*] a debt of $581 still remains on the church . . . *17 April* Went to Sabbath School met in the new church our room is the second from the south, number scholars 123, collection $22

27 May 1888: Rained very hard while we were in church, so dark had to light the gas.

Modern congregations accustomed to mortgages for capital improvements may marvel at this attitude toward indebtedness, but the

Gebbys were no doubt like other members in making a substantial donation. Their five hundred dollar contribution exceeded their annual family living expenses. They even made token donations to other church building drives in the community.

23 June 1889: The new Methodist church was dedicated to day, they raised $8,000 this forenoon. We were there this eve. they raised about $500 to help pay for the organ.

10 January 1891: Jerry subscribed 45.00 for a Dunkard church building near Jack Hudsons, Samuel Miller solicitor

Financial reports for these years show the Gebby family annually contributed one hundred dollars to the church, the largest family contribution in the congregation.[6] When the boys reached their twenty-first birthdays each began making his own five dollar contribution. Margaret's journal shows this pledge was paid quarterly and viewed as their contribution to the minister's salary. Margaret also contributed produce and labor to fund-raising activities of the Ladies Aid Society, which funded a variety of things from Communion supplies to church hymnals. During the economic depression of 1893–94 when some members failed to pay their pledges, Margaret's journal shows how the women intensified their money-raising efforts but were eventually forced to call upon the men of the congregation to solicit money to solve the problem of the minister's unpaid salary.

11 December 1889: gave Dunk Dow [*church treasurer*] a check $25 for salary

13 September 1892: paid Dunk Dow $25.00 salary . . . *14 December* gave D. Dow a check $25.00

10 June 1893: We took 2 chickens 5 loaves of bread, some cottage cheese and some butter to market for the benefit of the building committee . . . *21 July* The Ladies aid committee met here this afternoon agreed to hold a lawn fete in the park a week from to night, having Ice Cream, Lemon Aid, Lemon ice. Mrs D. Dow, Mrs McMillen, Mrs Dowell, and Mary McCracken were the committee . . . *24 July* I was at town this P.M. at Frank Dowells at a meeting of the aid committee . . . *5 August* I took six loaves of bread to the market some cottage cheese and chicken, the proceeds of the market was $14.66

2 June 1894: the U.P. church had a market to day, took in about $13.00 I took bread, cookies, cottage cheese, eggs and buttermilk . . . *21 July* I took 5 loaves of bread, two pies, cookies and some smearcase to the market . . . *30 October* Jerry was sick last night and to day. Orra &

Elmer are gone to a meeting of the men at the church to consider the best
interests of the S.S. & church and to raise money to pay the debt . . . *31
October* At the church the men raised $111.00 expect to get $50 more
from those not present last night . . . *6 November* Orra was soliciting
for the church debt but succeeded in getting $5.00

9 December 1896: All except Jerry attended an entertainment at the
church given by the Ladies Aid Society. They had a program mostly
musical, some literary performances, it was very good, 15 cts admit-
tance fee

MINISTERS

*Although the roles of men and women were clearly defined, Presby-
terians were democratic religious congregations. In this period women
could not hold leadership roles as members of the session or ordained
ministers, but Margaret's journal shows that they could and did cast an
equal vote on important issues such as the selection of a pastor. This
procedure was evidently accepted as routine several decades before
women were permitted to vote in civil elections.*

29 March 1888: All attended the congregational meeting this afternoon at the church.[7] Mr. I.P. Sharp of Sidney preached. Took an informal ballot on the candidates resulting as follows, Spencer 7, Marshall
31, Logan 78, Davidson 5, Livingston 7, Hamilton 2, Comin 1. Second
ballot Logan 94, Marshall 27, Spencer 2, Davidson 1. Made out a call for
Logan to be presented to presbytery next Tuesday . . . *20 April* Mr Logan declined our call . . . *7 October* had a congregational meeting after
S.S. took an informal vote for the election of a pastor first Ballot G.W.
Hamilton 70, W.W. Patterson 53, D.C. Stewart 4, George Scott of Mt.
Ayr, Iowa 1, total 128. 2nd Ballot Hamilton 86, Patterson 45, total
131 . . . *16 November* Rev Hamilton is in town [*preached sermon on
Sunday*] . . . *18 November* Rev. Hamilton agreed to accept the pastorate of the congregation. He goes back to Monmouth to finish his
work there then will be here the ninth of Dec. to remain with us . . . *12
December* All went to a reception for Mr Hamilton at the church. the
audience room was full. the choir sang three pieces. Duncan Dow make
the address of welcome on behalf of the cong. Mr. Kerr for the ministry,
Judge Lawrence for the citizens. Mr Hamilton responded in a very appropriate speech. F.R. McLaughlin presented Mr Kalb a gold headed

cane on behalf of the cong. for his kindness to it while vacant in a neat
little speech. Then we all were introduced to Mr Hamilton

*Devout Presbyterians respected a scholarly ministry and rejoiced
when a son of the congregation accepted the call to study theology.
Margaret's journal reflects this pride, especially when the young man
was her nephew Ralph Aikin. The proximity of Xenia Seminary frequently provided the Bellefontaine congregation with student ministers
and the congregation reciprocated with financial support. Margaret's
journals reflect nothing but encouragement for these provisional pastors
who were young enough to be her sons.*

22 January 1890: all went to church, heard Charlie Cleland preach.
he was licensed last evening at Silver Creek. he is attending the Xenia
Seminary. Text, "Keep they heart with all diligence for out of it are the
issues of life" he is the making of an excellent preacher.

6 December 1891: Collection for the Xenia Seminary (14 cts pr
member)

3 September 1894: I was at Aikins for supper, Ralph left for Xenia
on the 5.50 train to attend Seminary . . . *11 November* all attended
church this morning Ralph Aikins preached. Text "How shall we escape
if we neglect so great Salvation" Heb 2-3. A collection was taken for the
coal bill this morning. all there this evening. Ralphs text was "Open thou
mine eyes that I may behold wondrous things out of thy law"

21 June 1896: all at church to day Ralph Aikin preached from 1 Cor
15, 1-4, his theme was "The simple Gospel" a very sound clear gospel
sermon.

SUNDAY SCHOOL AND YOUNG PEOPLE'S GROUP

*Margaret's diary reflects the traditional role of the church in provid-
ing religious education for children and a wholesome social environment
in which the young adults of the congregation could interact.*

21 October 1890: went to church to a presbyterial convention of
young people, quite a good many delegates from other societies present.
Mr Church of Scotch Ridge our guest. Rev Hustin led a prayer meeting,
then Prof White of Xenia Se. made an address, then they had a social got
home at half past ten.

16 February 1893: Orra at prayer meeting, George intended going but forgot and eat onions for supper . . . *24 October* George went to Sidney this morning as a delegate to the Presbyterial institute.

23 November 1894: Nannie and I were at Duncan Dows at a S.S. Teachers meeting. they considered what they thought the best interests of the school and about making arrangements for a Christmas entertainment.

15 April 1895: Orra is gone to a meeting at Rev. Hamiltons arranging with other officers for the work at the young peoples meeting . . . *21–23 August* A little Company left on the 9.35 train to attend the Institute at Columbus. Rev. Hamilton, Ralph Aikin, Tom McCracken, George Gebby, Laura & Ellie Dow, Dadie Miller, Sallie & Mabel Aikin, others go tomorrow[8] . . . Elmer left for the Institute at Columbus on the 5.5 . . . *29 December* Orra, George & Nannie are gone to O.Y.P. and church. Elmer is sick with a cold

26 March 1896: Orra & Mattie called to night Nannie went with them to prayer meeting and election M.C. Boals Superintendent, J.M. Abraham Assistant Superintendent, E.R. Gebby, Sec. & Treas. . . . *11 October* All at church this morning, this was a rally day for the children, the church was decorated with Autumn fruits, flowers & leaves . . . *10 December* Was at church tonight. The young people elected George President of the O.Y.P.C. A committee agreed the next entertainment given by the aid society would be an old fashioned spelling school[9]

This family's involvement with the church extended to an automatic assumption that young people of the congregation who chose to attend college would attend Monmouth, a United Presbyterian school in Illinois. Margaret's diaries give no hint whether she ever wished one or more of her own sons could be among them.

22 December 1893: the Monmouth students came home this morning . . . *23 December* Elmer is getting better, Laura Dow & Arthur Mc-Cracken called to see him this evening.

9 January 1894: Our Monmouth students left for college this eve Arthur & Tommy McCracken, Laura Dow, Arm. Wallace, Annie & Will Wallace

PRESBYTERY MEETINGS AND MISSIONARY SOCIETY

The Women's Missionary Society had educational, social, and fund-
raising goals, but it perhaps served its most important function by giving
women an opportunity to practice organizational skills and assume
leadership roles. Margaret's entry for 22 May 1888 is cited in its entirety
because it gives an excellent picture of the hostess' entire day, including a
last-minute acquisition of new curtains.

22 May 1888: baked bread and pies, went to town had 6 lbs 9 oz of
butter and 9 doz eggs, got peaches, pineapple, apricots, 4 yds lace curtain 37½ pr yd $1.50, shoe polish 25, Jerry slippers $1.15, two rocking
chairs $6.00, came home put up the sitting room curtains, pieced the
parlor curtains, then milked, fed the calves got ready to receive the
parlor meeting of the missionary society which met here this evening had
a very interesting meeting, being led by the Pres. M McAra. Several
psalms were sung, prayers by McAra, Aikin, Smith & Rev. Scott, also
remarks by some members & Rev. Scott collection 80 cts.
    11 April 1889: Went with Anna & Lizzie Robeson to Mr Boals to
help with the Mission Quilt . . . *16 April* Went with Anna and Lizzie
Robeson to Mr Boals to work on the quilt, finished all we could do. Mrs
Stewart, Mrs Reid, and Mary McCracken were also there.
    23 August 1893: Elmer gone to a reception given to Lou Frey at the
M.E. Church. she goes as a Missionary to Corea the 1st of September
    31 January 1896: Nannie was at Missionary meeting at Duncan
Dows. they had a devotional and business meeting, then a social, had
refreshments, sandwich, pickle and coffee each member paying 10 cts,
18 present . . . *9 August* I took five loaves of bread, a crock of cottage
cheese and a chicken to a market for the Missionary society, every thing
was very nice and sold well, they cleared $20

The division between male and female roles in the church was most
evident when the Bellefontaine congregation hosted Presbytery or mis-
sionary board meetings. Visiting pastors and elders were guests in the
homes of the congregation and the women of the church prepared dinner
and supper at the church each day. Margaret's journals reflect an in-
teresting view of the practical arrangements behind these regular reli-
gious business meetings.
    The largest event during these diaries occurred soon after the new
building was completed when the Bellefontaine congregation hosted a
national missionary board meeting. Margaret boarded two ministers

from Kansas for an entire week, chaired the Monday dinner committee, and helped each day.

2 May 1889: Aunt Hannah, Lizzie and I went to Mrs Rankins to a meeting of our list for boarding the home mission board, made out our bill of fare, transacted all the business . . . *9 May* We were at a meeting of our committee at D. Dows this afternoon, a full attendance. saw Jim McCord about meat, offers good roast for 10 and ham for 12 cts . . . *15 May* The Board of home Missions met in the church this P.M. Jerry went at six Oclock brought home two Delegates Rev. Haggerty of Kansas City, and Rev. Jackson of Anthony, Kans . . . *16 May* was at the church, Mrs McBeth and I ordered 30 lbs of beef and 18 lbs ham of Jim McCord, went again this evening for conference at the church, Revs Jackson and Haggarty with us again to night . . . *17 May* went to the Church helped work for help in return took a gallon of cream and two gal. of milk. Went to a social in the church, speeches made by Dr. Paul, Marshall Boals, Dr. Robb . . . *18 May* [*Saturday*] baked bread for Monday at the church. was at the church awhile, the Huntsville cong. fed the preachers today. Rev Jackson gone to preach at Cannonsburg, Rev Haggarty to Bellecentre preaching to the Covenanters. dressed three chickens for Monday, packed and marked dishes, spoons, knives, &c . . . *19 May* all went to church Rev. J.S. McKee of Butler Pa preached. All went in the evening Rev. McKitteric of the Lombard St. Mission Allegheny city preached[10] . . . *21 May* I went to the church helped prepare dinner and supper for the committee of Missions quite a good many present, paid Oscar McLaughlan $1.16 for ice cream mixture, had a nice entertainment after supper speeches were made by Rev. McKee, Owens, Henderson, McNeal, Kyle, and elder McCandless . . . *22 May* the ministers went back to the church this morning, they all left to Springfield at three Oclock. paid Jim McCord $4.55 cts for meat for dinner on Monday at the church.

The regional Presbytery and Women's Missionary Society met concurrently, and the women of the congregation were able to prepare meals for one hundred or more and simultaneously complete their missionary business. These events were so routine Margaret's journal suggests the women took their management skills for granted.

3 April 1893: baked a cake and dressed two chickens to take to the church tomorrow . . . *4 April* took our things to the church for the entertainment of the Presbytery and Missionary Society. quite a full attendance. Rev. Buchanon made an address to the society this evening.

the thank offerings were handed in by the different societies amounting to over $400. Bellefontaines was $45. our guests to night are Rev. Oldham of Liepsic and his elder, Mr Lowry, Mr Stewart of Silver Creek, Mr Wiley of Piqua . . . *5 April* Grandma and I were at the church took our dinners there. 111 ate dinner some have gone home. the W.M.S. adjourned this P.M. the Presbytery was still in session when I left. A Mr Bovard was ordained by the Presbytery and two other young men (dont remember their names) were licensed . . . *6 April* I was at the church got my roasting pan and crock

26 March 1895: I was at the church with others arranging for the entertaining of the Presbytery and Woman's Missionary, all of the members west of main street entertain on Tuesday. we agreed on a bill of fare and adjourned

GOVERNMENT

TAXES

I n this time period taxes were levied on property rather than income. Farm families like the Gebbys were subject to both real estate and personal property taxes. Personal property was assessed annually. Margaret's diaries reveal that they usually had the same assessor throughout this period and that he was well enough acquainted with the family to stay for dinner.[1]

6 May 1887: Walter McPherson was here for dinner, made the chattles $5855

4 May 1889: Detwiler accessor enlisted. Horses $400, cattle 1200, hogs 175, carriages 70, watches 10, organ 10, money 60, household 100, grain 805 = $2830

22 April 1890: Walter McPherson was here for dinner, the assessment amounted to $2550

17 April 1891: the Assesser (Walter McPherson) amount of Assessment $3070

18 April 1892: The Assessor was here this P.M. 7 Horses $350, 53 cattle 1300, 14 Hogs 50, 4 Buggies 100, Farm Tools 100, Grain & Hay 810, 2 Watches 10, 1 Organ 20, Credits 1400 = $4140 Walter D. McPherson

30 April 1894: Walter McPherson was here for dinner, assessed the property total amt $3900

17 April 1895: Walter McPherson the Assessor was here and took property to the amount of $4900 just $1000 more than last year.

Logan County Courthouse. (From D. J. Stewart,
Combination Atlas Map of Logan County, Ohio
[Philadelphia: D. J. Stewart, 1875])

Jerry paid taxes in person at the courthouse semiannually or in later years entrusted the job to one of the sons. Taxes were frequently paid the same day they received a bank dividend, suggesting that the family had savings that they relied upon as a source of cash at the time taxes were due.[2]

3 January 1887: Jerry went to town paid the taxes $152.75

4 January 1890: paid Taxes $176.70, got bank dividend $120 . . . *19 June* Paid taxes $175.00

1 July 1891: Jerry paid the taxes $217.40, got Bank div. $140

4 July 1892: Jerry paid the taxes $217.29

3 January 1893: Jerry was at town got Bank dividend $140, paid Taxes $171.80 deducted road tax $13.76 . . . *6 July* Jerry paid the taxes $156.90, got the bank dividend $120.00 one pr ct less than usual . . . *30 December* Orra paid taxes $192.40

7 July 1894: Elmer paid the taxes $165.56

9 July 1895: Jerry paid the taxes $157.85

Like their neighbors, the Gebbys usually met their road taxes by working them off on an assigned stretch of nearby road. It is impossible from Margaret's diaries to determine how much credit was given for a day's work by a man with a shovel or a man with a team and wagon, but on average the Gebbys contributed two men with a team and wagon working two days per year.

15–16 August 1887: Orra and Cal working on the roads near the Colton farm . . . Orra and Cal worked on the roads again finished the Blue Jacket tax.

9–10 October 1888: Orra and Cal were on the roads hauling gravel from G.W. Aikins pit . . . Orra and Cal finished working on the roads to day

11 May 1889: Orra and Cal worked on the Blue Jacket road to day . . . *30 August* Cal worked out the road tax on the Miller land ($2.00) brought home a load of rails.

14 May 1894: Orra & George each had a team working on the Blue Jacket district, Wellie shoveled . . . *11 October* Wellie finished working on the road to day, the tax $7.05

16 October 1895: George worked on the roads with the little team, finished in the northern district . . . *19–20 November* Orra, George and Wellie worked on the roads to day in the Blue Jacket district . . . Orra and George worked on the roads this forenoon finished working out the road tax $10.00, had one team.

8 October 1896: Orra, George & Wellie worked on the roads to day. Orra drove, George and Wellie shoveled.

ELECTIONS

Although campaigns for women's suffrage were intense during the period covered by these diaries, readers receive the impression that Margaret took it for granted that men voted and women did not. She was aware of local and national candidates and knew who the men of her family voted for, but there is no indication that the family discussed politics very much or that women in her family and neighborhood resented their lack of franchise. This may, in part, be a reflection of the strength of the political party system and the general tendency to vote a straight party ticket. The Gebby men and most of their friends and neighbors were Republican and if Margaret could have voted she would undoubtedly have supported the same slate.

Ohio was a key state in national politics during the last half of the nineteenth century, nearly dominating the Republican party.[3] *Margaret's diaries contain interesting glimpses of pretelevision campaigns: political rallies with church ladies providing food as a money-raising activity, men congregating at the courthouse on election night waiting for the results, torchlight parades and fireworks to celebrate victory.*

10 October 1887: Elmer went to town to see and to hear Senator Sherman speak at the court House.

19 June 1888: Republican nomination day in Chicago . . . *25 June* the Republican convention nominated B.H. Harrison of Indiana for president and Levi P. Morton of New York for vice president . . . *24 July* the 1840 Harrison men met in town today . . . *31 July* the boys gone to the township house organizing an Harrison & Morton club . . . *11 September* Orra gone to Harrison & Morton meeting at the Township house[4] . . . *2 October* The boys gone to a Republican meeting at the Township house this evening . . . *19 October* Ben Butterworth made a political speech tonight, Orra and Elmer went to hear him . . . *6 November* Jerry went to the election a great many on the road to day notwithstanding the rain . . . *7 November* election returns, announce Harrison and Morton elected. Democrats crest fallen, Republicans rejoicing . . . *10 November* the Republicans jollifyed to day and this evening, fire works to night the boys up town now.

6 November 1889: Campbell elected Governor . . . *20 November* Elmer gone to town to a Democratic Jollification over the election of Campbell for Governor.

7–8 November 1890: Cal fed, went to the election. Jerry went to Badgers saw the cattle went to the election. Elmer and Orra went to town to hear the result of the election . . . the returns of the election are in this evening Repub. [*newspaper*] Sheriff Roach, Treasurer Rogers, Clerk Freemain, Prosecutor Odor, Probate Jug. Pettit

14 September 1891: J.D. McLaughlin & Mrs Dowell called soliciting for lunch to be held by the ladies of the cong. on McKinley day. I promised some Rolls, slaw, cream, pickles & pies, butter . . . *17 September* attended the McKinley meeting, quite a large crowd in town. McKinley a good speaker, he is at Piqua this eve. Orr of Mich. speaks here this eve. The ladies of the Cong. had lunch in the Hill storeroom. I was there this P.M. took bread, butter, slaw, pies, dont know how they succeeded yet

23 June 1892: Cleveland was nominated by the Democrats at Chicago for president to day . . . *8 November* the men built a fence across the railroad so they could feed the cattle in that field. this being Presidential election day, they voted. Harrison Republican, Cleveland Democrat. Orra worked in the barn this P.M. making a wagon bed . . . *9 November* the election returns are coming in claim a Democratic victory that Cleveland is elected.

7 November 1893: this was election day Harrison Tp gave 114 Republican out of 187 votes

2 April 1894: Orra and Wellie plowed all day. they voted the Republican ticket. Jerry voted before dinner, the boys all gone to town to hear election news . . . *4 April* the results of the primary election was Fergus, Commissioner, Inf Director Young, for treasurer it was a tie between Ebrite & Roach . . . *23 April* the men all were at the election voting for Ebrite. the results of Harrison Tp was Ebrite 64, Roach 43

18 June 1896: McKinley was nominated for president to day . . . *14 August* Elmer & George are hearing a speech by Judge West at the Opera house on the free silver question . . . *31 October* Went to a McKinley torchlight procession, it was certainly the largest one ever in Bellefontaine, a great many people in town all day . . . *3 November* Voted for McKinley for President. the boys are up town getting election news . . . *4 November* The result of the election returns so far is McKinley considerable majority . . . *7 November* A celebration of McKinley victory is going on to night a torchlight procession and flags & banners, too cold for us to go . . . *8 November* Cold winds, cloudy, spitting snow. all at church.

TEMPERANCE

Temperance was a very emotional issue during the period covered by Margaret's diaries and history generally credits the Women's Christian Temperance Union with the movement's leadership. These diaries, however, present a woman with strong temperance opinions who remained on the sidelines listening to men give speeches.[5] The United Presbyterian Church was strongly against alcoholic beverages and such spirits came into the Gebby home only when prescribed by a physician for medicinal purposes, so the family's participation in local temperance meetings was a public rather than personal concern. Although none of the Gebbys, male or female, were eligible to vote regarding Bellefontaine saloons, they supported the campaign by community churches to close the saloons.

16 February–18 March 1889: Orra and Elmer gone to temperance meeting at the opera house tonight . . . Orra and Elmer gone to Union temperance meeting at the Lutheran church . . . the boys and I were at the temperance meeting at the opera house. Tracy lectured and showed the view called the rock of ages a very crowded house got home ten minutes till ten . . . Held a gospel temperance meeting in our church at three Oclock this afternoon, the house crowded. Dr Tracy recited some of his experiences, gave some very good advice to young and old. the boys all gone to another meeting at the opera house the last of ten lectures given by Tracy . . . went to temperance meeting, Judge Bennett, John Stewart, Campbell, Brand, Singly, Dow and Tracy, a very full house . . . All attended the Union temperance mass meeting, prayer by Rev. Blair, the addresses were by Tracy, Hamilton, Christie, Williams, George Emerson, Judge West. Took unanimous vote that the saloons must go . . . Bellefontaine voted on Prohibition today. 1st wards majority was wet 26, 2nd 87 dry, 3rd 119 dry, 4th 3 dry. The bells rang out the news at 8 Oclock a very exciting day and hard working on both sides. Cal and Jerry went to town this evening to hear the news . . . *1 May* Saloons closed to day . . . *17 June* Jerry went to Tp house this being voting day on the whiskey question, the drys were 91 against 8 wets.

The rural township was obviously more strongly for Prohibition than the town wards, which contained saloons. It was an issue that was regularly revived, and this particular family evidently maintained their vigilance.

4–10 March 1894: Attended a mass Temperance meeting at the M.E. church. several persons spoke but Judge West made the principal speech of the evening.[6] are to have meetings this week as an effort is being made to repeal the ordinance . . . after church went to the opera house where Gen Custus gave a temperance lecture, the last of the series. the house was very much crowded. the people are aroused on the subject . . . the primary election was held this evening in the court house which will decide the temperance question in the corporation, the votes not near all counted out at 10 P.M. . . . The temperance cause triumphed

27 September–6 October 1896: A mass temperance meeting is to be held in the M.E. church this evening, the city council are trying to have the Local Option ordinance repealed. this meeting was called in opposition to it. it has rained nearly all this afternoon and is still raining very hard, I fear the meeting will not be well attended . . . Elmer and George are gone to a Mass Temperance meeting at the M.E. church to night . . . The vote on the repeal of the Local Option was lost.

CITIZENSHIP

In Margaret Gebby's world it was taken for granted that interaction with government was a male responsibility, not only in the regular routines of paying taxes and voting, but in all interactions between citizens and authority. The Gebbys' proximity to the county seat made them an atypical farm family, and Bellefontaine's decision to extend its boundaries in the 1890s created a concern that their house not be included within the corporation limits.[7] Margaret's awareness of the situation is reflected in her diary, but it was her husband who met with government officials.

24–28 November 1891: Town council voted to extend the corporation this eve . . . Orra & George took the tape line and measured from the present corporation line to our gate making it 550 ft. Jim Wonders claim the new corporation line will be between our house & barn

15–16 February 1892: The surveyors were running out the line for the extended corporation of Bellefontaine the mile from the public square came to our house . . . the surveyors finished running the new corporation line of the southwest quarter of town. it is a few feet east of our Garden fence . . . *17 May* Jerry met with the Commissioners and council about the extension of the corporation, they postponed action until the 21 of June

A dramatic example of the small population of male citizens available for community responsibility in rural county seats is the frequency with which Jerry served jury duty. Trial juries rarely lasted more than two days and on occasion seem to have been assembled rather casually.[8] *Payment was two dollars per day, the same as property owners were credited for a day's labor credit for their road tax.*

18–19 January 1887: Very cold and windy, mercury 4 deg below zero, had an invitation to Josh Doans birthday surprise but it was too cold to go.[9] Went to town got Orra a vest $1.00 pair of pants $4.00 at Honest Johns, called at Fathers, Jerry went to the courthouse got picked up on the jury. I came home alone . . . Jerry was on the Jury all day got home about 5 Oclock received his pay for the two days $4.05, got his dinner at the restaurant 25 cts

11–13 October 1888: Jerry was summoned as a Juror on the Moots, Vaughn, Williams and Daughtery stealing case at one Oclock did not get through . . . Jerry was again on the jury got through after noon, the jury found a verdict of guilty against Sam Vaughn . . . Jerry got his Jury money $4.05

3–10 May 1889: Jerry was at town summoned as juror in the case of Mckinnon against Cousins, case postponed until the 20th . . . Jerry went to the court house as a witness on the Hen Pash case but they have not reached it yet, Jerry was picked up as a Juror in the Grant Jackson case of West Liberty . . . Jerry attending court owing to the sudden illness of Judge Lawrence the case was dismissed until tomorrow morning . . . Jerry went to court, Judge Lawrence not able to attend to the case, jury dismissed.

15–18 January 1890: Jerry went to town was picked up on the jury, did not get home till after dark . . . Jerry was at court this forenoon, finished their business and were discharged . . . Jerry received his jury fees $4.25

8–11 May 1893: Jerry attending the grand jury . . . Jerry on the Grand jury . . . Jerry was on the Grand Jury again to day . . . Jerry got home from the grand Jury this afternoon got his pay (4 days $8.05)

11 January 1894: John Harner and wife were here for dinner. He & Jerry attended a trial before Justice Kelley, Harner Bros against W.T. Patterson. Patterson bought sheep at Fosters sale belonging to Harner Bros. claims the sheep had foot rot, claims damages. Jury: E.B. Dillon,

Sidney Nickols, John Richardson, E.S. Jackson, W.H. Neer. Attorneys, Howenstine for Plaintiff, Dow for defendant, did not get through.

As a landowner, with civic responsibility, Jerry was occasionally called upon to perform a farm estate appraisal. These were usually done by three local citizens whose only qualifications were a presumed knowledge of land and equipment values in the neighborhood. Even by nineteenth-century economics one dollar appears to be token payment, and one assumes there was a certain prestige in being asked.

18 February 1887: Jerry, John Gray & David Kaylor appraised the Royer estate today. Received $1.00 for services.

14 September 1892: Jerry was appraising Covers Butchering outfit this evening. Mr Dillon assisting

6–21 February 1894: Jerry received a notice that he had been appointed one of appraisers of the Huber farm . . . Jerry with John Grimes & John Longfellow appraised the Huber farm to day at $45.00 pr acre . . . Jerry received his pay for appraising the Huber property $1.00

The community involvement of a full-time farmer is obviously less than a county seat businessman, but as his sons assumed more of the farm labor it appears that Jerry accepted more community responsibilities.

30 January 1892: Jerry attended the meeting of the agricultural society for the election of officers. Harrison Tp elected Flickenger for manager . . . *23 May* Jerry was sworn in to day as a director of the bank to fill a vacancy by the death of J.M. Dickinson . . . *30 May* Jerry met with the bank directors this morning[10] . . . *31 December* Jerry met with the bank Directors they decided on a dividend of 7 pr ct

TRANSPORTATION and COMMUNICATION

⸺⸻◈⸻⸺

BUGGIES, SLEIGHS, AND BICYCLES

T*he house by the side of the road from which one can watch the world go by and be a friend to man[1] has been the subject of poetic romanticism. But compared to many farm families who lived in relative isolation, the Gebbys experienced this ideal daily. Margaret's home was on the "Sidney Pike," the main artery west from the county seat, and a variety of traffic could be observed on its way to or from town.*

21 May 1891: Rained several showers, two very heavy ones this evening, just what is needed. two ladies drove into the shed during the rain.[2]

14 June 1892: B.F. Royers huckster wagon upset in front of the house about noon, a wheel broke causing the accident. . . . *1–2 November* a boy tramp is sleeping in the barn, says he has been to Chicago and going to his home in Cleveland . . . gave the boy tramp his breakfast, told him to get home as soon as possible.[3]

Not all of the traffic on the pike was human. Livestock on the way to or from the railroad stockyards was driven on foot and it was not uncommon for the Gebby barnyard to offer temporary accommodation to a group on the move.

24 February 1887: Ed Patterson left some cattle here a while this afternoon till he went home to get his dinner. . . . *24 October* John Brown left some sheep in the Barnyard for a while this forenoon.

The Gebby men, too, drove cattle or hogs on the road and knew they could count on helping hands if they occasionally ran into problems.

5 September 1896: The men went to the Depot got the cattle from Chicago. they being range cattle they were very wild and hard to manage. one got separated from the rest became unmanagable. Wellie and Edgar Aikin followed it to keep it from injuring people. Jerry, George and Orra took the others (19) to the farm, then came back took Jersey with them found the Steer in a barnyard on the Blue Jacket road. they got them home about noon.

Most of the vehicles on the road, of course, were horse-drawn buggies, carriages, and farm wagons. When Margaret wanted to go somewhere she was quite comfortable driving herself in either the single-seat buggy or the two-seat carriage. Only once did she record a serious accident.

2 March 1889: Grandma and I started to Harrys met Kate going to church, we then called at Fathers, then at Harners, kept Lizzies baby for her to go to the store, came home about four Oclock, found a dog in our buggy brought him home with us. . . . 27 June Grandma, Aunt Clara, Aunt Hannah, Lizzie & I were at C.C. Cooks to day, had a pleasant visit. Aunt Clara staid with them. When coming home down McAra's hill Harry fell breaking a shaft, skinning a shoulder and knees considerably was except frightening us all the damage done.

26 February 1896: Mattie & I expected to go to town but were disappointed in getting a horse.[4]

This family had a variety of vehicles, but like families today there wasn't always one available when Margaret wanted it. As the boys got older and were traveling on their own the Gebbys acquired more buggies, much as modern families with teenage drivers need more cars. The 1892 tax appraisal credits them with four buggies.

7–14 October 1887: [during the county fair] Jerry bought a carriage from Harry Garwood . . . Got carriage from H.G. paid $100 whip 50 cts Straps 90 cts.

4–19 June 1888: Jerry was at Huntsville this morning wanted to trade old Fan and colt to H. McKinnon for a buggy. Henry was here this P.M. saw Fan, did not trade . . . Jerry got the buggy repaired at Millers $3.60 got paint and brush $1.80 then washed and painted it[5] . . . Orra and Elmer painted the old carriage today . . . Elmer and I put new oil-cloth in the buggies.

30–31 December 1889: Jerry and Orra went to town bought a buggy from Hartzler $90 . . . Orra and Jerry brought home the new buggy bought a set of harness $12, a robe and whip $7.00 making a total of $109 for buggy and attachments.[6]

30 April–19 May 1891: Jerry left the carriage to Garwoods shop to be varnished . . . Jerry was at town this P.M. got the carriage paid $10.00, looks swell. . . . *25 August* Elmer washed Orras buggy this P.M. gone now to a party at Hugh Newells.

27 May 1893: Orra washed his buggy this afternoon.

4 August–10 September 1894: Jerry sent $62.50 check to W.H. Murry of Cincinnati for Buggy & Harness . . . Jerry got the buggy he ordered some time ago, freight $1.00[7]

Of course the business end of a vehicle in the nineteenth century was a good horse. Some families had special carriage horses and larger draft animals for farm work, but like many farmers the Gebbys evidently considered this a luxury. Charlie and Harry were general purpose horses, evidently reliable enough to be handled by a woman driving her own buggy or a boy driving a team with a load of hay. Jerry usually broke his own colts to harness for farmwork, but when they bought a colt for Margaret to use with the buggy, they hired a trainer.

13 June 1893: Grandma, Jerry and I visited with Josie Leman at John Harners to day, went to Mr Fricks to see a family horse but she was not for sale . . . *21 June* three answers to Orras advertizement for a horse . . . *11 October* were at Tommy Cooks sale. there were a great many people there, things generally sold high. Jerry bought a colt for $40.00.

30 August–18 October 1894: Jerry left the colt at Mr McDonalds for him to break . . . Stopped at McDonalds got Maud, drove her to Johns, she is quiet and gentle, is a good traveler for a two year old colt.

To those of us who carefully remove keys from automobile ignitions and lock the doors, it seems amazing that people routinely tied their horses and buggies to hitching rails and almost always returned to find them as they were. Travel by horse and buggy did have its dangers, but for the most part accidents were relatively minor.

5–6 February 1893: The Aikin boys could not find their horse and buggy when they came out of church this evening . . . the Aikin boys got their horse in the livery stable. it had got loose and had been taken to the stable.

8 July 1894: the boys were at S.S. and church. they met with the misfortune of being upset while on the way to S.S. they were all in the buggy driving Charlie being blind of an eye he shied off at a board threw himself and the buggy down in the ditch completely overturning the buggy & breaking the two bows, bent the braces, split the seat some but did not do any other damage, the boys all escaped without injury.

When traveling any distance the Gebbys went by train. In the eleven years Margaret describes only one overnight trip by horse and buggy and this required much preparation. This trip is fascinating both for its travel details and for the extended family network it reveals.[8]

13–15 May 1886: Went to C.C.Cooks to day to make arrangements to visit Darke Co. expect to start Tuesday morn . . . Jerry went to town this P.M. got buggy repaired $13.00 . . . shoeing Charlie 25 cts; took Harry to the blacksmith shop to be shod. . . . *17–20 May* Charlie Cooks came about half past eight Oclock on their way to Darke County[9] . . . Got up at half past three started to Darke Co at five, passed through the towns of Logansville, Port Jefferson, Sidney, Hardin, Dobsons Corner, Berlin, Yorkshire, Tea cup town, North Star arrived at John Robesons at about five Oclock . . . Staid all night at John Robesons. Jerry, Charlie, Orrie, Lon, and Sam went to Weston to get Charlie shod 30 cts, he having lost a shoe, they then drove round the farm, in the afternoon they played Croquet, we went to see the pond then went to the wood and gathered some fern, brought some home . . . Started for home at six Oclock, eat dinner about two miles west of Sidney about half past eleven rested the horses a few minutes left for home reached home about half past five. Charlies turned north in Logansville to go home through Lewistown. Jerry plowed the Garden this evening.

It is easy to follow this route on current maps and realize that it took this two-buggy caravan twelve hours to travel approximately fifty miles, with a stop to rest the horses and eat the dinner they carried with them.

Roads in this community were graded and graveled, usually in both spring and fall. When winter covered gravel with ice and snow, families exchanged buggies for sleighs and for the most part seemed to enjoy the exhilarating change.

20 December 1886: Got down the Sleigh this morning, the sleighing good, but not extra. Orra & I went to G.W. Aikins in the sleigh this eve.

17 January 1887: Jerry was at town got 3⅓ yds of flannel and three yds of drilling to line the Buffalo robe $1.30. I lined it this evening does very well patched up the head part for a foot robe.

12–14 January 1891: Orra took down the sleigh. I patched 8 holes the mice had eaten on the sides . . . Grandma, Jerry and I visited with John Harner and wife, Harry & Kate and Paul at Uncle Johns. all were in sleighs. Sleighing good . . . Elmer gone to McCrackens to a party and enjoy a sleighride. . . . *3–4 March* the sleighing is very good this is the deepest snow of the winter . . . Orra and Sam Robeson took a sleigh ride this P.M. called on Cook and Harner at Rushylvania. Elmer got Harry shod this eve he is gone sleighing with a party to Dick Painters.

13–14 January 1892: enough snow fell last night to make real good sleighing . . . splendid sleighing, Orra took the horses to the shop had their shoes roughed up, 3 deg above this morning, 9 deg this evening, beautiful moonlight night, good sleighing

5–6 December 1893: cold south wind, everything covered with sleet. The boys all gone to church this evening Harry being smooth I could not go . . . Jerry got Harrys shoes pulled off. the blacksmiths were all so busy he could not wait.[10]

With the development of the "safety bicycle" in the 1880s a new mode of transportation began gaining rapid popularity, especially among the young people.

21 July–12 September 1891: a bicycle agent was here to see Orra this evening . . . Orra Cook was here this eve trying to sell the boys a bicycle. did not conclude a bargain, he left for the nine Oclock train . . . Orra & Elmer gone to town on bicycle business . . . Orra Cook brought the bicycle the boys bought of him, paid $69.00 for it. the boys are practicing riding it . . . Orra rode about 14 miles on his bicycle this evening. he rode east of Cherokee a short distance then back through Huntsville & home . . . Elmer riding on bicycle . . . Elmer took the bicycle to the shop for repairs, then took a ride to the lake . . . Orra came home about 4 Oclock ate supper at 25 min past 5 he left for Rushylvania, [*about ten miles*] got home at 20 min till nine. he made the trip there in an hour & 15 minutes, came home in an hour and 10 min . . . Orra went to Degraff on his wheel took supper at Lyman Doans . . . Orra rode the bicycle to church then to West Liberty & home again

Although their parents paid for the bicycle since the boys had no separate source of income, the decision about this vehicle was clearly made by Orra and Elmer. They must have ridden friends' bicycles before acquiring their own because a week after they received it Orra was taking a fourteen-mile trip. The similarity between the acquisition of this bicycle and a modern young man with his first car is remarkable: running off in every direction to show friends, testing out how fast it would go. The three Gebby boys shared one bicycle, but they were prized possessions and even girls worked to earn their own.

5 May 1892: Signed for a pound of baking powder for Sallie Dow helping her get a bicycle, 40 cts. . . . *10–24 August* George went to Huntsville on the Bicycle this P.M. . . . George went to Rushylvania this afternoon on the wheel. . . . *12–15 October* Orra left for Hamilton on his wheel at half past 2 this morning . . . received a card from Orra stating he had arrived at Hamilton at 6 P.M. Wednesday, making the trip in 16 hours . . . Orra came home this evening, came on the cars to Springfield, on the wheel from there

This trip of approximately one hundred miles over gravel roads in sixteen hours was quite a feat, but Margaret does not mention any mechanical breakdowns. Young men were setting bicycle records throughout the 1890s and Orra must have considered this a challenge. It was a grueling test of physical endurance, and he was evidently satisfied with his accomplishment for he came two-thirds of the way home on the train. The fact that he sent his parents a postcard announcing his arrival suggests they were a bit worried about this trip, but it also reveals the speed of mail communication when communities were served by several passenger and freight trains daily.

PASSENGER AND FREIGHT TRAINS

During this period Bellefontaine was a major rail junction. The Cleveland, Columbus, Cincinnati, and Indianapolis Railroad, popularly known as the Big Four, ran east to west along the Gebby farm intersecting the north to south Cincinnati, Sandusky, and Cleveland line on the west side of town about one-half mile from the Gebby home.

Such proximity to the railroad provided both advantages and disad-

*vantages. Discussions over the right-of-way were frequent, dry grass
fires along the line were a constant threat, train accidents could be fatal,
and trips to town had to allow for being delayed by a passing train.
However, the farm had a gravel subsoil, which brought a substantial
cash payment when the railroad bought gravel to make improvements in
the 1890s.*

30 August 1889: the dry grass in the field next the railroad took fire
burning over considerable bounds

27–31 January 1890: the C.L. & M. railway surveyors run a line just
south of the orchard and barn this morning . . . the railroad men were
locating the buildings along the line

25 September 1891: the railroad grass was on fire this P.M. our men
got there just in time to save the line fence between us and Cotters

16 March 1893: A railroad agent was here to day trying to get the
right of way through the farm. offered to build a road on the line now
ran and build two culverts and pay $500 in money, the distance 2133
feet. it leaves 4 acres 90/100 north of the railroad. Jerry did not accept.

24 February 1895: Owen McFarland Jr was killed by the cars at
Gretna [*a mile or so west*] this afternoon. this is the fourth of the family
that has been killed by the cars, one in 1888, one in 1891, one in 1894
and this one in 1895. he was in his 16th year.

13 April 1895: Jerry and a Mr Hays was out viewing the gravel bank
the R.R. Co wants to get some more gravel. they did not do any thing
definite yet . . . *14–15 May* S.W. Hayes, Engr M. of way of Cleveland
was here to night seeing about the gravel pit at the farm . . . Jerry and
G.W. Aikin looked over the gravel pit ground but could not make any
new suggestions. Jerry left the agreement with the agent . . . *27 May*
The men moved the fence back out of the way of the gravel pit men,
they are preparing to scale the soil off, have their teams, wagons and
tents &c. Jerry was at town got locks & keys to lock the barn at the
farm . . . *21 June* Jerry and I was at town signed the agreement with the
Big 4 R.R. selling them about 5 acres more gravel for the sum of $1500 to
be paid on or before the first day of August next . . . *10 July* The men
who have been working at the gravel bank left to day having finished
their job . . . *15 August* The fencing for the railroad at the gravel pit
arrived this morning

*Railroads provided passenger and freight transportation that seems
remarkably convenient even a century later. The Gebbys had no free
rural mail delivery, but someone was in town nearly every day and
brought the mail from the post office box. It was not unusual for a letter*

from relatives near Cincinnati to be posted in the morning and received in the afternoon, messages to and from Chicago cattle buyers were received the next day, and even England seems closer than modern readers would suspect. In emergencies, both messages and people moved quickly by rail.

28 July 1890: Father & Mother called this afternoon. I read a letter he received from G.W. Hamilton dated July 13 from London . . . 22 August this evening attended a welcome extended to Rev Hamilton on his return from Europe, had Ice cream, Lemon aid and cake, a large attendance

27 September 1890: Selected a box (302) in the new P.O. room paid 35 cts rent and 50 cts for the keys

18 December 1890: I intended going to Degraff to see Aunt Mattie but father had received a card from Joshua stating that she had died at 11 Oclock last night . . . 19 December Jerry & I attended Aunt Mattie Doans funeral at Degraff at 2 Oclock this afternoon. Dr Kalb preached from "Let not your heart be troubled neither let it be afraid, ye believe in God believe also in me" Father & Mother, Lyman & Mattie also Elmer went down on the noon train. Elmer rode home with Dow Aikin in his buggy. We got home about dusk.

2 June 1895: Ella Dow has been visiting in Pittsburg for the past two weeks is sick with Dipthera news came by telegram this afternoon. Mrs Dow left on the six P.M. Train. Duncan going with her as far as Urbana

The real bonus for the Gebby family's proximity to rail lines was the convenience of ordering a freight car so they might ship cattle and hogs to market by driving them to the station. Livestock markets fluctuated with weather conditions and excerpts from Margaret's diaries reflect the process of dealing with markets hundreds of miles distant in Buffalo and Chicago.[11]

1 May 1890: Jerry ordered a car to ship hogs next Saturday . . . 3 May Jerry, Elmer and George weighed the hogs (6250 lbs) drove them to the stockyards, hauled two of the fattest, took some straw & bedded the car. Mr Kaylors weighed 6725 they loaded them for the two Oclock train.

15 July 1891: Jerry was at town this P.M. saw Lorimer Kerr of Buffalo. John Riddle was here to see Jerry about shipping cattle . . . 31 July Jerry & George got a load of bedding at Uncle Johns for the cattle car . . . 1 August The men brought a load of cattle from the pasture to the stockyards for shipment at one Oclock, the train was an hour & a

half behind time. Train left here about five Oclock, Jerry going with them . . . *4 August* Jerry came home at half past 2 Oclock this A.M. sold the car load of cattle (18 head) which averaged 1300 lbs (shrink 50 lbs) for $4.65 pr hd, after deducting expenses received a draft on N.Y. for $1037.50. Expenses to Buffalo $10.00 . . . *15 August* John Riddle paid Jerry $5.00 for looking after his cattle to Buffalo.

15 December 1891: Jerry & Orra left at six Oclock this evening for Chicago in charge of six loads of cattle, three of Riddles, two of their own, and one of Culton Bros. the train was some two hours behind time . . . *19 December* Jerry got home about 11 Oclock this A.M. not well, sold the cattle straight for $4.70 pr hhd. Thursdays market bought 48 head for $2.90 pr hdd. they averaged 842. Those he sold averaged 1400 lbs $2264.04 net (expenses $87.84) bought two cars of stock cattle $1173, commission $20, balance to Jerry $1071. Orra came home with the cattle reached home at 11 P.M. 29 hours on the way home. Bob and family stayed here this evening he helping bring cattle here . . . *21 December* Jerry went to the Depot ordered a car to ship the hogs and remaining cattle to Cleveland tomorrow. settled with the Railroad Co. paid $48.24 freight on the two loads of cattle brought home . . . *22 December* the hogs averaged 237 lbs the big white weighed 460 lbs . . . *23 December* Jerry went to the stock yards to get a crowbar they left there yesterday. found a hog they had missed in the darkness last night when loading, sold it to John Grimes for $7.

NEWS

The infrequent comment on local or national news throughout these diaries is both a disappointment and an affirmation of the narrow vision of a farm housewife. Whether typical or not, her focus was on her farm, home, family, and church. Local events were occasionally mentioned, but even items that were thoroughly covered in local newspapers such as the brief gas boom in northwestern Ohio or the local arrival of electric lighting receive little mention. It was obviously Margaret Gebby's purpose to record family activities and finances, not her thoughts on newsworthy events.

27 August 1886: The gas well was torpedoed at noon today but failed to get any more gas, down upwards of 1600 feet

7 July 1887: Father & Mother were here for dinner Grandfather &

George went to see the gas well which is down 1700 feet . . . *6 August* a small gas vein has been struck at the Angel well . . . *8 August* they shot the gas well this morning not much gas, a little more than the first well . . . *9 August* gas well almost a failure.[12]

26 September 1894: all attended the celebration of the Memorial building, the corner stone was laid by the Masons, the box deposited contained a copy of all the papers of the town, a roster of some of the churches. the parade was a success. the trades display was splendid. the fire works this evening was grand.[13]

21 January 1896: The electric lights are burning for the first time[14]

18 June 1896: Jerry and Lon visited Piatt home near West Liberty. it has been bought and they are making arrangements to convert it into a sanitarium.

8 December 1896: The Grangers are having a convention here in the K. of P. hall about 300 members & visitors from abroad are here.[15]

Disasters such as fires were big news in the nineteenth century as they are today. Margaret's diaries provide interesting insights in how families coped when someone's home burned and how volunteer fire companies responded to assist each other in major fires.

9 April 1888: Orra was at town this evening heard that Tommy Cooks house was burned at noon to day, got no particulars . . . *10 April* I saw J. McCrackens this morning on their way to T. Cooks to help them put their goods that was not burned away . . . *11 April* called at Fathers helped Mary McC and M.A. Aikin, Mother make four shirts for Jim & Orra Cook they having gotten their others burnt . . . *17 May* Went to Tommy Cooks saw them in their temporary dwelling took them a half doz plates and a meat platter

29 October 1891: Quite a fire in Kenton to day, sent here for help but before our co. could get a Locomotive to take our engine there they got a telegram that the fire was under control

15 March 1896: There was quite a disastrous fire in town between one & two oclock this morning. the Lawrence Lockhart & Niven building were much damaged by fire & water. Abraham grocery, Osbornes Hardware, Eaton Restaurant & Carter Bros on the lower floors, the offices & rooms above are destroyed, roof fell in[16]

Petty crime was a fact of life in the idyllic countryside of a century past, but in neighborhoods where everyone was known to others and strangers were noticed it was relatively infrequent and insignificant. This seems particularly noteworthy on a farm adjoining a railroad that prob-

ably carried its share of vagabonds. These diaries make no mention of vandalism that wantonly destroyed property.

6 *September 1886:* Some person stole nine chickens Sat. night - 7 small, 2 large ones

22 *September 1887:* Some sneak thief stole a shirt of Jerrys last night off the line.

3 *May 1890:* Some thief stole Dillons horse, Buggy, robe, whip & harness last night. Albert and Simon Daily was out all day but got no clue

15 *February 1891:* Some sneak thief stole Elmers umbrella from church . . . 17 *May* some sneak thief cut the rings of Orra's martingale at church

2 *November 1892:* somebody husked some corn last night, part of three shocks

21 *June 1893:* Some person broke into Abednego Detricks house this afternoon got $40.00 in money and some clothing.

15 *October 1894:* Mr McAra called saying that some tramps had taken two shocks of our corn made a bed of them in his woods.

More serious crimes were recorded with a curious moral ambivalence. Margaret considered a prison term for forgery severe for someone she knew, but murderers who were lynched by mobs drew no expression of outrage from this Christian housewife. Ohio was a long way from the frontier by the last decade of the nineteenth century, but attitudes about frontier justice were not dead.

2 *October 1890:* the expressman on the four Oclock train between W. Liberty & Urbana was tied & robbed of $5,000, supposition points to himself.

8 *April 1891:* Bales the murderer of policeman Harper of Kenton was taken from jail and hung by a mob at 2 Oclock this morning

19 *December 1892:* Orra was at town this evening heard that A.L. Smith was in jail for Forgery to the amount of $1775 . . . 21 *February 1893:* Judge Price sentenced A.L. Smith to 3 years in Penitentiary at hard labor, a severe sentence.

15 *April 1894:* Seymour Newland was lynched and hanged by a mob at Rushylvania last night at 9.30

12 *July 1894:* Gus Weaver was arrested this evening on the charge of carrying concealed weapons. he had received notice to leave town by 7 P.M. but he declined doing it. a mob of about 200 had collected to tar &

feather him. to save trouble & probably bloodshed the Officials arrested him. he is charged with being an Anarchist.[17]

Two historic uprisings of national significance during this period are mentioned in these diaries but their very brevity strongly suggests that this rural homemaker was firmly on the side of law and order. When one considers the attitudes of individuals such as farmers and housewives, one must analyze the bias of local newspapers, which were their sources of information.

11 November 1887: Four of the Chicago anarchists executed today[18]

7 June 1894: Co F 2d Regiment from here was called to Cambridge O. to quell a difficulty with the Miners[19]

Margaret Dow Gebby shortly before her death in 1920.

EPILOGUE

S ome readers may be interested in a postscript regarding the Gebby sons, who were left on the brink of manhood as their mother's diaries conclude. Orra spent his entire life in Logan County, living in the house built just after his marriage, farming this land, and passing it on to one of his sons at his death in 1947. Elmer married his cousin Laura Dow and became a partner in Keller and Gebby, a grain elevator and coal supply business in the town of Bellefontaine, where he lived until his death in 1936. George married and had two children prior to his death during a blizzard in 1918 while serving as a missionary on an Indian reservation in Arizona.[1]

Throughout these diaries readers may sense that Margaret suffered fewer illnesses and enjoyed generally better health than her husband. Jerry died in 1901 at the age of sixty-two from pneumonia that brought on a fatal stroke. Margaret lived until the age of eighty-five, enjoying generally good health until a fall confined her to her home shortly before her death 29 November 1920.[2]

NOTES

*The original Margaret Dow Gebby diaries, 1886–1896, are in the
manuscript collection (MSS 964) of the Ohio Historical Society.*

PREFACE

1. The nineteenth-century term "housewife" is used in preference to the
more current terminology "homemaker." For rationale, see Glenna Matthews,
Just a Housewife: The Rise and Fall of Domesticity in America (New York:
Oxford University Press, 1987).

2. Current society places low value on homemaking roles, and the popular
media often convey the impression that this has always been so. The mid-nine-
teenth century, however, was recognized as the golden age of domesticity with
talents as strong as Catharine Beecher turning their attention to domestic education. Even Stanton's biographer admitted the staunchest women suffragists
found "it is a proud moment in a woman's life to reign supreme within four
walls, to be the one to whom all questions are referred." Elizabeth Griffith, *In
Her Own Right: The Life of Elizabeth Cady Stanton* (New York: Oxford University Press, 1984), 44.

THE GEBBY FAMILY FARM

1. Campbell-Dow genealogical research by author and correspondence
with descendants. Bellefontaine Cemetery lots #460 (Gebby), #473 (Dow-
Cooke), #503 (Aikin). Obituaries, *Bellefontaine Republican:* Martha Campbell
Doan, 30 December 1890; Sallie Campbell Dow, 8 March 1892; Peter Dow, 27
August 1895. U.S. Census, Logan County Ohio: 1840 Harrison Township, p. 53;
1850 Harrison Township, p. 189; 1860 Lake Township. Bellefontaine, p. 52.

2. Margarets were often nicknamed Maggie or Peggy a century ago, but
the only record in which Margaret D. Gebby signed anything less than her full
name was a deed for land sold in 1875 signed Maggie Gebby (Logan County
Deed Record 53, p. 23). Her grandchildren remembered her as Margaret,
perhaps reflecting a more dignified relationship or her wish to discard a childish
nickname later in life.

3. Fred W. Carter, ed., *Stories About Logan County Schools,* Bicentennial Project, Logan County Farm Bureau Council #22, 1976. Union School was the predecessor of Bellefontaine High School, which graduated its first student in 1867. Margaret would have been nineteen when it opened in 1854, but no student rosters have been found. An advertisement in the *Logan Gazette,* 6 September 1856, refers to its Teachers Class, Academic School, and Commercial College. One suspects that Peter Dow might have been involved in the Teachers Class since the Logan County School Examiners' lists show his occupation both as schoolteacher and druggist during the 1860s. No records for teaching licenses have been found from 1855 to 1868, but numerous female teachers were hired during the Civil War and it seems likely that Margaret might have been one. Logan County Marriage Record, vol. D, p. 74.

4. Robeson-Gebby genealogical research by author and correspondence with descendants. Tombstones at Mt. Pleasant Cemetery, Monroe, Ohio. Tombstones and Records, Bellefontaine Cemetery lots #460 (Gebby) and #766 (Robeson). Obituaries, *Bellefontaine Republican:* Mary Gebby, 10 July 1894; John N. Robeson, 21 July 1896. Warren County Supreme Court Minute Record, vol. 3, pp. 113 and 120, divorce petition. Logan County Common Pleas Court, Journal O., p. 500, divorce petition.

5. Logan County Death Record, vol. 1, p. 148, John C. Gebby, flux, 8, September 1875.

6. Biographies—Robert P. Kennedy, *Historical Review of Logan County, Ohio:* (Chicago: S. J. Clarke Publishing Co., 1903), G. W. Aikin, p. 731; Duncan Dow, p. 258; James E. McCracken, p. 664. *History of Logan County, Ohio:* (Chicago: O. L. Baskins & Co., 1880), Duncan Dow, p. 596; Lyman Doan, p. 775; Lyman Dow, p. 800; Thomas Cook, p. 818. D. J. Stewart, *Combination Atlas Map of Logan County, Ohio: Milton Wolfe* (Philadelphia: D. J. Stewart, 1875; reprint, West Liberty, Ohio: Liberty Printing, 1975), p. x.

7. Logan County Death Record, vol. 1, p. 148: John R. Gebby, consumption, 20 November 1875. D. J. Stewart, *Atlas of Logan County, Ohio:* biography and portrait, Abraham and Martha Harner, pp. IX and 5.

8. Mary Gebby purchased 107 acres in Union Township for $3,344, 3 March 1856 (Logan County Deed Record 30, p. 149). On 17 March 1862 she sold this property for $6,000 and bought 147 acres adjacent to Harner for $9,000 (Deed Record 38, 152–53). An advertisement to sell this property 4 January 1872 in the *Bellefontaine Republican* described this homestead where Margaret Dow Gebby began her married life as a "large, nearly new frame dwelling, with large bank barn, wagon shed, carriage house, corn crib, hog house, and other outbuildings." On 11 March 1866 Mary Gebby purchased twenty-one acres for $1,302 to complete her holding of Section 17, Township 4, Range 13 (Deed Record 43, p. 56). Jerry Gebby paid $7,000 for sixty-one acres in Harrison Township 1 October 1872 (Deed Record 50, p. 275). The tax assessment on this property in 1870 was forty acres plowland $2,994.75, 21.67 acres woods at $75 per acre, $400 house, $200 other buildings, total $5,220. This was the property on which the Gebbys lived during these diaries. On 20 March 1875 Mary, Jerry,

and Maggie Gebby sold the 168 acres in Union Township for $16,800 (Deed Record 53, p. 23) and 12 February 1877 bought the 62.37-acre "Huston" farm and 160-acre "Lord" farm from A. R. Harner who had apparently bought them for resale to the Gebbys after they sold their Union Township property. The Gebbys paid $6,262 for the Huston farm, which had an 1870 tax assessment of $3,101 including $300 for the house they would use for their hired man and $12,187.50 for the Lord farm, which had an 1870 tax assessment of $6,285 including a $300 house that may have housed a second hired man before the boys became old enough for farmwork (Deed Record 55, 268–69). The rapid inflation in land values during and immediately following the Civil War contrasts sharply with static and falling values during the depression of the 1890s.

9. The term "wheat houses" is from Helen Gebby Evans who was in her grandmother's home many times prior to her death in 1920. Jerry and Margaret Gebby may have done some remodeling to this $400 house, perhaps putting in the furnace that Margaret's diaries describe being replaced in 1895.

10. Non Population Census Schedule, 1880 Products of Agriculture, Logan County, Ohio, Harrison Township, ED 113, p. 12 #4 and p. 17 #4. The average farm in 1890 contained 93 acres (21.5 percent unimproved) in Ohio and 137 acres (42.6 percent unimproved) in the United States. (*Abstract of the Eleventh Census, 1890* [Washington, D.C.: Government Printing Office, 1894], 61).

11. *History of Logan County, Ohio* (Chicago: O. L. Baskins & Co., 1880); Robert P. Kennedy, *Historical Review of Logan County, Ohio* (Chicago: S. J. Clarke Publishing Co., 1903); D. J. Stewart, *Atlas of Logan County 1875; Atlas of Logan County, Ohio* (Philadelphia: D. J. Lake & Co., 1890); Henry Howe, *Historical Collections of Ohio* vol. 2 (Cincinnati: C. J. Krehbiel & Co., 1902), 97–117.

12. *Atlas of Logan County, Ohio* (1890). The township was formed in 1832 and had a population of 658 in 1840, 987 in 1850, 912 in 1860, 994 in 1870, and 978 in 1880. Harrison Township, with 329 scholars, had the largest township enrollment in the county in 1879 (Max McGowan, "History of Logan County Schools," Logan County Public Library, Vertical File 87–1479; Interview with Josephine Heminger, coordinator, DAR project on one-room schools).

13. What appears on contemporary maps as Indian Lake was referred to as the Lewistown Reservoir, a body of water covering over seven thousand acres and ranging four to five miles in length and width.

WEATHER

1. Margaret had no personal knowledge of Egypt, but Christian missionaries working among dark-skinned people of Africa made Egypt a colloquial symbol of darkness.

2. Farmers, like seamen, observed weather signs and placed credence in the

popular rhyme, "Red at night, sailor's delight, Red in the morning, sailors take warning."

3. Western Ohio residents frequently experienced mild tremors and recent research provides evidence that a billion-year-old geologic scar known as the Greenville front extends north and south directly beneath Logan County. ("Ohio's Basement Yields Secrets," *Columbus Dispatch*, 4 March 1988, B2).

4. "There was quite a quaking of the earth yesterday morning, which those who have quiet consciences and sleep well, did not have the pleasure of enjoying" (*Bellefontaine Republican*, 1 November 1895, 3). It apparently lasted less than a minute and caused no serious damage or injury.

BUILDINGS, EQUIPMENT, AND HIRED HELP

1. Margaret's brother-in-law who farmed less than a mile away.

2. Margaret's first cousin was a lawyer in Bellefontaine.

3. Logan County Deed Record 72, p. 223, records this sale at $5,110, implying the Gebbys paid $307.09, approximately 6 percent interest on this mortgage.

4. A distant cousin who spelled his name differently and was not considered a relative.

5. Logan County Deed Record 73, 309–10, records this sale from D. M. Kaylor to Hannah Robeson, 40.67 acres for $4,000. There is no mention of her living husband.

6. Margaret's sister and brother-in-law were retiring and moving into town.

7. Jerry's uncle John had died the previous summer and their equipment was sold in the spring when farm equipment often sold higher.

8. The house where the hired man lived.

9. This entry is unusual because it is in Orra's handwriting. Margaret might have shared his sentiments but she never expressed such thoughts in writing. It does provide an example of the obligations of the farm wife to provide meals for a wide variety of people: carpenters, painters, hay balers, threshers, cattle buyers, and tax assessors.

10. Various types of wind wheel technology had been used for years, but the replacement of wooden towers with metal in the 1880s permitted construction high enough to be effective in Ohio. The year the Gebbys installed their wind wheel was the industry's peak, with seventy-seven companies in operation. Technology improved for a number of years, but wind power was gradually displaced by electricity (R. Douglas Hurt, "Windcatchers and Eyecatchers: Technology Down on the Farm," *Timeline* 2, no. 2 [April–May 1985]: 26–39).

11. November 20 was Sunday and the Gebbys attended church. No mention is made of business, but one suspects Jerry talked with other men and learned where to get his casting repaired locally.

12. Farm wage rates for the United States from 1885 to 1895 ranged from $18.50 to $20.00 per month with a home provided. Single men who received room and board with the farm family averaged $12.50 to $14.00 during the same period (Bureau of Census, U.S. Department of Commerce, *Historical Statistics of the United States—Colonial Times to 1970*, part 1 [Washington, D.C.: Government Printing Office, 1975], 468).

13. Whatever the reason for delayed payment, it was treated as a loan at 8 percent interest.

14. Slang term for rail fence derived from its twisting appearance.

CROPS

1. Crop rotation was recommended as progressive farming practice in this period before extensive use of chemical fertilizers.

2. See Henry C. Taylor, *Tarpleywick, A Century of Iowa Farming* (Ames: Iowa State University Press, 1970) for comparable data on farm equipment purchases on the western side of the Corn Belt.

3. R. Douglas Hurt, *American Farm Tools from Hand-power to Steam Power* (Manhattan: Sunflower University Press, 1982), 11–13, plows; 31–33, planters; 59, corn-cutting sled; S. H. Rosenberg, ed., *Rural America a Century Ago* (St. Joseph, Mich.: American Society of Agricultural Engineers, 1976), 1–3, plows; 18–19, corn harvesters; 30–31, reapers; 34–35, hay loaders; Robert L. Ardrey, *American Agricultural Implements* (New York: Arno Press, 1972 reprint of 1894 publication), 17, Gilpin plow; 171, Brown corn planter; John T. Schlebecker, *Whereby We Thrive: A History of American Farming 1607–1972* (Ames: Iowa State University Press, 1975), 175, indicates sulky plows became commercially available late in the 1860s and were commonplace in the 1880s from Ohio to Iowa.

4. Hurt's *American Farm Tools* (pp. 94–97) shows a barn haymow very similar to the Gebbys' equipment and suggests that horse-powered balers were in common use well after the introduction of steam-powered equipment. Schlebecker, *Whereby We Thrive* (pp. 197–98), indicates the first hay loaders came onto the market in the 1870s but did not become popular until the 1890s. He dates the horse-powered hay press from 1853 and the steam press from 1882. Various models of forks for loose hay and presses for baled hay are pictured in *Farm Implement News, Buyer's Guide* (Chicago, vol. 6 [1895]: 104 and 114). Ardrey, *American Agricultural Implements*, shows various models of hay loaders (p. 99) and hay presses (p. 161). The *Ohio Farmer* (17 May 1890, 376) advertised that the Rock Island "Jewett Hay Rake and Loader" would take hay as left by the mower and rake it clean and deliver a ton onto the wagon every fifteen minutes.

5. Champion Reapers such as Jerry purchased at the 1889 Logan County Fair were manufactured by Warder, Bushnell and Glesner Co. of Springfield,

Ohio, which also manufactured mowers under the Champion brand. Their advertisement in the *Ohio Farmer* (3 May 1890, 330) featured President Harrison driving their two-horse mower with sickle bar.

6. The Gilpin plow was a popular steel-pointed sulky, or riding plow, which had been on the market for about ten years.

7. A man working hard with a corn knife might cut and shock twenty shocks per day by hand, but two dollars per day can be compared to the twenty dollars per month paid the hired man.

8. On many farms corn was husked by the shock in the field during the late fall and early winter. The Gebbys may have valued the stocks as fodder for their cattle, for they endured the backbreaking labor of hauling the cornstalks to the barn floor for husking.

9. Center braces for supporting shocks made by bending and tying four stalks from two adjacent rows.

10. Hurt pictures and describes various models of corn-cutting sleds (*American Farm Tools*, p. 59).

11. This was obviously a two-man sled, and with experience Orra and the hired man increased their productivity, but the three hundred shocks per day claimed by agricultural equipment dealers sounds like pure fable.

12. A knotted chain to guide the planter had to be staked to each side of the field.

13. Hay was far less vulnerable than wheat to a few extra days of sun or rain. If overripe, wheat shattered during harvest, and the economic loss quickly became severe. But beef cattle would eat hay that had been rained on even though it might have lost some of its nutritional value.

14. The *Bellefontaine Republican* (13 July 1894) was advertising McCormick Bros. hay tedder and Rock Island Hay Loaders.

15. Riding the horse that pulled the hay trip fork was a favored job for young boys.

16. Between 1880 and 1890 rail track in Ohio expanded from 5,415 miles to 7,903 miles (*Abstract of the Eleventh Census: 1890* [Washington, D.C.: Government Printing Office, 1894], 218).

17. This was evidently a horse-powered press from the Ann Arbor Agricultural Company. Local agricultural equipment dealers did not have sufficient demand to stock this machinery.

18. No baling was done the previous two weeks while spring plowing was done.

19. The reference to cloverseed is actually clover hay that will later be hulled for its seed.

20. Sometimes threshers worked other farms between the Gebby home place and farm, other years they might move directly from one to the other.

21. In these accounts the crew that cooked dinner for threshers usually involved only relatives. It seemed to require three or four women, and Margaret usually exchanged help with her sister Martha and one or more of the Robeson cousins. The ratio of three women cooking dinner for sixteen men and supper for eleven is typical of these diaries.

22. This suggests the Gebbys had a reaper model sold by the Warder Co. in Springfield, Ohio, which delivered the cut grain to a platform for a man to bind by hand into sheaves. At the 1889 Logan County Fair Jerry purchased a Champion reaper-mower for $170, no doubt because its automatic tying mechanism would replace at least one man's work in the field.

23. Numerous references to getting flour at the mill indicate the Gebbys exchanged their wheat for flour but not necessarily that they were receiving flour ground from their own grain.

24. Crop yields in 1891 were above average in Ohio, with averages from 8.53 to 20 bushels per acre from 1886 to 1896 (Ohio State Board of Agriculture, *Fifty-eighth Annual Report* [Springfield: Springfield Publishing Company, 1904], 80–81).

25. The price per bushel in Ohio ranged from fifty-one cents to ninety-nine cents between 1886 and 1896 with the peak in 1891 and the low in 1894.

LIVESTOCK

1. The Jersey milk cow could be led with a halter and entice the wild range steer to follow her home.

2. Without knowing how much corn these cattle consumed one cannot compute its value, but corn prices peaked at fifty cents per bushel nationally in 1890 and fell as low as twenty-one cents in 1896 (*Historical Statistics of the United States—Colonial Times to 1970,* 512). The Gebbys obviously felt it was an advantage to market their corn as meat.

3. The 1870 Census of Products of Agriculture, Logan County, Ohio (Roll 39, p. 3, no. 32) shows the J. M. Gebby farm with four horses, three cows, seven cattle, twelve sheep, and seventeen swine. Perhaps they eliminated sheep when they moved to Harrison Township near town.

4. Veterinary science was in its infancy when the Ohio Veterinary Medical Association was formed in 1883. It was 1895 before Ohio State University employed a trained veterinarian on the faculty (*A Century of Caring* [Columbus: Ohio Veterinary Medical Association, 1984]).

5. Hog cholera was first identified in Ohio in 1833 but there was no effective treatment except the destruction of infected animals. With national losses estimated as high as sixty million dollars annually, the disease was finally eradicated in 1978 after years of diagnosis, quarantine, and vaccination (Jack Hayes, ed., *Animal Health: Livestock and Pets,* U.S.D.A. 1984 Yearbook of Agriculture [Washington, D.C.: Government Printing Office, 1985], 299–300).

6. Despite Margaret's inconsistent spelling she must have been well acquainted with this tincture of opium, laudanum, which was frequently used as medication.

7. Morgan stock were highly favored as multipurpose horses in this area about that time, but there is no evidence the Gebbys ever sought purebreds.

8. Loyal Republicans may note the Gebby men not only supported the ticket with their votes, they named two of their colts for the 1888 presidential and vice-presidential candidates.

9. A few weeks after Shep's fatal encounter with Rough on Rats.

HOUSEKEEPING AND FURNISHINGS

1. 1880 U.S. Census, Logan County, Ohio, Harrison Township, p. 12, #86 records Maggie Hinkle, age 18, as a servant and Wm. L. Davis, age 26, as a farmhand boarding in the Gebby household.

2. Folk culture considered lye soap superior for heavy cleaning such as farm work clothes long after commercial varieties became available.

3. In 1895 the average wage rate per month for farm labor was $12.50 with room and board, suggesting that hired girls were paid less than hired men, but on a percentage basis the difference was less than one might have suspected (*Historical Statistics of the United States—Colonial Times to 1970*, 468).

4. Margaret cut fabric for carpet from old bedding or clothing and sewed it together in strips. She took these to a local weaver to have a carpet made.

5. The 1897 *Sears Roebuck Catalogue* (1897; reprint, New York: Chelsea House Publishers, 1976) pictured "mattresses" that would currently be recognized as bedsprings. All were made of wire, some flat and some vertically coiled. This probably explains why Margaret was filling a straw tick for George's bed two years after purchasing a "spring bed and mattress" for him.

6. Plasterer $3.00, Creamer $37.50, Lumber $7.85, Hardware $16.63, Lime $.86, Carpenter $4.45, Oilcloth $9.00, Table legs $.50 = $79.79

7. The nearby Logan County Children's Home.

8. Housework went on as usual during the kitchen remodeling project.

9. For two days work.

10. The Gebby hired man served as plasterer's helper.

11. The carpenter was building a wood cabinet to enclose an iron water tank.

12. The old hand pump to the well.

13. They had evidently temporarily installed an old stove from the washhouse.

14. The master bedroom had now been moved downstairs.

FOOD

1. There were many nurseries in western Ohio but the Gebbys preferred to deal with Jerry's uncle who had a nursery near Hamilton, Ohio.

2. Early April had been cold and snowy and they had obviously waited two weeks to plant these bare root plants.

3. Celery was a common crop in the muck soils just south of Lake Erie and the Gebby farm contained patches of similar soil, which Margaret refers to as damp places in the prairie.

4. Rain was frequent and the diary notes repeated dustings with paris green.

5. Logan County was too far north to depend upon a successful peach crop except in a few areas protected from late frosts.

6. Home preservation of fruits greatly increased after the Civil War when glass jars with self-sealing lids began appearing in country stores (Richard O. Cummings, *The American and His Food* [Chicago: University of Chicago Press, 1940], 85).

7. It would appear that this homemaker was simultaneously using tin cans sealed with paraffin and glass jars with zinc lids sealed with rubber rings.

8. Wine apparently refers to grape juice since the Gebbys did not produce or drink a fermented product.

9. Cider refers to apples pressed for juice that would be boiled down and used in making apple butter.

10. The birth of the "Banana Republics" began with the patent of refrigerated railroad cars in 1867. The first refrigerated car of bananas was shipped to Chicago two years later (Cummings, 62).

11. The hindquarter was the largest and most choice, but beef was mostly cut into chunks and roasted either dry in the oven or moist as with potroast. The Gebbys never ate steak as modern readers would know it.

12. Loaves of bread could be purchased in town from bakers but many housewives baked their own to save money and suit their family's preference. It appears that this family regularly consumed about a dozen loaves weekly.

13. Even experienced cooks evidently had difficulty gauging the uneven heat of a wood-burning stove.

14. No mention of a trip to town suggests this purchase was from a traveling peddler.

15. Sugar barrels evidently held 300 to 350 pounds and required the men to make a trip with the farm wagon as they did when getting flour at the mill. It is interesting to note that the price of sugar dropped from 7¾ cents per pound in 1888 to 4½ cents per pound in 1896.

BUTTER AND EGG BUSINESS

1. Jensen points out that farm families nurtured the butter trade as a secure source of income, which was often enough to buy most of the commodities needed for the household (Joan M. Jensen, *Loosening the Bonds, Mid-Atlantic Farm Women, 1750–1850* [New Haven: Yale University Press, 1986], 83).

2. In the school year ending 31 August 1888, Logan County paid male township district teachers an average thirty-six dollars per month and females twenty-six dollars per month for an average school year of twenty-nine weeks (*Thirty-five Annual Report of the State Commissioner of Common Schools* [Columbus: The Westbone Co. Printers, 1889], 49).

3. In Stadtfeld's memory of his farm childhood, "the poultry and eggs that sold earned pin money for the women, money never taken too seriously in the days when bookkeeping was casual and cost accounting unknown." But he was surprised in reviewing his father's account book to find cash income from poultry and eggs nearly equaled that for the dairy herd (Curtis K. Stadtfeld, *From the Land and Back* [New York: Scribner, 1972], 119–20). Butter and egg income was significant not only to individual farm families but as an agricultural industry. A Logan County history indicates that in 1902 some 600,000 pounds of butter were marketed, and that "does not include creamers but simply the product of the farm and household" (Kennedy, *Historical Review of Logan County, Ohio,* 154).

4. The Sidney churn was evidently a local model produced in the nearby town of Sidney, Ohio. The price and length of time to produce butter suggests this was a crank model of the box, cylinder, or barrel variety. Sears and Roebuck catalogs of the 1890s offered all of these versions in this price range as well as the older standing dasher churn. Box churns had been featured at the 1876 Philadelphia Centennial and various models of cylinder churns appeared in dairy equipment shows throughout the last quarter of the century. Margaret's pride in the time saved suggests that she very likely replaced an old dasher churn. Rosenberg indicates that it normally took forty to sixty minutes to churn butter (*Rural America a Century Ago,* 58–61).

5. Margaret's contribution of 20 percent to 30 percent of the family living income plus the value of home-produced food compares quite favorably with recent statistics that show that part- and full-time working women on average contribute about 26 percent of total family income (Valerie K. Oppenheimer, "The Female Labor Force in the U.S.: Demographic and Economic Factors," in Ralph E. Smith, ed., *The Subtle Revolution: Women at Work* [Washington, D.C.: The Urban Institute, 1979], 12).

6. The 1890 census was the first to provide data on women in the labor force with a total of 3.7 million: 37 percent of the single women but only 4.5 percent of married women. The 1900 Logan County census, however, shows all of the women earners referred to in these diaries were recorded at home without occupation except the hired girl. This perpetuates inaccurate myths regarding the economic contribution of nineteenth-century married women. For example, Hofferth and Moore emphasize recent increases in the labor force "including married women who traditionally have felt no economic need to work" (Sandra L. Hofferth and Kristin A. Moore, "Women's Employment and Marriage," in *The Subtle Revolution,* 99).

CLOTHING

1. Strasser states that the ready-made clothing industry late in the nineteenth century was dominated by men's wear, with less than one-fourth of the women's wear in 1890 being factory made (Susan Strasser, *Never Done: A History of American Housework* [New York: Pantheon Books, 1982], 134).

2. Son George could walk the mile to the neighbors but Grandma needed to ride in the buggy.

3. This sounds like a mother-of-the-bride dress, but there is no evidence in the diaries that it was worn for any special occasion. Perhaps it was simply a summer dress for church. When her oldest son was married two years later she made no mention of getting a new dress.

4. The middle Gebby son was by then a clerk at the bank.

5. Local newspaper advertisements and the 1897 Sears Roebuck catalog show various styles of blue denim overalls, which would today be referred to as jeans. The best quality of ready-made suits advertised for men were wool worsted, which could easily have been purchased for the prices cited.

HEALTH AND HOME NURSING

1. A sack of stones was evidently being used as a weight to counterbalance the hayfork.

2. This sentence is written in George's handwriting beside his mother's entry.

3. Most homes relied on one of the family medical guides published throughout the nineteenth century. It is not known which one Margaret Gebby owned, but for reference on contemporary diagnosis and treatment the editor has used R. V. Pierce, *The People's Common Sense Medical Adviser*, 6th ed. (Buffalo, N.Y.: World's Dispensary Printing, 1878) and E. Harris Ruddock, *Family Doctor: A Popular Guide for the Household*, 3d ed. (Chicago: Gross & Delbridge, 1889).

4. Cholera morbus was a common summer complaint usually related to food spoilage from inadequate refrigeration or sanitation.

5. The wording of this entry suggests Jerry may have suffered migraine headaches, but no other source confirms this.

6. Entry is in George's handwriting.

7. George is again writing for his mother.

8. At this price the Gebbys were probably buying gold rather than the less expensive steel frames. The 1897 Sears catalog contains an eye chart in its optical department, which probably represents choices in corrective lenses similar to those the Gebbys could purchase.

9. No mention of an extraction suggests these were a replacement set of false teeth.

10. Trained dentists capable of removing decay and filling cavities were relatively rare in towns such as Bellefontaine. This procedure was more expensive than an extraction and it would appear from these entries that the Gebbys reserved this option for front teeth.

11. Cousin.

12. Niece's infant. Such events must have reminded Margaret of her own child's death, but no comment is ever recorded.

13. Niece's daughter.

14. Dillons were neighbors.

15. Margaret's father's brother.

16. This death is not recorded and readers can only assume from diary descriptions that the cause was a combination of factors associated with age.

17. Logan County Death Record, vol. 2, p. 79, cause of death—typhoid fever. If accurate, it seems surprising that there is no mention of the disease in Margaret's record.

18. There is no record of the cause of death in spite of the fact that his son Lyman, who was a physician, was living with him at his death. Peter Dow evidently divided his property among his children before his death for his estate amounted only to two hundred to four hundred dollars (Logan County Probate Court Estate Packet D-8).

19. Appendicitis had been known for more than a century but the first surgical removal had been successfully performed in Philadelphia only a decade earlier. Lister's research on antiseptic procedures had dramatically increased surgical survivals during the last quarter of the century in urban centers, but Bellefontaine physicians were not qualified to perform this procedure. A physician was called in who had observed the surgery, although he had not previously performed the operation himself.

20. Bellefontaine had no hospital at this time, and family legend has it that the operation was performed on a table in the Gebby home. There are no further entries in Margaret's diary until 31 May, a fact so unusual it attests to the demands on her time and emotions. It seems certain from the time span and symptoms described that the appendix had ruptured and caused infection. The 22 May *Bellefontaine Republican* reported, "Mr. Orra Gebby, upon whom an operation was performed for appendicitis, a few days since, is in a critical condition, at his father's home, on the Sidney Pike."

21. This entry seems to indicate the invalid was moved to his own home, but the absence of further entries until 6 June suggests that his mother was spending every day there caring for him, perhaps allowing his wife the night shift.

22. A type of chaise lounge with wheels.

23. This is an early example of medical procedures that could produce economic catastrophe for a family. The $248 can be compared to the annual $200 paid the hired man. One can see why it was surgical procedures and then hospitalization that led to the need for medical insurance.

24. The degree of convalescence nearly two months after surgery can be judged from the fact that this was a Wednesday and all of the men were making hay.

25. This would appear to be a stomach upset unrelated to the surgery, but the speed with which the doctor was consulted suggests the family's continuing concern.

PARENTING

1. Farmers Institutes were a national adult education program operating in Ohio through the State Board of Agriculture. In format they were similar to county Teachers Institutes. For background on the concept see John Hamilton, *Farmers' Institutes and Agricultural Extension Work in the United States in 1913*, U.S.D.A. Experiment Station Bulletin, No. 83 (Washington, D.C.: Government Printing Office, 1914).

2. The 5 January 1892 *Bellefontaine Republican* mentioned that Elmer Gebby was in Cleveland studying civil engineering. This was a rigorous four-year course of study, which included algebra, geometry, trigonometry, chemistry, rhetoric, French, and mechanical drawing in its first year. It would appear that Elmer did not meet the examination requirements to begin his sophomore year (*Catalogue of the Case School of Applied Science, 1889 to 1895*).

3. The men were in the midst of hay and wheat harvest, but Elmer evidently secured a job as a draftsman for the summer. The 1892 *Cleveland Directory* lists Sidney R. Badgley, Architect, with offices in the prestigious Arcade Building. Perhaps this was an internship since the family seemed to be providing Elmer financial support.

4. The 1892 *Cleveland Directory* lists J. P. Walsh & E. A. Upstill as Miners and Shippers of Coal & Coke.

5. The Spencerian Commercial College established in 1848 was then offering a wide variety of day and evening classes. It appears likely that Elmer emphasized business accounting coursework.

6. While several Aikin and McCracken cousins acquired teaching licenses, there is no evidence that George Gebby ever took the teacher's examination (County School Examiner's Records, 1892–1914, Logan County School Superintendent's Office).

7. These entries in Orra's handwriting are the only time he wrote in his mother's diary. His reference to his brother Elmer as "the dandy" and his brother George as "the kid" is far more revealing than anything his mother ever wrote about roles of family members. It seems to be written with a touch of humor but with a candor that probably reflects teasing nicknames between the brothers.

8. Elmer was still working as a bank clerk when he and Laura Dow were married 17 July 1901 (Logan County Marriage Record, vol. 1, p. 318).

BUILDING A HOUSE FOR A SON AND HIS BRIDE

1. It is interesting that the men borrowed the township road scraper to begin digging the cellar before Margaret records any contact with a potential carpenter.

2. The Gebby hired hand helped mix concrete for the mason laying the stone cellar wall.

3. It would appear from these entries that green lumber from recently cut sawlogs was being used for framing.

4. According to the financial records this was a crew of three carpenters and the framework was raised their second day on the job.

5. Decorative L-shaped wood braces were by this time precut and ordered from a large urban lumberyard.

6. Standard wall construction involved wood lath, covered by a coarse plaster containing animal hair, and finished with a smooth "whitecoat" finish plaster.

7. For some reason, Margaret's 1896 diary was not purchased for two weeks and there are no entries until 13 January. Her financial records show that two carpenters worked every day except Sundays from 30 December to 13 January apparently doing the interior woodwork.

8. It seems unlikely to be doing exterior painting in January, so perhaps this reference is to interior painting and varnishing woodwork and floors.

9. The 1897 Sears Roebuck catalog offered English semiporcelain china dinner sets in this price range. A standard one hundred piece set included twelve cups and saucers, dinner plates, breakfast plates, pie plates, sauce plates, butter plates, one medium and one large platter, one open and two covered vegetable dishes, sugar bowl with lid, cream pitcher, pickle dish, slop bowl, covered butter dish, and sauce boat.

10. Bedroom suites at this time normally contained a full-sized (double) bed, dresser with mirror, and commode. These, as well as the extension table, six chairs, rocker, and stand were probably in the golden oak so popular in the 1890s.

11. Iron stoves in this price range usually had firepits that could burn either wood or coal, an oven, four to six burner holes, side and high shelves where food could be kept warm, and a reservoir to hold warm water. Helen Gebby Evans remembers this stove as having elegant steel trim and a door to cover the high warming shelf.

LEISURE

1. An excellent comparison can be observed in the 1884–1889 diaries of Mary Dodge Woodward who homesteaded near Fargo, North Dakota (Mary

Boynton Cowdrey, ed., *The Checkered Years* [Caldwell, Idaho: Caxton Printers, Ltd., 1937]).

2. It was most unusual for Margaret to be so dressed up that she did not drive herself.

3. Jerry's first cousin Eva Kitchen was twenty-eight years younger, and she frequently visited for a week or more, socializing with the relatives in this area and apparently developing a romantic interest in her cousin George Harner.

4. This is Margaret's niece Jennie Aikin Cleland and her sister Martha Ann Aikin.

5. Julia Robeson Steddam and her husband were obviously visiting her family.

6. William Bennett, the widower of Jerry's aunt Elizabeth Robeson Bennett, was probably visiting numerous relatives in the Bellefontaine area.

7. Nellie Patton was related to Aunt Hannah Robeson and obviously visiting in their home.

8. All three maternal aunts were visiting with their nephew's family.

9. The Lewiston Reservoir, now Indian Lake, at that time covered more than seven thousand acres, while Silver Lake about a mile from the Gebby home covered some one hundred acres.

10. It was dangerous and unusual for someone to go fishing alone. There is no evidence whether the Gebby boys or their companions knew how to swim.

11. Julia Robeson Steddam's husband was a professional photographer at Lebanon, Ohio, and he was evidently instructing George.

12. Perhaps the artist supplies referred to were materials for developing photographs. George seems to have been using some form of dry plate process rather than the Kodak introduced by George Eastman, which included a film roll to be returned for developing (Beaumont Newhall, *The History of Photography* [New York: Museum of Modern Art, 1982], 124, 145).

13. Margaret's brother-in-law had a maple grove, which was tapped each spring to produce maple syrup.

14. Teachers, especially high school teachers, were often referred to as professors in this time period.

15. This is an interesting indication that the older brothers no longer wanted the "kid" tagging along. When the circus came to town older teens preferred the evening show.

16. This was obviously a visit as guests rather than as members. The Harrison Township Grange Hall was on the Sidney pike between the Gebby home and farm. The diaries make no mention of weekly Grange meetings and the Gebbys either did not belong or were not active in this farm organization. Entries regarding Masonic and Catholic services lead a reader to suspect Margaret would have been uncomfortable with Grange secret rituals.

17. Margaret may have attended as her son's guest since Bellefontaine High School had its first graduate in 1867. The first alumni reunion was held in 1874 and by 1895 there were 212 graduates.

18. County histories refer to a library in Bellefontaine by this time but there is no evidence the Gebbys used it. The family did, however, own a number of

books and made frequent exchanges with relatives.

19. Like many county seats throughout the Midwest, the Bellefontaine Opera House annually hosted an educational entertainment series. Newspaper advertisements suggest the Star Lecture Series sold two hundred to three hundred season tickets, but they do not include a program of the year's features.

HOLIDAYS

1. There was no home mail delivery in the nineteenth century. Boxes were rented at the post office annually, and in the Gebby family, whenever anyone went to town they picked up mail.

2. Everyone worked at the wheat this holiday Friday, but no one worked on Sunday the sixth. Everyone worked on the wheat harvest again on Monday.

3. It sounds as though parents and youth of the 1890s had a bit of a generation gap about entertainment.

4. In commenting on the lack of a celebration in Bellefontaine, the newspaper indicated that Company F of the militia had gone to the Urbana parade and a great crowd of five thousand shared the festivities at Lake Ridge.

5. This pattern is so contrary to popular mythology that entries are presented for every year so readers may seek their own understanding rather than accuse the editor of distortion.

6. Margaret seems to have gone to her parents' early to help prepare dinner while the rest of the family went to church.

7. Elmer was away at school and the family received a letter on 25 November but he did not come home.

8. Jerry's first cousin, a house guest.

9. The family evidently had dinner and then scattered to work or socialize.

10. The United Presbyterian service was religious. Gifts were presented to children but the service did not include a visit from Santa Claus or Kris Kringle as newspaper accounts reveal the Lutheran and Baptist services did.

11. The more casual the acquaintance, the more anonymous Margaret's reference to women is. She frequently identifies them only as wives or daughters.

12. Houseplant in living room. The Gebbys did not decorate a tree at home.

13. One wonders whether Margaret really appreciated this "nice" present or knew that her sons might read her diary.

14. This entry assumes everyone knew the anniversary being celebrated was Columbus' discovery of America, little suspecting that a century later Columbus Day would be celebrated 12 October.

15. This is a dramatic skit for the local literary society.

CELEBRATIONS

1. This reception a week after the ceremony was probably when the couple returned from a wedding trip. The reference to getting home between one o'clock and two o'clock on Saturday morning when the family would normally be rising to do chores about five o'clock is worthy of note.

2. Local papers at this time often listed the presents received and the names of their donors.

3. The family evidently did not leave the grandmother home alone at night.

4. Local advertisements for the Knickerbocker describe it as an excursion train with buffet, parlor, and sleeping cars, which made regular runs to a number of lake resorts.

5. The implication is that the Gebbys contributed to a group present, perhaps the rocking chair.

6. It is interesting to compare this account with the *Bellefontaine Republican:* "Over a hundred of the friends of Mr & Mrs Jerry Gebby gave them a surprise call last week on their 20th wedding anniversary and had a splendid time. They took their own dinner and set a royal spread, and hugely enjoyed Jerry's discomfiture. It was handsomely done and most heartily appreciated."

7. The newspaper described the celebration in slightly more detail reporting that the celebration closed by singing the Twenty-third Psalm, no doubt very meaningful to this religious couple, but an ending that would be considered quaint at similar celebrations today.

COUNTY FAIR

1. Jerry's uncle who lived near Lebanon, Ohio.

2. Jerry's Robeson cousins were then living in Darke County, Ohio.

3. Margaret's cousin's daughters from Degraff, Ohio.

4. Local newspaper accounts cannot be taken objectively, but the 7 October 1887 *Bellefontaine Republican* claimed the Arts Hall exhibits were better than the Michigan State Fair and the grain better than the Ohio State Fair. It is certainly true that local farmers felt a loyalty to their county fairs that did not apply to the relatively remote state fairs. During these years Logan County usually had three thousand to five thousand exhibits, but newspapers made no special mention of premium winners. Fair directors were occasionally criticized for running horse races and games of chance, but the majority of fair-goers evidently approved for they remained.

EXCURSIONS

1. The Campbells were second cousins on Margaret's mother's side and this is the only mention in the diaries of interaction with this family.

2. This unexpected visit with Jerry's aunt and uncle lasted three days.

3. There is no indication what the subject of this exhibition was, but Springfield, Ohio, at that time was a thriving cultural center with two opera houses, which featured that same month international touring companies of the *Mikado* and *Faust* complete with orchestra and chorus.

4. This water and light show was the most publicized extravaganza of the exhibition, and one wonders whether it was an economic or moral restraint that limited its viewing to the two outgoing young men of the party (See Christopher L. Bensch, "Exotic Electric Delights: Cincinnati's 1888 Centennial Exposition," *Timeline* 1, no. 2 [December 1884–January 1885]: 42–53).

5. Perhaps no other entry in the diaries marks Margaret more distinctly as a farm wife. Most writers would mention exotic species seen, but Margaret was noticing their health.

6. Jerry's cousin Eva Kitchen was already showing signs of consumption from which she would die six years later. Her frequent extended visits in the Gebby home during these years emphasize the lack of knowledge about contagious disease.

7. There are no entries 29 August to 5 September except for Sunday when morning services at the First United Presbyterian Church in Chicago and evening services at the Second United Presbyterian Church in Englewood are described. This suggests the Gebbys spent a day traveling each way and five days in Chicago attending the fair, church, and perhaps contacting cattle buyers.

8. The Chicago World's Fair ended the last of October, and Logan County waited until after the county fair for this excursion train. Tickets were six dollars for transportation, and the 19 October 1893 *Bellefontaine Republican* reported 570 tickets sold requiring thirteen cars.

9. The exhibition advertised that visitors could see "the earth for fifty cents," and one suspects the Gebbys saw as much of the 633 acres, almost a third of it under roof, as they could (Julian Ralph, *Harper's Chicago and the World's Fair* [New York: Harper & Brothers, 1893]; David F. Burg, *Chicago's White City of 1893* [Lexington: University of Kentucky Press, 1976]; Strasser, *Never Done: A History of American Housework*, 73).

SCHOOL

1. Ohio's township schools became free for all youth from six to twenty-one in the middle of the nineteenth century, but in 1877 it became compulsory for all

youth eight to fourteen to attend a common school at least twelve weeks per year (Nelson L. Bossing, "The History of Educational Legislation in Ohio from 1851 to 1925," *Ohio Archaeological and Historical Society Publications* 39 [1930]: 133–58). In 1886 township schools statewide averaged twenty-nine weeks annually (Leroy D. Brown, *Annual Report of the State Commissioner of Common Schools* [Columbus: Myers Brothers, State Printer, 1887]).

2. Mr. Whitworth was principal of Bellefontaine High School and secretary of the Logan County School Examiners. Students went to the school and registered to attend.

3. The same teacher did not necessarily teach both autumn and spring terms.

4. Margaret's direct contact with the previous year's teacher suggests she was not pleased with the quality of the applicant. There is no record available to confirm who actually taught that spring, but this entry is an interesting example of women's influence even though women were not given the right to vote for school directors in Ohio until 1894. By then Margaret's children were through township school and the privilege probably meant little to her personally.

5. The percentage of real estate tax allotted to township schools could be credited toward high school tuition if the family had no children attending the township school.

RELIGION

1. This was the Reformed Presbyterian Church, which maintained strict linkage to its Covenanter tradition.

2. This expectation was obviously shared with her sons as well as her diary for some or all family members went every other night that week. Margaret seems to be fulfilling woman's historic role as guardian of the family morals.

3. This entry summarizes ninety-seven persons who were baptized and transferred into membership in five local congregations after two weeks of revival services.

4. The *Bellefontaine Republican* for 12 April 1887 carried a front-page photograph of the new building at its dedication with a description of its construction and a history of the congregation (See also the *United Presbyterian Church Centennial, 1831–1931*, published by Rev. George LeRoy Brown, printed by DeGraff Journal Press).

5. The newspaper described the auditorium as fifty-five by fifty feet with pews for 350 persons and lecture and classrooms for 350. These could be combined and chairs placed in the vestibule to accommodate 800 to 900 persons. The dedication article refers to 480 yards of carpet from Wissler Bros., apparently machine loomed in strips a yard wide, which the ladies of the church sewed together.

6. Financial Reports of the Trustees and Treasurer of the United Presbyterian Church of Bellefontaine, Ohio—1892, 1893, 1895, 1896. Total receipts exclusive of missions these years ranged from $1,162.22 to $1,440.05.

7. The centennial history of this church indicates it had a membership slightly less than 200 when Reverend Hamilton was called to the pastorate and reached its zenith at 250 during his ministry. The membership roster in the 1892 financial report contains 250 names, 101 male and 149 female, including teenagers such as the Gebby sons. When Margaret records 130 or more persons voting there can be no doubt that this included the women of the congregation.

8. The fact that eight of the nine young people attending this regional meeting were Dow family cousins dramatically reflects a small congregation relying on family networks for its support.

9. This is certainly a clue that spelling bees were no longer common practice in centralized schools such as Bellefontaine.

10. The regularity of Margaret's daily entries and the absence of any entry on 20 May suggests just how busy this day was and how late Margaret probably got home.

GOVERNMENT

1. Although the Gebbys sold livestock throughout the year and there would be fluctuations in the number on the farm, this does not explain the wide variations in the total assessment from $5,855 to $2,550 three years later from the same assessor. There must have been valuation adjustments tied to the economic situation.

2. Harrison Township consistently had one of the lowest property tax rates in Logan County at 12.40 mills compared to 26.60 for Bellefontaine in 1886, and 14.00 mills compared to 30.40 in Bellefontaine in 1896. These 14 mills were distributed: 2.84 to the state for general revenue funds, schools, and poor relief; 7.10 to the county for roads, bridges, elections, soldiers' relief, and county children's home; and 4.06 to the township for schools, roads, and bridges.

3. This dominance included Presidents Hayes (1876) and Garfield (1880) and contenders like Senator Sherman who led on the first ballot at the 1888 convention. Governor McKinley's election was a fitting culmination to this strength throughout the post-war era (H. Wayne Morgan, *William McKinley and His America* [Syracuse: Syracuse University Press, 1963], 92 and 114).

4. According to the *Bellefontaine Republican* the Harrison Township delegates to the county Republican convention that fall were Margaret's cousin Peter Dow and brother-in-law George Aikin.

5. One of the most significant pieces of legislation in Ohio during the temperance movements of the late nineteenth century was the Dow Law of 1886, which began the policy of taxing the liquor traffic. It was introduced and shepherded through the legislature by Margaret's cousin Duncan Dow, who was

a Republican representative from Logan County (Eugene H. Roseboom and Francis P. Weisenburger, *A History of Ohio* [Columbus: The Ohio Historical Society, 1986], 245).

6. Judge West was a local lawyer with a national reputation as the "blind orator" whose eloquence in nominating James Blaine was credited with swinging the 1884 Republican National Convention in his favor.

7. There may have been local ordinances regarding livestock, which would have caused them problems, but the primary concern was undoubtedly the tax millage, which throughout this period was twice as high in Bellefontaine as in Harrison Township.

8. Several entries refer to her husband being "summoned" to jury duty, undoubtedly referring to his name being drawn from voter registration lists as it would be today. However, references to being "picked up on the jury" suggest that some civil trials obtained juries from men who happened to be in town around the courthouse on any given day. If so, the potential for bias is obvious.

9. This would have involved a trip near Degraff eight or ten miles west.

10. This became a regular Monday morning event through the rest of this year, but was apparently an interim position that did not continue beyond this term. There were two banks of similar size in Bellefontaine. Jerry served as director and Elmer became a teller in the People's National Bank. Margaret's cousin Duncan was for a number of years a director in the rival Bellefontaine National Bank.

TRANSPORTATION AND COMMUNICATION

1. Sam Walter Foss, "The House by the Side of the Road," in *Masterpieces of Religious Verse*, ed. James Dalton Morrison (New York: Harper and Row, 1948), 422–23.

2. Strangers obviously or Margaret would have noted who they were.

3. Breakfast served with a motherly sermon!

4. Margaret usually drove Harry, who was also used for pulling farm wagons.

5. They evidently gave up trying to trade for a new buggy and decided to fix up an old one.

6. This sounds like a new buggy for nineteen-year-old Orra.

7. This was a special sale price advertised in journals such as the *Ohio Farmer.*

8. Margaret's nephew Charlie Cook, oldest son of her sister Jane, had married Lizzie Harner, Jerry's first cousin. They farmed about four miles north and although they were about fifteen years younger than Margaret and Jerry the families seem to have been quite close. The object of this visit was Jerry's uncle John Robeson, who was then farming in Darke County, Ohio.

9. The Cooks lived north of Bellefontaine and their overnight stay with the

Gebbys so the two-buggy caravan could get an early start the next morning confirms this was a major trip.

10. This sounds remarkably similar to the rush a century later at service stations when the first storm of the season caught car owners without snow tires or chains.

11. Agricultural freight was a large and profitable business. Ninety-five rail companies competed in Ohio with 8,767 miles of mainline track by 1899 (R. S. Kaylor, "Ohio Railroads," *Ohio Archaeological and Historical Society Publications* 9 [1900]: 189–92).

12. Northwestern Ohio experienced a natural gas boomlet late in the nineteenth century climaxed by the Karg well near Findlay in January 1886, whose flames could sometimes be seen at night some forty miles away, perhaps as far as the Gebby home (Russell McClure, "The Natural Gas Era in Northwestern Ohio," *Northwest Ohio Quarterly* 14 [1942]: 83–105). But reality often failed to live up to expectations and Logan County was on the edge of the dream. The 31 August 1886 *Bellefontaine Republican* reported a large crowd assembled and twenty gallons of nitroglycerine used to shoot this well at Belle Centre, but the next day they decided to abandon it.

13. This was the largest local celebration during the years covered by these diaries. The newspaper described its 1¾-mile parade with marching units from several nearby towns and a crowd of ten thousand people greeting dignitaries such as Governor McKinley.

14. The *Bellefontaine Republican* 24 June 1895 was more effusive, headlining its story "Out of the Darkness." It reported, "The electric light plant was put in operation Tuesday night, and at the sound of the whistle our people rushed out of their houses to see the town beautifully lighted for the first time, by electricity."

15. The newspaper claimed four hundred delegates for this statewide meeting and referred to their lodging in homes as well as hotels. The Gebbys' lack of participation compared to the Presbytery meetings reflects a lack of support for this farm organization.

16. Margaret's description concurs with the newspaper account on 17 March. It reported that five hoses were on the fire within fifteen minutes of the alarm and commends "a colored man," Otto Jackson, who mounted a ladder and directed the hose through the roof. The newspaper listed $23,900 of insurance on the businesses in these two buildings erected in 1832 and 1834 and concluded with an attitude that would make modern preservationists cringe. "They had served their day and it will be a great improvement to the town to have beautiful modern structures put up in their places."

17. This incident derived from the miners' uprising in southeastern Ohio. The *Bellefontaine Republican* reported Weaver's arrest for carrying a concealed weapon. After making a number of insulting remarks including an expression that he hoped the militia came home in coffins, he apparently stood by the restaurant with his hand on a gun in his pocket.

18. The instigators of the Haymarket riot, which drew worldwide attention in May 1886.

19. Governor McKinley called out the militia statewide to quell the protests of southeastern Ohio miners regarding working conditions. The response of newspapers who supported the governor is typified by the *Bellefontaine Republican* of 12 June 1894: "The miners were mostly Huns and Slavs and other foreigners, who jeered and taunted, and blackguarded and cursed the troops in their various tongues, and showed a very bad spirit."

EPILOGUE

1. U.S. Census, Logan County, Ohio: 1870, Union Township, p. 14; 1880, Harrison Township, #86; 1900, Harrison Township, #36. Interviews and records of Helen Gebby Evans, daughter of Orra D. Gebby, born 1900 at Bellefontaine.

2. Obituaries, *Bellefontaine Republican:* Jeremiah M. Gebby, 14 May 1901; Margaret Dow Gebby, 30 November 1920.

GLOSSARY

Basque: tight-fitting woman's shirtwaist.

Bright's disease: chronic kidney infection.

Chatterbox: noisemaker for celebrating.

Cholera morbus: noninfectious intestinal disease causing cramps and diarrhea, usually associated with contaminated food.

Comfort: bed covering made by inserting a warm filling such as old blankets into a fabric cover and securing all layers with knotted yarn.

Consumption: tuberculosis.

Corn Belt: midwestern region suited by soil and climate for corn production—generally recognized as western Ohio, Indiana, Illinois, Iowa, and fringes of adjacent states.

Cradle: scythe for cutting grain that has bar extension to catch and hold cut stalks until tied into a sheaf.

Creamer: container for storing milk and separating the cream, which rises to the top.

Delineator: adjustable pattern for cutting a garment.

Duck: strong cloth of linen or cotton, lighter than canvas, used for work clothing.

Extended family: persons related by blood or marriage who interact as kin.

Family farm: unit of land producing crops and livestock owned and operated by a nuclear family.

Fascinator: woman's head scarf usually knit in an open, lacy style.

Flux: bloody diarrhea.

Fresh: reference to a dairy cow that has calved and is producing milk.

Furrow: row of plowed soil.

Gallus: center brace to support a cornshock, made by bending and tying four cornstalks from two adjacent rows.

La grippe: influenza.

Laid by: term to describe cornfield that has been cultivated for the last time to remove weeds.

Laudanum: tincture of opium in alcohol, used as medication.

Martingale: leather strap of horse's harness that runs down between forelegs.

Militia: citizen volunteer defense force that preceded National Guard.

Muleys: range cattle without horns.

Neuralgia: nerve pain.

Pieplant: rhubarb.

Pleurisy: inflammation of the lungs causing chest pain and cough.

Plush: fabric finished with long cut pile, very popular for wraps.

Polonaise: skirt with a divided front that is looped back to reveal underskirt.

Pongee: soft thin fabric of Chinese or Indian silk.

Prairie: grassland that had never been plowed.

Sham: underlining for skirt to make it stand away from the body.

Sheaf: bundle of wheat or oats bound together with stalks of straw.

Shock: corn or grain stacked in fields to dry.

Sickle: crescent-shaped cutting tool with short handle.

Signal service: predecessor of the National Weather Service that operated by telegraph messages and signal flags.

Smearcase: homemade cottage cheese.

Sugartree: maple.

Veranda: front porch.

Whitewash: inexpensive coating made from lime and water, used to clean and brighten work areas such as washhouses and storage cellars.

Worm: rail fence laid in a zigzag pattern without fasteners.

INDEX